BEARS & FLOWERS

Books by the Author:

THE EDUCATION OF A BEAR HUNTER
BEARS & FLOWERS

Bears & Flowers

by Ralph Flowers

BEARS *and* FLOWERS

Copyright © 2003 by Ralph Flowers

ISBN 0-9741366-0-3

All rights reserved. No part of this book may be reproduced in any
form, or by electronic/mechanical means, including information
storage and retrieval systems, without
permission in writing from the publisher; except by
reviewer who may quote brief passages in a review.

Illustrations by Ralph Flowers
Cover illustration by Dave Sanders

Printed in the United States of America

To Velma

*Who has endured these many years
as a bear hunter's wife—*

*who has so patiently listened to all of these stories
after each hunt—*

*whose faith in me, encouragement, and assistance
helped bring my experiment in supplemental feeding of bears to
successful fruition—*

I dedicate this book.

Acknowledgements

I am grateful to my granddaughter, Cammy Flowers, as well as Kathleen Shaputis for their faithful assistance in typing the original manuscript of this book. Thanks to Dave Sanders for providing the cover drawing. And to Ron Munro for his many kind words in the Foreword, thank you. A special credit goes to my wife Velma for her insistence that I complete this work.

Contents

Foreword *by Ron Munro* / ix

Preface / xiii

1. Unsolved Mysteries / 1
2. The Transition / 13
3. Canyon River / 23
4. A Real Cliffhanger / 39
5. A World of Mud / 55
6. The King Creek Jinx / 73
7. Hungry Hunters Spare the Cook / 79
8. Snares, Bears, and Scares / 113
9. Japan / 131
10. Austria / 155
11. Hungary / 173
12. Africa / 213
13. Bosnia / 229
14. Alaska / 247
15. Austria Revisited / 263

Epilogue / 269

Foreword

I FIRST HEARD THE NAME RALPH FLOWERS SOMETIME IN 1976 when I browsed a list of recently published outdoor books that were for sale. One book on the list was titled *The Education of a Bear Hunter,* and was authored by a man that lived in Aberdeen, Washington. His name was Ralph Flowers. I am a life-long resident of Washington State, an avid hunter, and a hunting book written by someone living within a 100 miles of my house is always of interest to me. I showed the list of offered books to my wife, and suggested that the one that was heavily circled with a felt pen would make a nice Christmas present. How pleased I was on Christmas day to find Ralph's book among my presents, and I started reading it that very evening. What fascinating reading!

Ralph Flowers was born in Maryland among a family of hunters, and shot his first deer at age fifteen. By the time he was seventeen years old he had an itch to see more of the world, and he and a friend joined the army. He went to boot camp in Alabama, and was then shipped west to Fort Lawton, Washington on the edge of Puget Sound. Arriving in the early spring of 1946 Ralph was amazed at how green and fresh the hills around him were. He took an instant liking to the country. One weekend he went to Aberdeen, a small logging and fishing town in southwest Washington, to visit a cousin who had docked there on a merchant ship. Aberdeen was surrounded by timbered country that abounded with fish in the rivers and streams, and deer, elk and bears in the forest. For a young man with a burning desire to hunt and fish, Ralph realized that this could be the land of his dreams. Over the next few months he made several trips to Aberdeen, and soon met Velma, a local girl raised among a family of hunters. Romance came quickly, and in March of 1947 they were married. Velma was sixteen years old and Ralph was eighteen.

For the next 13 years Ralph and Velma were busy carving their home site out of the forest, building a house, and raising a family. Ralph worked in the local mills at night, and spent as many waking hours as possible hunting and fishing. Bears were so numerous in western Washington they were considered predators. While you could only hunt deer and elk in the fall, you could hunt bears at any time of the year, and Ralph took full advantage of this wonderful opportunity. He hunted them with hounds, hunted them in the cascara stands and berry patches when the berries were ripe, and when these opportunities weren't available he would climb to the top of an old growth stump, and sit there till dark if necessary, in hopes of spotting a bear on the opposite hillside. With a keen eye, and astounding accuracy with a firearm, he was deservedly gaining the reputation as one of the finest bear hunters around.

By 1960 many of the old-growth timber stands in western Washington had been harvested, natural stands of second growth timber were taking their place in the forest, and bear damage to these younger trees was increasing at an alarming rate. Bears in western Washington usually hibernate for a few weeks in the coldest part of the winter, but as the weather warms up they are soon out of their dens and roaming for food. Usually it is too early in the year for berries to be ripe, and the grass to be green, and a hungry bear will rip the bark off of a young tree to get to the succulent cambium layer.

Some bears, especially a sow with an infant cub, will stay in one area for several days, attacking as many as 50 trees in a day. Sometimes the tree is totally girdled, and eventually dies, and sometimes the tree is only partly girdled, and as the tree gets older the wounded area is exposed to insect and fungus damage. The Washington Forest Protection Association, an association of the larger industrial forestland owners in the state, had hired a bear hunter to eradicate bears, but he just couldn't keep up with the job in such an expansive area of timberland. They were looking for a second man to help out, and it was suggested that Ralph Flowers should be a candidate for the job. With great trepidation Ralph applied, and was overwhelmed when he was selected from a long list of applicants. He said that when he walked out of the meeting where he had been assured of the job he had to pinch himself to make sure it wasn't all a dream. He just couldn't believe that he was now going to get paid to hunt bears, the very thing he wanted to do in his life more than anything else.

It was through Ralph's affiliation with the Washington Forest Protection Association that I had the opportunity to meet the man whose book I had enjoyed so very much. In 1982 a friend by the name of Stu Bledsoe was the Director of WFPA, and I asked Stu if he could arrange for me to meet Ralph Flowers, the man by then known as the "Bear Man". It was arranged that a friend and I would meet an employee of WFPA in Olympia, and we would drive to Ralph's house just outside of

Aberdeen. I remember the event very clearly. We drove around the house to the back yard, and through the door came this tall, thin, bespectacled, redheaded fellow. He approached us with his hand extended and immediately wished us a warm welcome in a quiet voice, and almost shy demeanor. You could have knocked me over with a feather, as he sure didn't look like a guy that had more than once fought a wounded bear hand to hand, and over a career of nearly 30 years had harvested somewhere in excess of 1,100 bears. I immediately liked him, and we have been friends ever since.

So, Ralph's new book, *Bears and Flowers*, picks right up where the first book ended in 1975. Over the last 28 years Ralph's love of the outdoors, and the creatures that abound there, has not diminished one bit. His knowledge of bears is astounding, and it is my opinion that he knows more about black bears than any man alive.

As Ralph Flower's job of controlling the black bear population progressed, he continually tried to come up with ideas that might satisfy the bear's need for nourishment in the spring. He urged the Washington Forest Protection Association to help radio collar some bears, and through this study he determined that it was the sows that did most of the tree damage. He then convinced his employers to fund an experiment where 3 caged bears were fed a variety of food mixtures. With help from Washington State University, and after many experiments, he was convinced that if he could somehow feed the bears a food supplement in the spring they might leave the trees alone. This led to establishing feeding stations in the areas where the most tree damage was taking place, and lo and behold the idea worked. What a story! The man who was hired to kill the bears that killed the trees had almost single-handedly found a way to save both the trees and the bears.

By 1986 Ralph's feeding program was so successful that he was featured in a front-page article of the *Wall Street Journal*. In August of 1993 he was awarded a CERTIFICATE OF MERIT by Washington State University *"in recognition of a lifetime of study, understanding and admiration of black bears in Washington State."* Also, as word of the success of the bear-feeding program expanded he was invited to go to several foreign countries, including Japan, Bosnia and Croatia, to help foresters with bear damage problems. He was no longer just the "Bear Man" of Washington State.

While Ralph and I see each other at events of mutual interest from time to time, we also exchange letters every now and then. He is a terrific writer, and I find his letters both informative and enjoyable to read. In a recent letter he mentioned that during the summer he had cut his usual *twelve cords* of firewood for the upcoming winter. Twelve cords of wood is a lot of firewood. In fact, it is equal to a supply of firewood stacked four feet high and 192 feet long! He stated that over the years all the easy firewood close to the house had long ago been harvested, and he now had to pitch the pieces of wood several times to get them to an area where he could transport them to the woodshed. He chuckled that his firewood warmed him many times over, even before it got to the stove. In parting he stated that it seemed that cutting that much wood every year was getting more difficult than it used to be, and he mused whether being 74 years old had anything to do with it. Ralph Flowers is an extraordinary man.

Bears and Flowers is a book I think you will enjoy reading. Ralph Flowers is a man of his word, and you will find no exaggerations or wild, untrue tales. It is the continuing story of a young man who came west, fell in love, and spent a lifetime learning about, and enjoying, the wildlife around him. It is a book everyone who loves and appreciates the great outdoors should have in their library.

—*Ron Munro, forester*
Woodinville, Washington

Preface

"**B**EARS AND FLOWERS" IS A SEQUEL TO THE 1975 WINCHESTER Press publication "The Education of a Bear Hunter" and its second printing in 1989 by Binford and Mort Publishing (Hillsboro, Or.).

In "The Education of a Bear Hunter" I shared the experiences of my unique career as a professional bear hunter, employed by the Washington Forest Protection Association to help control tree damage inflicted by black bears. In much of western Washington bears do considerable damage to the woods, girdling and killing conifers in their quest for nourishment, in this case the cambium layer just under the tree's bark. One bear can destroy as many as 60 trees a day. To help curtail this damage it became my job to remove as many bears from the endangered areas as I could.

I accomplished this by the sport hunting methods of still hunting and tracking with hounds, as well as the use of cable foot snares, and had taken nearly 1000 bears when "The Education of a Bear Hunter" was first published in 1975.

Since then some significant changes have taken place in the management of black bears in Washington state. In 1973, a "spring damage" bear season was initiated in western Washington by the State Game Commission, restricting bear hunting to sixteen bear damage units in twelve counties, totaling 2520 square miles. The purpose of this move was to funnel all the sport hunters into the actual damage areas during the months that damage was occurring, and by concentrating their hunting reduce the tree damage.

It was agreed that no snaring would be done in those locations during the special season. I would continue to hunt and snare, but only in those areas where fresh bear damage was discovered outside the established spring hunt units and in different areas where the sport houndsman refused to hunt.

These spring damage bear seasons were continued into the early 1980s and bear populations plummeted alarmingly in the control areas by 1984. Nevertheless, intolerable levels of tree damage continued to occur. I wished for a solution other than killing bears, and in late 1984 I developed a plan that would revolutionize the way we control damage to forest plantations here in the Northwest. "Bears and Flowers" carries on from where "The Education of a Bear Hunter" left off bringing the reader up to the date and sharing many more hunting adventures.

At this writing I am nearing my 75th year and although the "bear fever" that has burned within me since my first bear encounter 55 years ago is somewhat diminished, my respect and admiration for the black "ghost of the woods" continues to grow.

Chapter 1

Unsolved Mysteries

Old Johnny Walker, who lived at Axford Prairie, always contended that the bears woke up from their "hibernatory sojourn" on St. Patrick's Day. Accordingly, each year he would make his way down Walker Road to the Deep Creek swamps on that day and seldom failed to capture a bear with his pack of hounds. These early rising bears were generally boars; the females tended to stir slightly later.

St. Patrick's Day, 1974, marked the end of a 35-day stretch of rain here on Grays Harbor and was followed by several days of sunshine. This lured me out of my "den" for an early season cruise through my hunting area to determine the condition of the old roads and bridges after the winter's storms. The new spring damage sport bear season had diminished my control area to encompass primarily the Promised Land, a flat, marshy, cedar country that nurtured a dense jungle of salal and huckleberry brush. It also nurtured a goodly population of bears that was continually replenished by an influx from the adjoining tribal lands.

On Joe Creek I found the first bear track of the season and set about placing foot snares there and at other established locations and crossings, but it wasn't until April 24th that they began to produce. The first bear caught was a yearling, followed a few days later by a large boar that measured six feet from nose to tail.

I also had a few snares set in some isolated locations outside the Promised Land boundaries and as the spring days warmed, these also started to produce bears.

I had made a trail set on lower Joe Creek, and to reach it I had to walk across a high and dilapidated logging railroad trestle that was too rotten to drive over. On reaching my snare, which was placed a considerable distance off the old grade in a stand of limby hemlocks, I found that it held an adult female bear. By her fierce raging on the cable, which was solidly secured to a tree, it appeared that she had just been caught. After dispatching her with my revolver and resetting my snare I noted that she was a pretty bear, heavy bodied and well furred, and was worth salvaging.

Quickly removing her entrails, I formed her into a pack by tying her left hind foot to her right front foot, then crossing and tying the remaining two feet. Thus her legs became my "pack straps". I then laid down on my back on the bear's body, slipping my arms through the crossed legs, and with some effort managed to slide first one set of legs over my right shoulder, and after much squirming and forcing, finally locked the remaining legs over my left shoulder. When I attempted to rise to my feet with my load I found that I couldn't get up! The bear's weight held me down like an anchor! With no tree close enough to grab to help lift myself, I was trapped in the bear's embrace!

Frantically, I tried to remove my arms from between the bear's legs, but they were forced onto my shoulders so tightly I couldn't slip them off. I tried to roll sideways in an effort to get my legs under me, but the bear's body extended too far on either side of me to allow it. I then realized that I was in a serious predicament if I couldn't free myself from the bear's carcass. If I expected anyone to find and assist me, I would be in for a long wait. I wasn't too anxious for anyone to see me in such an embarrassing situation anyway! I had visions of someone years later, stumbling onto my molding bones intermingled with the bear's skeleton, and that set me to struggling all the harder to free myself. After several minutes of jerking, flopping, and straining, I finally managed to change my position enough to allow me to use my hands to pull myself to a sitting position. I eventually was able to stand with my load and, nearly exhausted, staggered off down the trail with my bear, all the while wondering who had trapped whom? This experience taught me a valuable lesson - Always elevate a bear onto a stump or log before attempting to shoulder it as a pack!

April, May, and June are the months that bears peel trees, and those are also the months that they can be attracted to meat baited snares. By the end of June I had caught 16 bears, but as the wild berries began to ripen it was next to impossible to attract a bear to meat. Bears will eat meat when there is little else to be found, but when berries appear in abundance it is "forget the meat, pass the sugar!" From the end of June until early October I concentrated on unbaited trail and log sets in the bears' feeding grounds, and these were very effective. You just had to think like a bear and imagine where he would walk.

One of my trail set snares was placed in an old Promised Land cat road that had overgrown with brush to the point that it had now become a barely visible path. Bear tracks of all sizes in the mud showed it to be an established bear travel route between a mature stand of hemlock timber, and an old clear cut that had grown into a brush thicket jungle. I maintained this set each summer, and over the years it captured many bears for me. To keep the site from being torn up and destroyed by snared bears, I attached the foot snare's cable to a drag pole which allowed the bear to leave the area of capture and enter the adjacent timber or the brushy area in his efforts to escape. There he would become entangled and after I had dispatched him I could reset the snare in its original location with very little effort.

On one occasion my young daughter Jacky was with me when I checked this particular snare and found the snare cable and drag pole to be missing. Following the route the bear had taken was easy for he had ripped his way through bushes and rotten logs with the drag pole flailing behind him. We would find places where he had become temporarily entangled before freeing the drag pole from its impediment and moving on. His drag mark led us down to and across the old logging road and onto a huge pile of rotting logging debris at the timber's edge. Here the trail seemed to end until I spotted the snare's cable and drag pole lying on the logs and limbs of the debris pile. The cable was relaxed, and I assumed our bear had slipped the noose from his leg and escaped.

Jacky was standing by my side when I reached down to retrieve the snare cable. The moment I started to lift the cable and put pressure on it, I felt resistance on the other end and heard a loud snort as an enraged bear came tearing out from a dark recess under the log pile! I dropped the cable like it was red hot when the bear rushed at us, all bristled and blowing loudly through his nostrils. Grabbing my .357 magnum revolver I blasted four rounds into him in quick succession while Jacky stood paralyzed in fear at what was happening.

Even though all the bullets had entered the bear's head, I quickly eviscerated him, removed his heart and placed it, still beating, on a stump. Jacky was astounded at this until I explained to her that even though the bear appeared dead, his heart was still influenced by the high level of adrenaline that had surged to its coronary muscles, causing them to continue pumping blood through the bear's system. I had removed its heart quickly so the bear couldn't function and deal us any surprises, especially with Jacky on the scene. I think that was the last time she accompanied me on any of my snare checking forays!

I had some snares set on the middle fork of the Hoquiam River, on the ridges that sloped toward the east fork. After checking them on a late afternoon in June and finding them empty, I decided to stay in the area and still-hunt until dark. I settled myself on a log and watched my favorite canyon for several hours but when no bears appeared by dusk, I left my vigil and started the two-mile hike to my truck, hoping I might surprise a bear on the way before darkness set in. The smallest sounds of late-foraging woods creatures were magnified in the cloudy stillness that had settled over the woods. Hurrying along, I neared a hillside between the forks of the old dirt road that was overgrown with a dense thicket of vine maple, alder, and hemlock. Just inside the thicket, and ten feet from the road, stood two hemlocks, about eight inches in diameter and approximately 30 feet tall.

Suddenly, about 50 feet within the thicket in front of me, the stillness was broken by a horrendous uproar. It was a sound like no other wild animal that I had ever heard; a terrific growling and roaring that raised the hair on my neck and brought my rifle to the ready.

The bushes were crashing and cracking as the sounds of an apparent death battle drew nearer to me. The growling resembled that of a couple of mad dogs intent on killing each other.

At that moment, the top of one of the big hemlocks began to shake violently as if some large creature was making haste to climb it. I brought my rifle up, half expecting to see a bear appear in the upper limbs, but although the tree shook for several seconds, nothing revealed itself.

Just then the sound of the fight retreated the way it had come. After a few more seconds, all was quiet.

Rushing up the road and around a bend in case the creature should cross it and disclose its identity, I soon came to a dead-end on an old logging landing. Being determined to unravel this mystery, I entered the woods and slowly moved toward the battleground. Within 50 feet I found the soil and leaves churned up and an abundance of deer hair clinging to the vine maples.

Two does appeared and approached within 20 feet before withdrawing. Beside a log at the bottom of the large hemlock lay a dead fawn, warm and limp, with it's neck broken and one ear torn off. The doe's hoof-prints were indented in the log from striking at her attacker. About eight feet above the ground, on the tree's trunk, I found some of the fawn's hair, but I was baffled by the absence of claw marks on the tree that seemed to rule out a bear or a cougar.

What was it? I don't know. My wife believes in Bigfoot, Sasquatch, that abominable monster of the deep woods whose very name strikes fear to the faint-hearted. According to Indian legend it has roamed our coastal forests for centuries. I have never seen one.

In 57 years of stomping over the greater part of western Washington's wooded real estate, I have seen no evidence of the elusive Sasquatch. I'm not saying the Bigfoot isn't out there; I just haven't been fully convinced that it is. But if you want to believe in old Bigfoot, take it from here.

If I had to choose between the existence of UFOs and Sasquatches, I undoubtedly would decide in favor of the UFOs. That doesn't mean that I believe in the existence of extra-terrestrial space ships (sorry, E.T.), it simply means that I have seen some flying objects that I couldn't identify. Strangely enough, one such encounter occurred at almost the exact location as that of the mysteriously slain fawn, although 16 years earlier in 1968.

It was a dark, rainy April morning at 8:20 a.m., according to my diary, and I was near the end of a muddy logging road, on a ridge between the east fork and the middle fork of the Hoquiam River. Suddenly, far off in the direction of the east fork and well above the horizon, I saw a dark object that I couldn't identify with the naked eye hovering in the grey, rainy sky.

Quickly focusing my binoculars, I was surprised to see that it was some sort of a round object with a protuberance on one side, shaped very much like a Christmas tree ball. It was moving through the air at approximately 40mph, rotating as it came, and losing altitude. I lowered my binoculars as it dropped below the treeline and moved up the canyon that lay below the ridge that I was on. As it passed within 600 yards of me, I tried to determine the size through the dark, driving rain and guessed its diameter at less than four feet.

Just when I thought it was going to crash in the timber at the edge of the clear cut, it unexpectedly changed direction, made a left turn, and headed in my direction up a side canyon about 1000 feet in front of me. It appeared to be gaining speed as it dropped below a ridge that lay between us and disappeared from sight. Since it was well below the main ridgeline when I last saw it, I assumed that it had crashed into the thicket of 15-year-old- dog-hair hemlocks that grew in the draw.

Hurrying down a side road, I gazed wide-eyed into the draw, expecting to see the object, but to my surprise it was nowhere in sight. I searched the thicket for two hours, hoping to find the thing and solve the mystery. I found nothing. The object had disappeared as silently and mysteriously as it had come.

Yes, Virginia, there are UFOs. I have seen one. While to me it was unidentifiable, flying, and definitely and object, to someone more learned it may have been readily recognized as a weather balloon. I'm glad I can't explain it; it's fun to leave something to the imagination!

As the summer wore on, my snares continued to produce. I had made a trail set in an old cat-road near the Indian reservation boundary at a spot where I repeatedly saw the tracks of a medium-sized bear. The branches of a big, limby fir hung over the trail and from these limbs I hung a couple pieces of putrid beaver meat for bait. Placing limbs and branches on either side of my set to block off the trail, I left no place for the bear to pass except over my snare. Thick salal brush grew up to the edge of the trail on both sides and, to me, the path that led over the snare looked like the only logical place for a bear to travel.

The first time I checked this snare I found that I was dealing with a bear that was either extra smart, or just plain lucky. His tracks in the mud revealed that when he approached within three feet of my snare, he wallowed his way into the salal thicket, climbed the tree, and stole the bait, and departed through the thicket, making a complete detour around my snare. I replaced the bait and on two subsequent visits I found that he had repeated the same tactics as before, stolen the bait, and avoided my set.

I was determined to capture this fellow and knew I had to devise a way to lure him through the opening in the trail where my snare lay waiting. After digging a small hole in the trail about 12 inches from my snare, I placed an egg-sized chunk of beaver meat in the hole and covered it with dirt except for a very small bit that protruded above the surface. Then, on the other side of the snare, I repeated the process. On my next trip to the snare I found that I had captured my bear, a subadult male. He had sniffed out the buried bait, dug it up, and devoured the first piece, then his nose told him "Hey, there's another piece buried over there!" One step in that direction and the snare snapped around his leg.

I caught two more bears that day; one an adult female and the other a male yearling. I dragged all three of the bears from the woods, hauled them home and within 40 minutes had them skinned. I always had a waiting list of folks desiring bear meat and it was no problem to dispose of the carcasses.

In August, I hiked a mile on an old grade that led into the headwaters of the Wishkah. A dense thicket of cascara grew there that drew bears from miles around to gorge and fatten on the ripening berries. I made a couple of log sets, using no bait, and on a subsequent visit to my snares three days later, found a large and very fat female bear in one of them. I also saw the tracks of a larger bear in the area and decided to move one of the log sets to a nearby trail that the bear was frequenting. I found an ideal spot where the trail was narrowed by a broken bush and after placing the snare to my satisfaction, I dressed out my bear and started the long drag back to my truck. After logging was completed on the upper Wishkah drainage in the early 1950s, the steel and crossties had been picked up and the grade abandoned. Where the grade crossed the narrow but deep Middle Creek canyon, a huge earthen fill had been placed, but beavers had plugged its culvert in the mid-sixties, and the fill had been washed away. Dragging my bear down in the gorge was easy enough, but getting it up the other side was something else. It was hard to get firm footing and I only gained about six inches with each tug. (When dragging bears, I always turn them onto their back and poke a hay hook between their lower jaws.)

I arrived at my truck tired and sweaty, but seeing it was a fine evening for a still-hunt, I loaded my bear and headed for old Camp 3. I hunted from canyon to canyon until 8pm and although I saw 10 cow elk, 2 bull elk with nice racks, 2 rabbits, 6 grouse, 4 mallards, 1 bobcat, beaver, and a red-tailed hawk, I saw no bears.

Some weeks went by and bear activity seemed to have moved up-river from Middle Creek to the Larson Creek cascara thickets. Hiking into my trail set on Middle Creek with the intention of removing it for the season, I was surprised to find it held a big male cougar, freshly caught, and not very happy about the circumstances he now found himself in. Even though it was legal to take him, I didn't want to kill him. Hiking the mile back to my truck, I drove 20 miles to the Humptulips store and phoned my friend Rich Poelker, a wildlife biologist with the Department of Wildlife. Rich agreed to make the 100-plus mile drive from his home, bring his chemical-immobilization equipment, and go with me to release the big cat.

When Rich arrived at Humptulips, we returned to the hills, hiked back to the snared cougar, and proceeded to tranquilize and release it. The cat was in his prime; 140 pounds and seven feet, seven inches, from nose to tip of tail. After ear tagging him and placing an identification collar on him, we started back to my truck as darkness fell.

Two days later I returned to the scene to make sure the cougar had revived without complications and found his tracks heading west, toward Cougar Mountain. (Incidentally, this cougar was killed two and a half months later by a hound-hunter, eight miles north of Middle Creek, between the upper east and west forks of Humptulips river.)

When I ceased my bear hunting activities in early October, I had captured 43 bears, bringing my total up to 913. Up until this time my employment had been April through mid-October; the termination date coinciding each year with the opening day of deer season, which necessitated the removal of my snares from the woods. I passed the rainy fall and winter months with deer and elk hunting and beaver trapping until mid-January 1975. On that date my WFPA supervisor Bob Matthews offered me year round employment. My new position would be to serve as supervisor of WFPA's animal damage control service. I would continue to hunt and snare bears as well as coordinate the activities of five control hunters whose combined area of operations covered all of western Washington. I would also be required to make aerial survey flights each year over all this area to document concentrations of bear damage and use this data to set boundaries for the spring damage bear hunt units. (From the air, trees that had been girdled or damaged by bears during the previous years were easy to spot; the girdled trees appeared bright red and the partially girdled trees looked yellowish from stress.) It would also be my duty to draw, print, and distribute maps of the spring hunt units; attend game department and commission meetings; give slide-show presentations at meetings, sportsman's clubs, social clubs, schools, and colleges to educate the public about bear damage and our control objectives.

I could see that actual bear hunting or snaring activities would now become a lesser part of my job, but the prospect of year-round employment, vacation pay, and other benefits sure sounded good after 15 years of six-months-per-year work. I accepted his proposal and entered into my new assignment with great enthusiasm.

By the end of March I had completed the chore of drafting the spring hunt unit maps and had them printed and distributed. Port Blakely Mill Co. had been experiencing bear damage on their Kitsap Tree Farm near Bremerton, and it had increased in intensity to the point that control was necessary. This tree farm lay adjacent to the Bremerton municipal watershed lands where public entry was prohibited. As a consequence the bear population in this "sanctuary" was excessive, with the overflow filtering out through Port Blakely's holdings. And over-flight of the area showed me thousands of red trees, dead trees, and dying trees that had been ravaged by bears. After spending a day inspecting the area with the tree farm's forester, it was agreed that I should snare the area adjacent to the city lands.

At one spot, the forester said he had found a big nest on the ground and wondered what had made it. From his description I was sure that he had found a bears "nest". They often times will build a nest close to the base of a big limbed tree immediately after emerging from their winter den and utilize it while their metabolism returns to normal after their winter's sleep. The nests that I have found were generally located on a well-drained point above a stream. They will leave the nest to drink but will often snooze in their nest for a week before beginning to forage for food.

The forester led me up the ridge, and as we neared the nest we passed the upturned roots of a windfall tree. Glancing at it, I saw a hole leading under the root wad and immediately recognized it as the bear's winter den.

"Here's his den, Ed," I remarked. Ed turned and with a look of alarm on his face said "Do you mean I walked right by his den when I located this nest?"

The nest looked like a huge robin's next and was made from sword ferns, salal, hemlock and cedar branches, and other small bushes. It looked very comfortable, much more so than the cramped hole under the tree roots.

I set about placing my snares in early April, and on April 18th caught the first two bears of the year—an adult sow and a yearling, both on the Kitsap tree farm. The following week I captured three bears in the Promised Land.

I was impressed by the size of the bears I captured at Kitsap; even the females were large when compared to the coastal Promised Land bears. I took eleven bears from the Kitsap tree farm that summer—four males and seven females. Three of the males were adults six to ten years old and their weights were 367, 250, and 300 pounds. None of them had any body fat, yet the hide from the largest boar weighed 52 pounds.

One day while checking my snares at Kitsap I found a 40-year-old fir tree, freshly peeled by a bear, with its exposed sapwood shining white from top to bottom. Strips of bark that had been removed by the bear were draped over the tree's limbs like tassels. Three hundred yards up the road I found the culprit, a large female bear, tied up in my snare. She was freshly caught and full of energy which was plainly evident as she raged and tugged at the cable securing her front foot. After dispatching her with my revolver, I set about removing her entrails and found her stomach packed with tree cambium from her morning feeding. Being the bear's mating season, I wasn't surprised when I found her to be estrous. After rebuilding my snare setting and loading my bear, I continued on my route.

Three days later I returned and upon approaching this same snare I could see from a distance that I had caught something. The snare setting was a baited "cubby" set, using a tall stump as backing, making it necessary for a bear to step in the snare loop if he wanted to get to the meat bait.

The set was completely destroyed and the area around it torn up and leveled to the bare ground. Realizing that my snare had been anchored solidly to a large standing alder tree and seeing no bear at the scene, it was evident that my prisoner had escaped. When I reached the snare I found the tracks of a huge bear in the soft dirt and my eyes nearly popped out of my head when I saw that this behemoth of a bear had snapped the 3/16" snare cable! He had broken the cable between the swivel and the tree and had escaped with the snare "bracelet" around his foreleg! I followed his departure route but soon lost his trail in the dense salal thickets. It was hard for me to fathom how he could snap the cable without snapping his leg in the process. He would eventually be able to loosen the locking angle-slide that held the snare to his wrist by worrying it with his teeth. Apparently he had been traveling with the estrous female bear that I had caught in the same snare three days earlier.

In mid-May I hiked a mile into the Bear Creek drainage north of Aberdeen to check out a report of fresh bear damage. I had carried a snare and some bait with me and when I discovered newly peeled hemlocks and alders on a hillside above the creek, lots of skunk cabbage dug up in the creek bottom, and found the bear's freshly-used bed, I set about placing the snare. I knew that if I caught the bear it would be a real chore to get it out of the canyon, but I decided to figure that out when the time came.

A few days later, on my regular snare route in the Promised Land area, I found eight snares tripped by coyotes, two tripped by bears, and one snare on the middle fork of the Hoquiam River holding a sub-adult bear. I brought the bear out and gave it to a friend that lived along my travel route. I saved the Bear Creek snare until last, and to be on the safe side, carried a bait with me. On reaching the snare, I found that the bear had stolen the bait and tripped the snare without getting caught. After rebaiting and resetting the snare I hiked back to my truck, the round-trip taking two hours.

My friend Jim Cowan accompanied me on my next hike in to check this set, and we arrived apparently only minutes after the bear had stepped into my snare. The snare cable was secured to a drag pole which the bear had pulled down the hill to the creek. On hearing our approach, the bear crashed off through the dense salmonberry bushes and skunk cabbage at full speed with the big drag flailing behind him and adding to the racket. We could see the bushes swishing crazily and hear the commotion and even though we couldn't see the bear we knew we had snagged a big one. Hearts pounding in the excitement, we plowed through the swampy thicket in hot pursuit. Then, just ahead of us, we heard a tremendous splash as the bear dived into a beaver pond. We reached the pond just as the snare's drag pole became entangled in some bushy debris. The bear snorted and flopped and water flew in all directions as he tried to gain release. Not wanting the bear to get any farther down the canyon and make our job of retrieval more difficult than it already was, I managed a headshot with my .357 revolver that put an end to the commotion. Now the work began. Dragging the bear out of the pond and onto dry land, we removed his entrails and dragged him up the creek to the trail. The "trail" in reality was an overgrown natural gas pipeline right of way, and the first half-mile up from the creek was extremely steep and muddy. The bear was a 200 pound male and the thought of dragging him up that muddy hill didn't appeal to me at all. Hiking out to the road, I drove my pickup to the top of the gas-line hill and then, with not a little trepidation, I pointed it's nose down the steep, greasy-muddy hill and soon reached the creek. After loading the bear, we attempted to drive back up the hill, but even with 4-wheel drive we gained only a few yards. We had to use the truck's winch and 4-wheel drive the full half-mile to the top of the ridge and then, with a sigh of relief, made our way down the other side to the road. I gave this bear to Jim, feeling he had well earned it!

Later that season, returning from a bear damage survey in the Forks area, I decided to leave the highway and travel the old logging grade through the Promised Land. It was mid-morning of a very rainy day that showed no sign of improving. I left the highway in the Cook Creek area and, traveling slowly in second gear, had gone about two miles when I saw a bear about a half-mile ahead of me walking down a long, straight stretch of the old grade. Seeing that he was walking away from me, I eased my truck ahead, hoping to close the gap between us. So far, the noisy downpour of rain had muffled the sound of my approach, but when only 500 yards separated us, the bear stopped, turned sideways, and looked in my direction. I immediately turned off the ignition and waited for his next move. With the wind in my favor, the bear turned and resumed his walk down the road. Grabbing my rifle, I eased out of my truck and ran down the road, cramming shells into the magazine as I went. Now, a man has to run just to keep up with a walking bear, and to gain ground on this one I had to give it all I had. I was starting to puff from this sudden exertion and knowing this wasn't going to help my aim, I stopped within 300 yards of the bear, squatted in the road, and took aim just as he turned to enter the brush. When the gun roared, the bear flounced and flopped in and out of the brush, his hind leg broken above the foot. Jumping to my feet, I ran 75 yards closer, shot again, and broke his neck, laying him dead in the road. This was very handy and so I drove my truck forward, dressed out the bear where he lay, loaded him, washed my hands in a puddle, and continued on my way. The bear, a 125 sub-adult male, was fat and well furred.

In mid-August of that year I ceased my hunting and snaring for the season with 35 bears to my credit, and concentrated on my preparations for next season's control activities. Aerial surveys had to be conducted, damage reports collected from all the participating forest land owners, recommendations made for spring hunt unit boundary revisions, maps to be drawn and updated, reports from my professional hunters to be analyzed, and meetings - lots of meetings. By year's end, I could see that managing and supervising the bear control program was taking more and more of my time and I needed to find another hunter to take over my hunting and snaring responsibilities. This would be no easy task, for although there were plenty of hunters eager to have the job, very few would qualify. First, in order to minimize our snaring activities, I needed to locate a hound-hunter. Not just any hound-hunter, but a woods savvy one with a pack of well-trained dogs that could perform like a bear-catching machine. Secondly, the hunter needed to be a man of good reputation and integrity since credibility was a prerequisite if we were to have a sound working relationship with the Department of Wildlife. Thirdly, would such a man be willing to accept April though October employment?

I found such a man in Jess Caswell, a 31-year-old carpenter-construction foreman living in Newport, Washington. Jess was an accomplished carpenter, but his first love was his pack of well-trained hounds. Jess was an excellent dog trainer who could bring out the very best in a dog, sometimes taking a hound deemed worthless and turning it into a top-notch dog. After a day in the woods with Jess I was convinced that he was the man for the job. Consequently, in mid-January of 1976

I informed him that he could begin work in April, a decision that left us both pleased.

The old bear hunter, Bill Hulet, even though 14 years retired, still maintained a deep interest in the bear control program and hardly a day passed when he didn't phone me or stop by for an update. When I informed him that I was accepting the job of supervisor he was shocked and blurted out "Who's gonna take your bear huntin' job?" When I assured him that I had found a good replacement, and a hound-hunter at that, Bill seemed pleased. After all, hounds were his first love, too! A few days later, on January 15th, Bill suffered a stroke and on January the 20th he had two more, leaving him hospitalized, paralyzed on his right side and unable to speak. I went up to see him at the hospital that evening and found him alone and awake in his room. I hated to see the old timber beast in this condition, and told him so. His eyes met mine intently as I told him how much his advice and guidance had meant to me in my first years on the bear hunting job and how he had been like a dad to me. I told him he was tough and he would beat this thing, but before I could say more he reached up with his good arm and pulled me down close to him in a one-armed bear hug. Then he squeezed my hand, looking me directly in the eye, as if saying goodbye. I could tell he desperately wanted to talk and tell me something, but was unable. I'm sure he knew he wasn't going to win this one.

I made several more visits to Bill's room, but he had slipped into a coma and was listed in critical condition. After church on February 8th, my wife and I bought a pretty potted plant and took it to Bill's hospital room. His bed was by the window, but being a gray, rainy day, not much light filtered in. Bill looked terrible, but when we reached his bedside we were surprised to see his eyes were open and focused on us. He had come out of his two-week coma! I could tell he recognized us.

Now when Bill would stop at our house to visit, he had three subjects to discourse upon; bear hunting, politics, and religion - and in that order. He loved to bring up something that would get Velma expounding on Christian ethics and theistics. Once he got her going, he would chuckle, put on his hat, and say "See you in church!" as he headed for the door. Needless to say, we never saw him there.

But on this dreary February day Bill had no hat to put on, and he sure wasn't able to escape out the door. It wasn't surprising then, that he felt comfortable as he held Velma's hand and looked her in the eye when she spoke to him. She told him that we wanted to see him again someday on the "other side of the wall." Even though he couldn't talk, she asked him to pray in his heart as she prayed with him. Bill never took his eyes off her as she prayed, and when she had finished, he gave her hand a tight squeeze.

A short while later, he lapsed into another coma and didn't revive. He died on February 15th, at age 78.

Chapter 2

The Transition

After a long rainy spell, April arrived with blue skies and sunshine and I set about acquainting my new hunter with his control area which encompassed Grays Harbor, Jefferson, Mason and Kitsap counties. Since Jess was unfamiliar with most of the area I was glad to assist him in identifying bear crossings and traditional bear-damage hot-spots, just as Bill Hulet had done for me 17 years previous. This also gave me an excuse to participate in his hound-hunting and snaring activities, to be sure that tree-damage in "my" old area would continue to be kept at a tolerable level.

A new game department policy required that as many of the bears taken on control hunts as possible be brought out of the woods, the meat distributed to non-profit organizations (Boy Scouts, jails, prisons, missions, etc.) and the hides retained for sale at auction by the Department of Wildlife. Generally, this was done easily enough with the carcasses of snared bears, but removing hound-hunted bears was a different story.

More often than not these bears were treed in remote, roadless areas and necessitated much time and hard labor to retrieve them. On one of my first hunts with Jess his hounds started a bear in the Joe Creek area of the Promised Land and treed it after only a thirty-minute chase. Even so, the tree the bear decided to climb was far from the road and in a jungle of salal and wind-fall hemlocks that made dragging the bear an impossibility. In the early days of the control program the bear would have been opened up and as much of it fed to the dogs as they could consume. On this hunt it was necessary to cut the bear in half and, each of us loaded with all we could carry, struggle through the downed trees and towards the road.

On a subsequent hunt in the same area, Jess's strike dog, Wanda, started a bear off a freshly-peeled cedar tree along an old, brushy grade near Joe Creek. This bear lined out across Joe Creek and the sound of the chase faded away toward old Camp Six.

As we drove north, the sounds of the chase could faintly be heard, always in the distance and in an area of no roads near the tribal land boundary. This went on for five hours until we lost the dogs completely. While Jess stayed in the area where we had last heard the dogs baying, I returned to Joe Creek where the chase had started and had just arrived there when I heard a hound bawling as it bayed the bear. It was Cora, who had lost out on the chase at its start and was still in that area (with one other hound) when the bear decided to return, far ahead of the main pack. Cora was really putting pressure on the bear, since she was still fresh. I ran down the old grade, keeping parallel to the chase for a half-mile until the baying of the hounds told me the bear had either stopped to fight or had treed. The going was fairly easy under the hemlock timber and I found the bear treed about 40 feet up on the second limb of a young hemlock. When he saw me he chopped his jaws and "blew" and I could tell he was very unhappy after his five-hour run through the almost impenetrable boondocks. The tree being too small for him to climb higher, he swung around its trunk and started down, intending to jump clear of the dogs and escape. Finding him in the sights of my .270, a bullet to the head ended the chase. After opening the bear and feeding the liver to the dogs, I was able to drag the bear to the trail by myself.

One day in early June, Jess and I took the hounds for a hunt in the brushy Aloha area, about a mile inland from the beach. The dogs struck a bear immediately, red-hot, and the chase was on. Ten years previous, this had been one of my favorite "still-hunting" areas but the reproduction had now reached 17 years of age and the thick growth of fir and hemlock now melded into a continuous sea of green. The young timber had recently been pre-commercially thinned and a thick growth of salal and evergreen huckleberry now grew up through the downed trees. This made tough going for man or beast and put the dogs at a disadvantage on a bear chase. The bear could walk on top of the rotting jumble of felled trees while the dogs had to fight their way through it.

The hounds couldn't crowd the bear enough to make him "tree" or leave the reprod and after three hours of listening to the chase, I plunged into the thicket to help the dogs. I immediately began seeing lots of hemlock and cedar trees, freshly peeled by bears. Crashing and thrashing through the jungly mess, I finally caught up with the dogs, who had the bear bayed up in a thicket of huckleberry and salal bushes higher than my head. I was within ten feet of the dogs and the bear, but the vegetation was so dense I couldn't see the bear. Scenting my presence, the bear broke and ran and in short order he climbed a huge cedar-snag den tree that stood 150 feet tall. I had just reached the snag, which was located at the edge of a 50-year-old stand of hemlock timber when Jess arrived.

While Jess tied the dogs back away from the snag, I circled it, looking for the bear. There was a big hole at the snag's bottom that led into its hollow mid-section and another hole about thirty feet up. Figuring the bear must be inside the snag, I beat on the side of the tree with a short club. This stunt often would cause a bear to vacate a snag, for the noise must have compared to being inside a drum, but in this case, no bear appeared. I then crawled in the den hole at the snag's bottom and using a pole, probed the cavities under its roots, but got no response. Turning over and laying on my back I could see the daylight all the way to the top of the snag's hollow interior. Still no bear! This puzzled me. Jess and I circled the snag several times, trying to get a clear view of its top through the limbs of the hemlock that crowded it. We were just about to untie the hounds and abandon the snag when I spotted the bear's head peeking over a whitened limb at the very top of the snag. The limb was sprouting vegetation from the duff that had accumulated on it over the years and served to conceal the bear's body. Taking aim at its head, which was the only target I had, I knocked the bear from his lofty perch. This bear proved to be a yearling female around 60 pounds, and when we surveyed the bushy terrain we would have to travel, we were glad it was no bigger.

On July first of that year the general bear season opened and my supervisor, Bob Matthews, indicated that he would like to bring his son Mark and some friends down for a bear hunt. With the regular season being open, this meant we could hunt in areas other than the control units if we desired. Consequently, we decided on a hunt in the Donovan-Corkery area between the Wishkah and Wynoochee rivers. This area was brushy but much easier to hunt than the dense jungles in the Promised Land, a decision Bob and his friends were to appreciate before their adventure was over.

Around 9 a.m. on the appointed day, Bob and his crew arrived. My Maryland friend, Homer Myers, was visiting me and along with Jess and I our gang now numbered eight. In two vehicles, we headed for the hunt, and around noon Jess's strike dog Wanda struck bear scent. The chase was on and headed west into a roadless area. The sounds of the chase soon faded over the first ridge, and then it was anybody's guess where they might go. Jess headed north, up the grade, taking some of Bob's gang with him. Homer and I stayed near where the chase had started and soon heard the hounds' voices coming our way. Again the chase turned, and the baying grew fainter until its music was drowned out by the noisy spatter of raindrops on the underbrush. After contacting Jess on the C-B radio, Homer and I dived into the wet bracken ferns and salal and headed across country in the direction the chase had gone. The rain now became a downpour, making it very hard to listen for the hounds. Soon we heard the hounds in a canyon ahead of us, and their excited bawling told us they had the bear "bayed up" or stopped on the ground. By now we were soaked to the skin but the excited barking just ahead of us sent us crashing through the wet salal with reckless abandon. Just as we were nearing the fight, the bear broke and ran and the hounds' voices faded over the next ridge. Homer and I kept running in the general direction of the chase and when we topped the ridge it was apparent that the bear had treed about a quarter mile ahead of us. We hurried to the tree, which was a sizeable fir with bracken ferns growing six feet tall around its lower limbs. Climbing on a tall old-growth fir stump I was able to see the bear, hanging onto the tree's trunk, about 25 feet up. The bear spotted my movement, and started backing down the tree, intending to vacate his perch and run. It was a large adult bear and I hoped to keep him up the tree until our companions arrived, so I leaped from my stump, pushed my way through the ferns and limbs and made my way under the tree. The bear was coming down the tree, and though I yelled at him in hopes of changing his mind, he kept coming. The rain still came down in torrents and my glasses and rifle scope were wet and fogged, but by now the bear was so close I fired point-blank and the bullet struck him between the eyes. He fell the last eight feet and landed with a thud among the bawling hounds. In time, Jess steered the rest of the crew to the tree and we were glad for our numbers when it came to carrying the meat from the woods.

 A couple of weeks later we took the hounds for a hunt on upper Black Creek, a tributary of the Wynoochee. This was an area that had a history of tree damage and the appearance of freshly peeled firs indicated the current year was to be no exception. Near the end of a brushy cat road Wanda struck, the hounds were released and we grinned in anticipation as the canyon echoed with the noisy uproar of their departure on the chase. After a few minutes it became apparent that we had a split race; two of the hounds had crossed Black Creek and were already barking "treed" on the opposite hill while the rest of the pack were just fading from our hearing and heading in the opposite direction.

 Splashing across the shallow creek, we climbed the hill and headed toward the sound of the treeing hounds. Hearing our approach, the dogs really turned up the volume. The tree was a medium-sized, sparsely-limbed hemlock and at first glance it became apparent that no bear was up it. A closer look revealed a big bobcat crouched on a limb near the tree's trunk, its hackles raised and a low rumbling emanating from its voice box. Leashing the two hounds, we led them from the tree and headed back across the creek, leaving the bobcat up the tree to puzzle over his unexpected reprieve. Nearing our vehicles, we began hearing the main pack barking treed a short distance down the creek. We released the leashed dogs and they raced off to join their compadres at the tree, with Jess and I following close behind. We found all the dogs under a limby fir tree that stood in a large opening, apart from the other trees. Scattered among it's limbs and in plain view of the dogs were three bears; a sow and her young. These three were not as lucky as the bobcat and we left the woods with the entire bear family stowed in our trucks. It had been determined that female bears and their offspring inflict the heaviest concentrations of bear damage to young tree plantations since their home range encompasses only 3 to 6 square miles. Bears live to be thirty years old and it is easy to see how a tree plantation could be heavily damaged over the years by these resident bears. Killing cubs wasn't a fun part of the job, but it was required if we hoped to control bear damage by controlling bear populations.

After several more successful hound-hunts, Jess and I loaded eight of his dogs and drove directly to the Camp 3 area on the headwaters of the Wishkah. All the old-growth timber had been logged, the last of it taken out in the early 1960s. Much of the area from the earliest logging efforts had been aerial seeded and the hills were reforested with 30-year-old trees. The later logging areas had been hand-planted to Douglas fir and these trees were now 16 years old and prime targets for tree peeling bears. The plantations on Parker Creek were being hit especially hard and that is where Jess and I headed on this warm July morning. Within thirty minutes the dogs struck red-hot scent in the Parker Creek canyon and went roaring off on the track like a room-full of first graders at recess time. Almost immediately the dogs had the bear "jumped" and the sound of the chase moved off into the draws on the far side of the canyon.

Just as the bawling of the hounds was drifting into the distance, the chase split; three dogs went one direction and five continued in the original direction until they topped various ridges and their voices could no longer be heard. At this point we had to make a decision; do we drive several miles around to reach the area where they were headed or do we stay put in case the chase turns and heads back toward the point of beginning?

Jess opted to stay in the canyon while I drove several miles around to the divide between Parker Creek and the west branch of the Wishkah. An old road ran a mile down this divide (which we called Windy Pass) and ended, and I drove down it, stopping frequently to listen for the hounds. Near the end of the old grade I began to hear the three hounds, still running and on the Parker Creek side of the divide. Another few minutes and their voices changed to the familiar "treed" bark. I called Jess on my C-B radio and waited on the ridge until he arrived. We had just reached the dogs, who were barking up a 30-year-old hemlock, when the bear detected our approach and started backing down the tree's trunk. Before he could vacate the tree I shot and he tumbled down to the excited hounds who set about tugging and pulling on his hapless carcass. This bear was a male and being the mating season we assumed that the other dogs were after a female. We had almost reached our vehicles when we heard the voices of the other 5 hounds, barking "treed" far down in the timber on the West Branch Wishkah side of the divide.

Hurrying down to the end of our road we fought our way along an overgrown skid trail that led around the mountain until we reached a point where we could hear the dogs far below us in some big timber. Leaving the trail we headed downhill, the sound of the hounds growing louder, until we spotted them bouncing around the base of a solitary old-growth hemlock. The tree was around 160 feet tall, growing in a stand of 40-year-old trees. About 125 feet up was a large sucker-limb and the bear had chosen this for her perch. Jess tied the dogs back so the falling bear wouldn't squish them and when all were secured I took aim at her head and put a .270 bullet between her eyes. I was still using my old .270 Remington, Model 721, and a 2½ power Lyman-Alaskan scope equipped with a tiny Lee dot. This made for accurate shooting at small targets, near or far.

The bear was a female, as suspected, and in heat. She was one of the smallest adult female bears I had ever seen, weighing only 75 pounds. When we finally reached our vehicles we took the dogs to the creek for a drink and then headed home with our spoils. The day had turned rainy and the wet bushes had us soaked to the hide and the thought of dry clothes and a warm meal spurred us on our way.

We made five more hunts during the next ten days and treed eight bears and a bobcat. I was really impressed with the proficiency of Jess's hounds as well as with their master. I was sure I had made the right choice in selecting him for the job.

On a wet morning in mid-August we took the dogs back to the Camp 3 area for another hunt and started a bear on a ridge between Parker Creek and the main Wishkah River. The bear headed down the river almost to the mouth of Parker Creek, then climbed the ridge and dropped into the Parker Creek canyon. Crossing the creek, the chase headed in the direction of Windy Pass. As quickly as we could we made the long drive around and reached the end of Windy Pass road just as the dogs crossed the divide and dropped into the West Branch Wishkah County. This put the bear in the same block of timber where I had shot the little female bear from the old-growth hemlock a month previous. Jess and I headed down the old skid trail on foot until we heard the dogs again. They had the bear at bay so we ran down through the timber that was thick with underbrush, hoping to shoot the bear on the ground. Just then the bear broke free from his tormentors and headed uphill directly toward us. We squatted where we were but though the bear came so close to us that we could hear him panting, we couldn't see him because of the thick undergrowth.

The bear had been walking, bristled and defiant, just ahead of the snapping dogs but when he suddenly caught our scent he raced off back down through the timber at full bore. After a half-mile run, he slowed to a walk and the dogs' voices now rose to a roar as they followed him. We ran through the timber, following the chase, and after a bit we separated, hoping that one of us could get close enough for a shot. Jess went to the right, I to the left. The timber was more devoid of underbrush at this point and after a short run I heard and saw the dogs heading toward me. Then I saw the bear walk through an opening just ahead of the dogs, but I couldn't get a clear shot. The next time I saw the bear he came from behind an upturned root wad, and just as his head disappeared behind a big hemlock I got a bead on his shoulder area and squeezed the trigger. At the sound of the shot both the bear and the dogs disappeared behind the tree.

Jumping over a small log, I ran to the tree where I had last seen the bear, expecting to find him dead, but I received a surprise when the bear got to his feet and came tearing down the hill at me. When he was barely 8 feet from me, I pointed my rifle at his brisket and shot, with no time to aim. The bear rolled up into a stiff ball and his speed carried him on down, right at me. I ran and jumped clear and, just as the dogs nailed him, I stuck the rifle in his ribs and gave him another shot.

After the excitement I discovered that my first shot at the walking bear had grazed the tree, breaking up the bullet before it hit the bear. Although it knocked the bear down, he was only stunned. This was a close call and got my adrenaline going much more than shooting a bear out of a tree! The bear was an adult male, the kind that loathes climbing trees, and will walk and fight the hounds for hours. On this kind of bear you have to go into the woods and help your dogs if you intend to hang his hide on your wall.

When Jess's seasonal employment was terminated in September he loaded up his hounds and returned to his Newport, Washington home. He had surpassed all my expectations as a hunter, as well as a friend. His tally for the summer was 67 bears; 17 of which were taken in snares and 50 by hound-hunting. I had shot 20 of the hound-hunted bears and had enjoyed the summer immensely.

In early October I was visited by my brother's boy, Butch, and his co-worker

Jim, from Michigan. They had been sent to Seattle on an auditing assignment by their employers and it offered them an opportunity for a weekend visit to Aberdeen. On the morning of October 2nd, a typical rainy-foggy fall day, we set out in my Blazer for a combined ruffed-grouse and chanterelle mushroom hunt. My Yelm friend, Art Weller, arrived just in time to accompany us. After checking a few bear snares and shooting three grouse I decided that we should take a drive through the Promised Land country. Arriving there in mid-afternoon I drove slowly down the 8000 line to the old Elk Creek grade. The drizzly rain had stopped and the sun had appeared, hanging low in the south and casting long shadows. It had the feel of a perfect afternoon for game to be moving. After traveling in low gear about a mile down the old grade I parked the Blazer at the intersection of an old cat road and suggested to Butch and Jim that we take a walk down it. Art, who had been experiencing some heart problems, opted to wait by the vehicle.

I had brought my .270, as well as my shotgun, and we carried both of these as we walked along the primitive trail; the boys watching for grouse and I looking for bear sign. We had just rounded a bend in the trail when we met a bear, face to face at twenty feet, walking toward us. I got the .270 to my shoulder but before I could get a shot off, the bear dived into the dense underbrush to our right. Whispering to the boys to "Wait here!" I ran back down the trail at full bore, and as I passed Art at the Blazer I said, "Bear!" and kept running, turning to the left when I reached the main grade. I was playing a hunch although I was sure my friends were befuddled to see me running in the opposite direction that the bear had gone. But I knew something that they didn't; about one-quarter mile down the grade from where the Blazer was parked was an established bear crossing. No path or trail was visible there to mark it as a crossing, but I had seen several bears in the grade at that point over the years and also had captured some there in snares.

The bear that we startled was walking toward the old grade, and even though he had turned into the brush I felt that he would continue on his original direction once he found we weren't pursuing him. Running at full speed down the grade, I rounded a curve in the road just in time to see the bear bound onto the grade, 150 yards away, and on the crossing. I started to shoot, but he turned his rump to me as he ran between two big water puddles in the road. When he turned broadside to go into the brush, I fired, hitting him in the brain, and dropping him dead in his tracks.

Hearing the shot, the fellows brought the Blazer down the grade and Jim looked dumbfounded when he asked "How did you know that bear was going to come here?" I grinned and told him that I and the bear had this all planned ahead of time.

After gutting and loading the bear, we continued on down the grade to its end and were on our way back when I spotted another bear running across the grade.

This one headed for the tribal lands off to our right and escaped with his coat intact.

Near the end of October, Art Weller again visited me and we set out for the Palix River area in the Pacific County to locate some plantations that had been damaged by bears. After completing my work, we drove to Raymond and on up the Mill Creek road. I knew of a logging clear cut behind Granny King's old homestead and planned to spend the balance of the day deer hunting there. Art waited on the landings while I walked a mile through the canyon, but though I saw lots of deer sign and beds, I saw no deer. I did find a lot of bear sign including some day beds just inside the timber at the clear cut's edge.

When I reached the landing where Art was waiting, I suggested that we wait there and maybe get a shot at the bear. The bear's tracks and trails led me to think it had been visiting an apple tree at Granny King's. It was now 5:50pm, and I told Art the bear would probably show itself around 6pm.

My suggestion was almost prophetic, for I had hardly spoken the words when I looked off to my right about 500 yards and saw the bear walk over the point of a hill! I ran up the road and got 50 yards closer, sat down, rested my rifle over my knees and squeezed the trigger. At the rifle's report, the bear took off into the brush and disappeared. I waited a few moments and, seeing no more of the bear, I hiked across the canyon and climbed the ridge to the spot where I had last seen it. Daylight was fast fading when I reached the point and found the bear, a large female, lying dead in a downed treetop. She was five feet in length, nose to tail, and very fat. I decided it would be easier, though farther, to drag her down hill to the county road, so I yelled to Art to take the Blazer and meet me down there. I didn't open the bear up because I knew the cavity would get filthy while dragging her through the thickets in the dark. Rolling the bear where I could and dragging her through the tough places, I was nearing the road when it became so dark I could see neither the bear nor the route to take. Art made his way to me and brought my hay hook, which made the drag much easier. Gutting the bear near the road, we got her loaded and headed for home.

This pretty much ended my bear hunting for the year, and after killing a nice buck and an elk, I hung up my rifle and kept busy finalizing my recommendations for the next year's spring damage bear season.

Chapter 3

CANYON RIVER

THE WINTER DRAGGED ON, AND AFTER MEETINGS, NEGOTIATIONS, mapping, public information work, reports, and so forth, I was ready for a change of pace. And that brings us to a fish story. In this one the fish doesn't get away, although everything else does, including the pole, the boat, the gear, and, to a great extent, the enthusiasm of the fishermen.

The incident I am about to relate not only dampened my zeal for piscatorial endeavors, but it made bear wrestling seem tame by comparison.

Two friends, John Fillmore and Don Castle, had been encouraging me to accompany them on a Chehalis River sturgeon fishing trip, and had so nearly persuaded me that I purchased a new saltwater rod and reel for the occasion.

The morning of March 16th, 1977, dawned crisp and sparkling after seven days of rain, giving no hint of the unpleasant circumstances it held for me. At noon, I was pleasantly surprised by a phone call from John, inviting me to meet them at the Cosmopolis dock for an afternoon on the river.

Being only mid-week and having 33 hours work behind me already, I welcomed the chance for some relaxation. After a stop in Aberdeen to fill my new reel with 50-pound test line, I met my friends at 1pm just in time to help launch their 18-foot inboard boat.

The river was murky from the recent freshet, and being near high-tide, looked exceptionally wide. The boat's motor roared into action, the bow raised from the thrust, and proceeded to cut a silvery swath in the dark, brooding face of the river as we headed upstream.

After a couple miles, approaching a favorite fishing spot, John cut the engine and dropped anchor near mid-river. The water was deep here, around 50-feet, and the current swift, making it necessary to use 1-pound sinkers to keep our lines and bait on the bottom of the river.

Now, from my experience, fishing for sturgeon is about as exciting as counting flowers on the wallpaper. Once your line is in the water, you just sit back and wait.

And wait.

And wait.

This day was no exception. Even though the sun shone brightly, after an hour or so the sharp, cold breeze moving up the river made me glad that I had worn lots of warm clothing. A heavy hickory shirt, an insulated nylon vest, and a long, blanket-lined denim jacket kept me cozy-warm as I sat in the back of the boat holding my pole.

The boat's nose was pointed downstream, giving me an excellent view of the river until it made a bend far below us. John, hunkered below the windshield and fiddling with some gear, had removed his coat. Don was seated on the motor box. After awhile, an object appeared downstream at the river bend, too far away to be immediately identifiable.

"What in the world is that coming up the river?" I asked.

"Gravel barges," was Don's reply.

As they approached, hugging the south shore of the river, I saw that there were indeed two huge steel barges, high-riding and empty and attached end-to-end, being pushed upstream by a tugboat, the mast of which was barely visible above them.

Since this was definitely the most exciting thing that had occurred all afternoon, I watched with interest as the barges, still hugging the shoreline, quickly closed the gap between us. With a great expanse of water separating us, I felt no concern at their approach until the tug suddenly changed course in an apparent effort to "cut the corner" in the river. This maneuver caused the two barges, extending far in front of the tug, to suddenly sweep toward mid-river, quickly eliminating the safety zone of water between us.

To my horror, I watched as the barges headed for us on a collision course, as if aimed, and realized that the tugboat's captain was unaware of our presence on the river.

"John!" I yelled, "He's going to take us!"

Leaping on the bow of the boat to gain a little height, John yelled and waved his arms in a futile effort to make our presence known, but the barges continued on, straight for us.

Knowing that the heavy anchor was firmly snagged on the river bottom, John fired up the engine in an attempt to drag it free. The barges, now towering high above us, bore down relentlessly on our little craft. One quick lurch against the anchor rope, and our engine stalled. There was no second chance, for the gap between us had narrowed to ten feet.

"Jump!" John yelled, and without a second thought, I followed him overboard into the ice-cold depths of the murky Chehalis.

As soon as my head bobbed above the surface, I attempted to propell myself toward the north shore that flicked in and out of sight across the undulating expanse of water.

I had no doubt as to my ability to swim the distance, but to my dismay I found it impossible to assume a horizontal position. My heavy clothes and 8-inch-top work shoes, now saturated, threatened to take me to the bottom.

It was imperative that I put some distance between myself and the oncoming barge, and I flailed with all my strength to move out of its path. Suddenly, I realized that I was holding onto my new fishing pole with the line anchored to the bottom by a 1-pound sinker, causing me to swim in a wide arc. I dropped the thing and immediately made better headway.

John, a strong swimmer and unencumbered by a coat, was far in front of me. Flipping over on his back, he looked in the direction we had come, and yelled "Don didn't make it! Don didn't make it!"

Glancing over my shoulder, I saw the steel hulk of the front barge slicing through the water only 15 feet behind me, continuing on its way upstream. I also noticed that both Don and our boat were gone.

"Good Lord," I thought, "He doesn't even know he has hit us! He's not going to stop and help us!"

My main objective now was to reach the shore alive. My water soaked coat and vest were restricting my arm movements, and I attempted to remove them. Just then the wake from the passing barges hit me, again and again, going over my head and causing me to take water into my lungs and stomach. It seemed like the waves would never stop sloshing over me.

Straining my neck, I reached for air, only to take in more water.

I thrashed the water desperately, gaining precious yards, although I was being carried downstream by the current. If only I could get horizontal, I thought. With the cold 40-degree river water chilling my blood, it became more and more of an effort to stay afloat.

Suddenly I realized that I wasn't in control of the situation. I was sinking, although I could still see sunlight on the surface of the water above me. Fighting my way to the surface, I inhaled a mouthful of air and water, only to sink once again. This time the light went out above me, and all became black. I couldn't bring myself to the surface and the seriousness of the situation became all too apparent - I was drowning.

At first I was mad; what a stupid way to die, I thought, out here in this dirty river! Then I thought of my wife and daughters and the grief I would cause them, and in my mind I cried out, "God, save me!"

I didn't want to die; not like this.

I felt suspended and strangely peaceful in my dark, water tomb. There was no pain.

Then, in an instant, my head was above the water and I could hear loud voices somewhere around me. Although I could see nothing, I realized that I was staying afloat, and help was at hand.

I learned later that the barge had sunk our boat, taking Don down with it. The barges then passed over him as he bounced along their bottoms, until he popped to the surface alongside the tugboat.

Seeing Don, as well as buckets and seat cushions bobbing on the water's surface, the captain stopped the tug and pulled him aboard. Learning that two others were in the water, he cut the barges loose and headed to the rescue.

Meanwhile, John had made it to a point near shore when he saw me go under. Although full of water, he was bravely attempting to come to my rescue until he saw the tugboat heading for me.

Using a pike pole, they snagged my nylon vest but lost me when the fabric tore. Then, with one fellow holding on to him, the other leaned far overboard and fished for me again, this time they snagged my jacket and pulled me to the surface.

Towing me like a gaffed sturgeon, they brought the tug to the muddy shore. Leaving the barges adrift they took the three of us, gagging, coughing, and shivering to Cosmopolis and, subsequently, to Community Hospital.

By this time we were suffering from hypothermia and I was admitted to the hospital for the night. Within 2 1/2 hours my body temperature returned to normal but I was kept on oxygen all night in an effort to "dry" my lungs.

At daybreak the following morning I had an experience that I will never forget.

As dawn broke, I gazed out my hospital window, past the parking lot to the dark outlines of timbered ridges in the distance; hills that I had walked and followed hounds over so many times. I watched as the night shadows receded into the dark canyons, bringing the hills into sharp focus. It was a new day, a new beginning, the most meaningful dawning that I had ever witnessed.

And I was alive to enjoy it! I thanked God for it, realizing I had been snatched from death and given another chance. My outlook on life wouldn't be the same from that moment on.

Oh yes, I almost forgot—while dragging the river bottom a few days later in an attempt to locate their boats' anchor rope, John and Don pulled up two of our broken poles, their lines tangled together. Each line held a sturgeon; one a keeper, the other just a mite short of legal size!

That's catching them the hard way!

After the long, rainy winter, springtime's arrival seemed a little more welcome than usual. To me, spring is the headiest season of the year and by far the prettiest, especially here in coastal Washington where the foliage becomes so lush you can almost hear it growing.

By mid-May, the woods and swamps were showing a thousand hues of green, none of which clashed harshly with the others, but blended into soul-soothing landscapes, or as the Roman poet Horace put it, "poems without words." Spring is an inspiring time for me; a time of renewal and new beginnings, an effervescent stimulus that causes me to enjoy life to its fullest, savoring it, sip by sip. Though its sparkle fades in summer's heat and flattens in the winter rain, the month of May promises a cleansing of the dregs and a fresh cup of nectar!

Spring was here, no doubt about it. I savored it, basked in it, and made every day count, for I knew it wouldn't linger long. If it did, we probably wouldn't treasure it so highly.

Just like life.

Springtime's appearance coincided with the arrival of damage reports and I was glad when my new hunter, Jess, returned from his winter in Newport. These damage reports came from all parts of western Washington and a great part of my time was consumed in inspecting these areas and directing my hunters to them. Bernie Paque, who was now in his 16th year as a WFPA hunter, was assigned to the North Olympic area of the state, Bob Payne to the Central area and Jim Bryan hunted the Southwest area of the state. I was finding less time to personally participate in many of these hunts but still accompanied each of my hunters as often as possible. Once, when I returned from a successful hunt with Paque at Sekiu, I learned that Jess had treed and killed a hermaphrodite bear- one with both male and female genitals! This excited me until I learned that he had dressed, skinned, and quartered the animal and donated it to the mission without realizing its significance.

Shortly after this, on a rainy, windy day, Jess and I took the dogs to the Promised

Land for a hunt. We hunted through the Aloha area, up Joe Creek and past old Camp Six to Bear Creek and had just started up the Hall Creek road (that parallels the Tribal Land boundary) when the dogs struck, red hot. The chase headed to the east, away from the reservation's boundary, and into an area of dense salal and brush, which is typical terrain in the jungly Promised Land. The dogs had the bear "jumped" and were pushing him deeper into the swamps when we were surprised to see a yearling bear dash out of the salal, cross the road, and head for the reservation boundary. This was not the bear being chased but one that had been routed by the sound of the hounds. Our chase turned to the north, then headed west and crossed the Hall Creek road. From there the bear ran parallel to the road until it reached Hall Creek, then headed down to the north fork of the Moclips River. By now it was raining hard and blowing and we lost track of the dogs. The chase had started at 1:40pm and although we searched until 9pm, we couldn't locate the dogs. We were sure they were treed somewhere in that vast, roadless area, but where? I returned home, arriving there for a 10pm dinner and some dry clothes. Velma packed a lunch for Jess and I returned to Hall Creek around midnight. I located Jess, who was happy for the sandwiches, coffee, and dry socks that Velma had sent. Then we separated to search for the dogs. The rain persisted.

Jess picked up two of the hounds on the reservation mainline road but when I had seen nor heard nothing of the dogs by 2:30am I decided to catch a nap. I dozed until 4:15 and when dawn started breaking I set out once more on my search.

Jess learned by C-B radio that an Indian had picked up one of his pups and had taken it to Moclips. While Jess went to retrieve it, I continued my search, stopping every few hundred yards to listen for their voices. Around 9am, near the end of the 8000 road, I heard the dogs barking "treed" in a stand of timber about 200 yards away. Grabbing my .270, I crept into the woods and found not one, but two bears looking at me from among the trees upper limbs. I shot the bears, then loaded them and the hounds in my Blazer. After locating Jess, I left him there to locate one dog that was still missing and I headed for home, a little tired after this 30 hour hunt.

By mid-June Jess had taken 20 bears; six of these by snaring and 14 by houndhunting. On June 22, I joined him and a mutual friend, Bob Diamond, for another hunt in the Promised Land. At 10:30 that morning the hounds started a bear on the Aloha logging road near Joe Creek. This bear ran down Joe Creek, crossed it, and headed northwest toward the Aloha mainline, then doubled back into the Joe Creek area. It was a pretty day but as so often is the case in the Promised Land, a slight, but steady northwest wind came up, making it difficult to hear the dogs. I had nicknamed the area they were running in "No Man's Land," due to the absence of roads. Jess and Bob drove toward Camp Six in an effort to locate the dogs but I remained on a ridge above Joe Creek. Finally, at 4pm, I heard the dogs, still in "No Man's Land" and baying the bear. I radioed Jess and Bob but they were miles away so I headed into the almost impenetrable jungle of salal, huckleberry brush, and old logging slash, hoping to get close enough to the chase to get a shot at the bear. The salal was so tall and sturdy that at times I became trapped and had to retreat to find a way through it. I ran after the dogs for an hour and could get close to them when they stopped and held the bear at bay, but invariably the critter would catch my scent and run before I could catch sight of him. This happened several times until finally, at 5:00pm the bear treed. I could hear the dogs "tree-song" only 300 feet ahead of me, but could see neither dogs or bear until I climbed up on a broken tree top that protruded through the salal. Then I spotted the bear in a small hemlock, on a low limb, looking nervous and ready to come down from his perch. One jump and he would be swallowed by the underbrush, so I quickly shot him in the head, ending the chase.

The bear was a skinny yearling, and so I opened him up and fed the hounds the shoulders, flank meat, rib meat, and both hind quarters, plus the heart and liver, hoping to stuff them to the point that they would follow me from the woods. In a place like this it would be impossible to lead a leashed dog. After all the circles I had run, following the chase, I still knew the general direction I had to go to reach my truck, which was over two miles away.

Calling the dogs together, I started back through the brushy mess, but had gone only a short distance when the hounds "struck" another bear, red-hot!

Away they went, heading northeast toward the Camp Six area. I tried to follow, but the chase was so fast I soon lost them. The wind still blew, causing me to realize I had better give up on this chase and try to find my way out of this wilderness. By now it seemed that my easiest way out would be to head west down Joe Creek to the old trestle and then walk the logging roads back to my truck.

The farther I went, the thicker the brush became, but finally, to my relief, I reached the old trestle, crossed the creek, and headed down the road. After a 10 mile hike, I finally reached my truck and drove back down to lower Joe Creek, where I met Bob Diamond coming out of the brush. The dogs, with their stomachs stuffed from the kill, had given up on the second bear, and by 9:15pm we had them all loaded and headed for home.

One day in June, while looking for fresh bear damage in an area near the north beaches, I discovered 30 sets of bear tracks in the dirt on a half-mile section of logging road. I returned to that area twice and spent six hours sitting and watching that stretch of road in hopes of getting a shot at the bear, but the ocean breezes wafted my scent about, betraying my presence.

When, after the second hunt, I had seen nothing of the bear, I proceeded to place a foot snare on a log that lay back in the timber, 100 feet from the road.

Ten days later, when the snare had failed to produce, Jess and I took the dogs there to see if we could stir up a chase. His strike dog, Wanda, was tethered on the hood of his truck and when we reached the area near my snare-setting, Wanda raised her head, wagged her tail, and a couple of gruff "woofs" from her let us know she smelled bear. Before we released the dogs, I ran into the woods and found our bear caught in my snare. This cheated us and the dogs out of a bear chase, but we had worried about releasing the dogs in this area, anyway. Should a chase head west, the dogs could be killed crossing the beach highway. To the east lay miles of roadless, brushy, almost impenetrable jungles where it would be practically impossible to follow a chase.

On another Joe Creek hunt that summer, we had started a bear chase when one hound split from the pack and ran a bear in a different direction while the remainder of the dogs ran a bear in many circles in the "No Man's Land". While Jess was following the lone dog on its chase, I stayed with the pack. Eventually, they crossed to the south side of Joe Creek and treed the bear in a stand of mature timber.

I walked in to the treeing dogs and found them looking up a huge cedar snag. Although no bear could be seen on the outside of it, about 40 feet up the trunk I could see a sizeable hole which told me our bear was inside the snag. I beat on the snag with a club, but the bear wouldn't show himself. The dogs roared in anticipation, but the bear wasn't about to give them any satisfaction. After two hours, Jess appeared, leashed the dogs, and took them back to his truck. Settling myself into a comfortable spot where I could watch the hole in the snag, I sat quietly waiting for the bear to leave his sanctuary. After thirty minutes of silence and expecting to see the bear at any moment, one of Jess's pups showed up and I was forced to give up my vigil.

My annual aerial survey to document areas of bear damage curtailed my hunts in early July. I never looked forward to these flights with eager anticipation, preferring to keep my feet on the ground. Nevertheless, they were a necessary tool for locating and identifying damage areas and comparing damage levels, year after year.

Areas that had experienced damage during the previous year could easily be identified by "red flags", as we call them; trees whose needles had turned red because they were dead from girdling by bears. Trees that were only partially girdled were in stress, and their needles would be pale yellow. The areas with the heaviest levels of damage would be included in my recommendations for the following year's spring damage bear hunt units. Thus, as you can see, control was implemented two years after the damage occurred. It was easy to identify areas that would experience bear damage, but difficult to persuade the Department of Wildlife to issue a permit or include the area in a spring hunt until damage had actually occurred. Thus, the hunts were usually after the fact, and the bear was killed to punish him for peeling the trees instead of preventing the damage. Under this process, both the trees and the bears were lost.

For the survey I chartered high-winged Cessnas that provided good visibility, but it wasn't always possible to get the same pilot each year. Some were good, some were not so good. I needed to fly at 600 to 1000 feet elevation, depending on the terrain, moving up and down the different river drainages to enable me to keep oriented. With hundreds of square miles of trees, clearcuts, logging roads, and no buildings, it was easy to get disoriented. While making notations of the bear damage on my maps, I would look up and realize that the plane, traveling 90mph, had crossed a divide into a different drainage. Nevertheless, after many years of these flights, the areas became as familiar to me as my own living room.

One year the flight service sent me a young pilot who had just attained his license. He picked me up at the Elma airstrip near my home and, once we were airborne, he did just fine during our five-hour flight. Returning to Elma that evening, the air was cooling after a warm day and a stiff side-wind from the south buffeted our plane as we made our landing approach. We skimmed along, only a few feet above the runway, but the wind rocked the little Cessna so severely my novice pilot couldn't set the plane down. I stared in alarm as the end of the runway drew nearer and nearer and thought that surely he would take the plane aloft again for another try at any moment. But he didn't!

At the last second, the wheels touched the tarmac and we screeched off the end of the runway, stopping only a few feet from the fence, the county road, and a deep pond that lay on the other side.

At the sound of our noisy landing, the folks came running out of the terminal, expecting to see a disaster. My pilot taxied me up to the terminal, dropped me off, and then took off for his home field in Olympia.

I learned later that when he landed there, both tires blew out, being worn thin from the screeching stop at Elma.

One summer, during a fuel crisis, I scheduled a flight from Hoquiam to the North Olympic area near Sekiu. Arriving safely at the remote Quillayute airstrip, we picked up a WFPA employee, Bernie Paque, and spent quite a few hours doing aerial reconnaisance of the timber stands in the area. When we returned to Quillayute to drop Bernie off, the pilot remarked that we were dangerously low on fuel.

Since the Quillayute airfield had no fuel facilities and there was no guarantee that any fuel would be available at the Forks airfield, we found ourselves in a dilemma. If we flew to Forks and weren't able to obtain fuel there, we definitely wouldn't have enough in our tanks to take us to Hoquiam. I suggested that we forget Forks and follow the coastline on our homeward flight, allowing that we could make an emergency landing on the beach if we ran out of fuel.

Once at the ocean's edge, we skimmed over the beach at 100 feet altitude, watching with anxiety as first one, then both fuel gauges pointed at the empty mark. By this time we had reached the mouth of the Chehalis River, and when we turned the plane's nose upstream toward Hoquiam, nine miles distant, all conversation stopped at this point, for there was no place to set the plane down except in the river.

What a welcome sight when Bowerman Field appeared just ahead. And what a relief when we touched down on the tarmac!

I had another experience at Bowerman Field a few years later that I shall relate here. I had arrived there just after sunup on a foggy December morning to meet a forester who was flying down from Port Angeles in his private plane. I was to accompany him on his flight to Bend, Oregon, to attend a meeting concerning aerial photography of bear-damaged areas. Since the fog was so dense at ground level, I hardly expected him to arrive. But to my surprise, his little plane materialized out of the fog, right on schedule.

After topping off the fuel tanks I climbed aboard and we roared down the runway and were soon pushing our way upward through the enveloping fog. At 600 feet altitude we broke through the fog into clear blue sky and sunshine. Banking the plane to the south, which put us directly over the wide Chehalis River, the pilot, Jim, then pointed its nose upward and continued to climb. Just then, the plane began to shudder and shake violently, and the engine vibrated as if it would stop. Jim quickly switched fuel tanks, but to no avail; the plane was losing speed and altitude. Quickly radioing the terminal that we were going to attempt a return landing, he made a wide and slow turn over Hoquiam, all the while the plane sputtering and shaking and losing altitude. The approach to the airfield took us directly over Hoquiam's sewage lagoon, and as we skimmed just yards above it and managed to successfully clear it, I loosened my grip on the plane's instrument panel.

Almost immediately the tarmac appeared and Jim did a super job of setting the plane down. He managed to taxi it to a parking spot and I wasted no time getting my feet on terra firma!

On inspection, it was found that an engine valve had broken off. Jim informed me that he would have the engine repaired in about two weeks and we would reschedule our flight. I told him that, if he didn't mind, I would drive down and meet him at Bend!

Quite often on hot dry days, Jess would wait until late afternoon to take his hounds on a hunt. On one occasion, we were hunting in the Canyon River area, Jess in the lead with his strike dog, Wanda, on the hood of his truck, and I following in my Blazer. On one dead-end spur I waited as Jess drove down it, disappearing into a stand of timber. Finding no bear scent, he turned his truck around and was heading back toward me when I saw a bear cross the road ahead of Jess and out of his vision. In a few seconds his truck reached the point where the bear had crossed and the whole pack of hounds exploded as one in an excited roar of voices. Jess opened the dog box and the chase was on, red-hot from the start. I looked at my watch; it was 5:00pm. Twenty minutes later, the chase had crossed the Canyon River road and the bear was treed in a tall hemlock. Luckily, it was a downhill drag, for this bear weighed 267 pounds.

This hunt primed us for another, and the next day found us in the same area, arriving there around 9:30am. At 10am the dogs struck a bear in an area of heavy bear damage, just north of the Canyon River road. This bear was a runner, and since the young timber had been pre-commercially thinned, it was tough going for the dogs.

After a two-hour chase, I located the dogs baying the bear near the river. I started into the thicket of pre-com to try to get a shot at the bear, with my nephew Wayne, and Jess's son Rip following me. Our noisy approach alerted the bear and he broke and ran, cutting one of the dogs with his claws in the process. In short order the sound of the chase left our hearing and we returned to the road. A little while later I heard the dogs baying the bear again about one quarter mile back in the same thickets. This time I left my companions on the road and plunged into the woods, jumping from one downed tree to another, my feet seldom hitting the ground in the mess of thinned trees. The dogs and bear were moving slowly through this mess as well, and I caught up with the chase just as the bear climbed a small ten-inch diameter hemlock. He was only a few feet up, hanging on the side of the tree, when he winded me and made a movement to jump. I shot at the same moment and the bear fell dead among the dogs just as Jess appeared. This bear was a male and weighed about 125 pounds.

On a hot afternoon in late July, my daughter Sylvan arrived from Oregon for a visit. She gets as excited as I do about a bear hunt, and twenty-five minutes after her arrival we were headed out for a hunt with Jess. Rendezvousing with Jess and his son Rip, we drove once more to the Canyon River area, arriving there at 5:30pm. The devil club berries were ripe and usually grew in the cool, deep canyons near the river; a good place for a bear to feast on a hot day. At 6:45pm the dogs struck a hot track and the race was on.

The chase made many circles in the area of the river, constantly going in and out of our hearing. Jess and I separated to try to keep up with the chase and keeping in touch with our C-B radios. At one point I lost radio contact with Jess, just as I located the dogs, who were baying and walking the bear in another patch of pre-commercially thinned timber near the river. Grabbing my .270, Sylvan and I dived into the jungle of downed trees and headed toward the sound of the chase. As we fought our way through the timber stand we found lots of freshly peeled fir trees; stuff that had been done the previous month. The dogs and bear kept moving and while they made their way down into a deep side-canyon and up the other side, we managed to close the gap between us. Just as Sylvan and I reached the canyon's edge, we saw the bear go up a big-leaf maple on the opposite top-side of the canyon. A steep dirt cliff dropped off directly before the tree. The bear had found a perch only 20 feet up the gnarled, limby tree trunk, and one of the hounds had managed to elevate himself eight feet up the tree. The rest of the hounds roared at the bear from the ground. Taking careful aim, I shot the bear in the head and watched in dismay as he fell from the limbs and tumbled over the cliff all the way to the creek in the canyon's bottom. The dogs followed him in short order and were tugging at his hide by the time Sylvan and I reached them.

Opening the bear, I fed the dogs all they could hold, then cut strips of the bear's hide to make leashes for the hounds. We had just climbed up out of the canyon and started in the direction of the road when we met Jess and Rip hiking in. While Sylvan and Rip took the dogs to the truck, Jess and I returned to the canyon and carried out the hind quarters of the animal. This bear was a boar, around 240 pounds.

The Canyon River country is bordered on the north by National Forest lands; a vast area of deep canyons and high, timbered hills, and these lands joined on their north by the Olympic National Park. This creates a natural sanctuary in which bears propagate without much interference from humans.

During the bears' three month mating season, many of these adult boars travel many miles in search of romance. A great number of them traveling down the west branch and the Nuby branch of the upper Satsop River, and also the Little River drainage to the Canyon River country. As a consequence, the majority of the bears we killed in that area were males.

One September morning, two friends of mine - Art Weller and Jack Miller Jr. - joined Jess and I on another hunt in the Canyon River country. We arrived at the hunting grounds around 7:30am, while the fog still lay deep in the canyons. We hoped for a quick chase, for the day promised to be a hot one. With Jess in the lead with his hounds and my friends and I following in the Blazer, we drove higher and higher up the mountain between Little River and the Satsop's west branch. It was a beautiful, crisp morning, and now that we were above the fog, the sun sent fingers of light across the huge, wooded canyons, painting the distant ridges in gold. Little wisps of fog spiraled up from minor drainages and evaporated in a shiny haze. While I was admiring this view and reminding myself how fortunate I was to be alive and healthy enough to enjoy all of this, Wanda struck bear scent, red-hot, in the morning dew.

Jess dumped the hounds and they roared off down the mountain toward the west branch of the Satsop. Just as the chase started, a second bear ran across the old road in front of Jess's truck. I looked at my watch; it was 9:30am.

The chase traveled down the mountain and headed into the "bite" country — an area that lies between the junction of the Canyon River and the Satsop's west branch. The bear circled through the upper part of this area twice while Jack and I ran through the timber, hoping to get a shot. On the bear's second circle, he crossed the main line road and headed north, up Canyon River. Driving up a side spur, Jack and I made ready to ambush the bear, but when the chase came within 200 yards of us the bear turned uphill through some old-growth timber and the hounds' voices soon faded from our hearing. Quickly driving to the top of this hill where our road ended, we heard the dogs circling back down into Canyon River.

By this time it was late afternoon and the sun was scorching hot on the rocky hillsides. One by one the exhausted dogs began to drop out of the chase. When the bear crossed Canyon River and headed northeast into the Nuby Branch, only one dog, a blue tick female, remained on the chase and its voice was soon lost in the distance.

Joining Jess, we drove up the Nuby Branch trying to locate the hound, who by now was only howling once every fifteen minutes as it continued to walk the bear up the river canyon. Once, Jess saw the bear in a small opening, but couldn't get a shot. I drove up the road, and both Jack and I posted ourselves where we thought the bear might leave the canyon. The bear must have winded us, for he climbed a near perpendicular hill and crossed the road just around a curve from us. After crossing the road, he continued straight up the steep mountainside through a stand of young Douglas firs. When the dog reached the road, Jess caught it and called off the chase. It was now 6pm, an eight and a half hour chase that had covered 21 miles, airline.

Jess loaded his hound and roared off down the road to Canyon River, picking up dogs as he went. I turned my Blazer around and headed out a half hour behind Jess, keeping an eye on the mountainside up which our bear had escaped. At a sharp bend in the road, where a small creek roared over the rocks, I took one last look up the mountain and saw the bear nearly at the top, walking slowly across a broad open area, headed for the old-growth timber. Jumping out and cramming some shells in my .270, I held high over the bear that I estimated to be about 600 yards away and squeezed the trigger. The bullet struck the bear and he tumbled 50 yards down the steep slope before regaining his feet and continuing towards the timber. By this time Jack was out of the truck and we both fired again, one of our bullets hitting the bear's foot. A couple more steps and the brush at the timber's edge swallowed him up.

Jack and I were both about as tired as the hounds, but without a second thought, we started up the hill to try to locate our bear. The hill was nearly vertical and the rock slides and shale made it necessary to "switchback" our way up to it. We finally reached the spot where we had last seen the bear and immediately found a trail of blood.

We followed the trail into the timber and down into a steep canyon where we could hear the creek roaring below us. I knew the bear was badly wounded, for we would find places where he had tried to walk big logs and had fallen off into the high sword ferns. We trailed him cautiously, all the way to a thicket of salmonberry bushes by the creek. A large log as high as my chest blocked my path, and when I looked over it, I saw the bear, standing about 25 feet away. He had fought and wallowed the salmonberry bushes until he had formed a small clearing. The roar of the creek had prevented him from hearing his tormentors approaching, and I quickly put a bullet in him and ended the chase.

We were now only 200 yards up the creek from the truck and, this being the easiest path, we rolled the bear in the water and dragged him downstream to the road. This bear was also an adult male.

In October of that year, with visions of fried grouse breast and chanterelle mushrooms whetting my appetite, I made a trip to the upper Promised Land to see if I could find the ingredients for such a feast. I was accompanied by a young Mexican nicknamed Chaparro, who had come to Aberdeen on a student visa. With Chaparro carrying a shotgun and I my old .270, we walked down an old grade where I had shot a bear the previous fall. We walked along quietly, picking mushrooms as we went, and soon had enough for a meal. It had been a rainy morning, but the evening hours were beautiful; a good time to see some game moving about.

Around 5:45pm, we rounded a bend that gave us a clear view down the old grade for nearly a half mile. My eye detected a dark object in the grade, but it was so far away I couldn't be sure what it was. Looking through my little 2 1/2 power scope, I saw that it was a bear, but in the distance I couldn't tell if it was coming or going. A couple of steps to the right or left would put the bear in the roadside brush, and since he hadn't as yet detected us, I decided to try an off-hand shot. Aiming about four feet over the bear's form, I squeezed the trigger. Cranking another shell into the chamber, I looked through my scope and was surprised to see that the bear was still in the same spot. I couldn't understand why he hadn't run into the woods after my shot, and since I could still detect movement, I held a little higher and shot again. Still, the bear remained at the same spot and continued to move. Then, like a flash, the bear ran into the woods and disappeared. Chaparro and I ran down the road and when we reached the spot where the bear had been we found the road scuffed up in a wide circle and much blood. I had hit him the first shot and the movement I saw after that was his efforts to regain his footing.

The stunted growth of cedar and hemlock timber that crowded the road had a thick understory of winter huckleberry brush and salal that grew up through a maze of downed and rotting trees. The soil was swampy-wet and little lakes of water had collected on each side of the slightly elevated grade. I tracked the bear across one of these soup-holes by walking a fallen tree, and after going 75 feet into the woods, found the bear on a mossy spot, and very dead. It was a fat yearling female, and my bullet had struck it in the brisket.

After dressing out the bear and carrying it to the grade, we left her there and started hiking back up the road to get my Blazer. I stepped off the distance from the bear to the spot that I had shot from, and was amazed to find that I had killed the bear at 626 yards!

That was my last bear kill of the year, and after killing an elk and a nice black tail buck, I hung up my rifle and settled into the much less exciting routine of office work and preparations for the coming year's bear control work.

Chapter 4

A Real Cliffhanger

Ever wish you were a bear? It would have some advantages, especially for a lady: You would have that fur coat you've always wanted, you could sleep all winter, and best of all, you wouldn't have to watch your waistline.

With the high cost of groceries and heating fuel, sleeping through the winter doesn't sound all that bad of an idea.

You could "hole-up" just after the football season (the ladies would probably opt for a date preceding it) and emerge in time for a skunk cabbage feast before trout season.

Sound far fetched? Don't dismiss the idea. When I was a kid, Buck Rogers and Flash Gordon seemed preposterous, but in retrospect they were virtually prophetic. Now a trip to the moon is old hat, and is read about after you've completed the crossword puzzle.

If you still think I'm kidding, let's take a look at the denning habits of black bears. Generally, they enter their dens during a five-week period between October 21st and November 29th, with the adult male being the last to hole-up. There is some controversy as to whether bears are "true" hibernators.

The ground squirrel, woodchuck, and hamster are considered true hibernators because their body temperatures may drop to where it is only slightly above freezing.

During this period it is hard to arouse them, and they are practically incapable of movement. Even so, these "true" hibernators emerge from this state every few days, their body temperature returns to normal, and they feed (on caches), urinate, and defecate.

In comparison, bears move much more slowly into a state of hibernation, and remain in that state for extended periods. Their body temperature drops by less than 15 degrees, but their heartbeat slows to eight beats per minute. Even so, they are easily aroused and are capable of rapid movement.

During the month before hibernating, the bear begins to eat like it is going out of style, consuming 20000 calories a day. While hibernating, its body uses only 4000 calories a day. At this ratio, during one late fall day of feeding, the bear will consume enough food to sustain him through five days of hibernation.

While hibernating, bears might not feed, drink, urinate, or defecate for periods of up to six months. For a person, to retain body wastes that long would be fatal. The staple retention of urine would result in uremia, an accumulation in the blood of materials normally passed off, resulting in a poisoned condition, and death.

Somehow, during hibernation, the bear's body marvelously recycles the urine and uses it to maintain the proper level of body fluids.

How they do this, no one knows, but Mayo Clinic scientists have been studying hibernating bears to try to unravel their secret. Should they be successful, they hope to utilize the results in treating human diseases such as kidney failure.

Since researchers also suspect that a hormone controls a bear's winter sleep patterns, discovery and proper use of this hormone could be helpful in enabling obese humans to lose weight.

Imagine going into an induced hibernatory sleep weighing 300 pounds in November and awakening to a svelte 115 pounds in March! Limits of weight loss could be controlled by shortening the period of "hibernation". Presumably, insomnia could also be treated with this same hormone.

I can see comparable bear tendencies in myself already; I eat like a bear just before retiring and, like an adult male bear, I am usually the last one to bed. Something I couldn't do would be to be in one position without moving for six months; I would be a candidate for a humungous charley-horse!

But who needs induced hibernation? I'm usually in a semi-torpid state during the grey winter months anyway.

Besides, I couldn't survive six months without my strawberry sundaes!

By mid-March 1978, the salmonberry and elderberry bushes were leafing and blooming, and the grass was six inches high. The spring-like weather continued through the remainder of the month, but changed drastically on April 1st, opening day of the spring damage bear season. That day was greeted with rain and hail that continued until evening, but it didn't seem to dampen the enthusiasm of the sport hounds-men who had waited all winter for this event.

Jess and I had gone to the Promised Land that morning, and we found the area not only saturated by rain but by hunters as well. We encountered 27 pickup loads of dogs, two rigs with "still" hunters, many cedar shake cutters, and a few trucks that had met each other on the narrow roads and gone over the bank. Needless to say, no bears were taken that day.

The cold, rainy weather hung on throughout the month of April and although Jess hunted hard, he captured only three bears by month's end. Bears tend to spend alot of time close to their nests during April; I don't think they like the cold, wet days any better than we do!

After the first of May the bears began to prowl, and reports of fresh tree damage kept my phone ringing. After checking out the damage locations on-site, I then contacted the game department's regional biologist in the area affected and obtained a permit for a sport hound-hunter to go after the bear. If the hunter wasn't sucessful, I followed up his hunt with one of my professional hunters. All this was time consuming and often frustrating, especially if the sport hunter didn't solve the problem and the bear continued to peel.

Jess and I had set some foot snares for bears in Mason and Kitsap counties, and these produced six bears during May while Jess racked up 8 more with his hounds in Grays Harbor county during the same period.

On June 2nd, I accompanied Jess to the Bremerton area to check some snares. One of them held a large female bear, and after resetting the snare we loaded our animal and continued on our route. As we were approaching our last site, a bobcat bounded across the road ahead of us. Just as we neared our snare a yearling bear ran across the road and into the timber. Grabbing my .357 revolver, I ran after it, and although I glimpsed him once, he escaped without being shot at.

On checking the snare, we found an old adult female bear waiting for us. On our approach she took off with the drag pole and climbed a large cedar tree, stopping on a big limb about 30 feet above the ground. I shot her with my revolver, reset the snare, loaded the bear, and we headed out of the woods.

We had gone perhaps a quarter mile when Jess's truck developed transmission trouble and left us "dead in the water". While Jess walked the 2 1/2 miles to a telephone, I took my rifle and returned to the spot where I had seen the yearling. I settled myself on a log, hoping that he might reappear to seek his mother, who was now reclining in the back of Jess's truck. When he didn't show himself by nightfall, I gave up my post and walked out to the highway. A friend arrived after 10pm and towed our crippled rig home.

In the next ten days I caught four more bears in that same area, but the yearling wasn't among them.

After some unsuccessful sportsman hound-hunts failed to take any bears from a damaged unit near Snoqualmie, Jess and I took the hounds and headed there for a hunt. Once there, the Dept. of Wildlife's regional biologist accompanied us. Almost immediately on reaching the bear-damaged area, the dogs struck and, after a short chase, treed a female bear and cub. After taking care of these bears, we continued our hunt and soon started another bear. This one gave us a long, hard chase, but it finally treed. On arriving at the tree, we found a brown color-phase black bear waiting for us. This bear was a male.

Four days before this hunt, I had gone with Kelly Lund, who was a wildlife damage control agent for the game department, on a couple of damage complaints in Pacific county. One of these bears had been stealing chickens, the other raiding a motel's garbage bins. When Jess and I arrived in North Bend that evening after our Snoqualmie hunt we received a phone call from Kelly saying I had caught both of the problem bears in my snares. This made for a good day - eleven hours and five bears.

The next morning we returned to the Snoqualmie tree farm and hunted until noon, but when the day turned hot and we struck no bears, we terminated our hunt. Loading the dogs, we drove to Kitsap County to check our snares on the way home. One of the snares held a yearling bear, and the last one we checked held an adult female. Since there was evidence that she had at least one yearling with her, we turned Wanda loose to see if we could get a chase. Sure enough, Wanda opened up on the yearling's scent and the chase was on.

The bear ran three circles in the area, always returning to the spot where the sow had been caught. We had reset the snare, a trail set, and on the bear's last circle Wanda got caught in the snare. After the excitement of catching the dog in our snare, the remaining hounds lost the yearling's spoor and we pulled them off the chase. We made it home after a 15 hour day, and were happy to crawl in our friendly beds.

Lots of fresh damage was occurring on Gold Mountain near Bremerton, and although we had taken quite a few bears from the area, each visit showed us more trees peeled. There was evidence of an especially large bear, but he tended to keep out of our snares. I had set a snare on a big, rotting log near fresh damage and when I checked it a few days later I found an adult sow bear tied up and waiting for me.

While dressing her out I noted that she was estrous (in heat) and so I saved the urine that was in her bladder. After resetting the snare on the same log to my satisfaction, I saturated a couple cloths with the sow's urine and hung them on limbs above each end of the log. I also sprinkled a little of the stuff on the log.

Not many days later when the snare was checked, it held a 360 pound boar bear.

About a week after our Snoqualmie hunt, we returned for another "follow-up" hunt after an unsuccessful sportsman hunt in the Proctor Creek country. This area was a rough one to hound hunt, being extremely steep and rocky, and also because the noisy North Fork Tolt River roared through the canyons, making it tough to keep track of the hounds' voices.

We arrived at the permit area around 6:45am, and while Jess drove up a long straight stretch of road to see if he could get a "strike", I waited in my Blazer for his return. Just as Jess's truck disappeared at the far end of the straight stretch, I saw the bear come out of the woods and cross the road.

When Jess reached that spot on his return, the dogs opened up in a roar, and another chase was on. I drove north to a fairly open spot by a dry lake bed, but loggers were falling timber there and turned the bear. I ran as fast as I could around a bend in the road and got there just in time to see the bear cross the road. I quickly drove down a side road and radioed Jess where to wait for the bear. Nearing that spot, I ran up the road and got a quick glimpse of the bear running up a log. Jess was waiting near the other end of the log, and his quick shot grazed the bear and convinced it that it should vacate the premises.

The bear now fled down into the canyon of the North Fork Tolt, swam the raging river just below the mainline bridge, crossed the road, with the dogs hot on his heels, and treed on a steep hillside in an old-growth cedar tree. The bear was a large boar, and well furred. This had been a quick chase, and we were in North Bend in time for lunch.

Hound-hunting for bear can be exciting. In fact, some hunts can be more hazardous to the hunter than to the bear. That was the case on a subsequent hunt in the Proctor Creek country when we went after the "cliff bear". This bear had been devastating a young fir plantation, girdling the trees and scraping the sweet sapwood from the trunk with his teeth. Jess and I were called upon to remove the bear, and we arrived at the damage site on a drizzly, foggy morning in early July.

The dogs struck the bear's track immediately, and the chase was on. The bear led the dogs in a six mile loop into the Yellow Creek drainage, returned to the point of beginning, and with the hounds hot on his heels, started climbing one of the steep, rock faced ridges that are characteristic of this area. From a great distance we could hear the rocks rolling and clattering until the sounds of both rocks and dogs faded into the foggy clouds that shrouded the hills.

After a two-mile drive up the valley road, we once again were able to hear the dogs, high up in the clouds on a main ridge that dropped off into the Skykomish River country. Although we could but faintly hear them, it sounded like they were "treeing".

All roads ended here, so we set out on foot up the near-perpendicular mountain, making our way over rockslides; thickets of snow-downed vine maples that lay with their tops pointing downhill at us, these interlaced with devilclubs, logs, and thorny-stemmed briar bushes, all dripping wet from the drizzle. Soon we were in the cloud cover and could neither see below or far above us.

After climbing steadily for 3 1/2 hours, our ascent was blocked by sheer rock cliffs. We had long since ceased to hear the dogs, but this far committed, determined to continue on a search of the mountain tops that lay somewhere in the clouds above us. Following the base of the cliff, we came to a high waterfall that had cut a divide in the rocks. Here we were able to find some footholds and made our way up onto the face of the cliff, working our precarious way along it until, reaching a "bend" in the hill, we once again heard the dogs.

They definitely were treeing, but their voices were drifting down from high up on the cliffs above us. Spurred on by their excited baying, we threw caution to the wind and started scaling the cliff like a couple of monkeys. I had no sling on my rifle, and this left me with but one hand to climb with. Jess, with his rifle slung over his shoulder, was soon high above me.

Sparse vegetation and a few hardy trees grew out of the rock face, providing toeholds and handholds, but as my weight dislodged these one after another, I was struck with the terrifying realization that it was now impossible for me to get off the cliff the way I had come. And I didn't know what lay ahead of me. Looking down, I saw the tops of huge, old-growth trees below me. The scene was eerie and scary with the enveloping clouds swirling about and limiting my visibility from 50 to 100 feet.

I could hear Jess above me and, as he made his way, his progress loosened or eliminated many of the protruding rocks and bushes, until I found myself in the horrifying position of neither being able to go up nor down. I was clinging to the cliff with one foot in a niche, one hand gripping a spindly bush, my body pressed tightly to the rock to keep from falling backwards, and no handholds ahead of me within reach.

Suddenly I heard a great commotion from Jess's direction and a shower of rocks came rattling down the cliff towards me, ricocheting off the steep face like bullets and disappearing into the cloudy nothingness below me.

I looked through the fog in the direction that the rocks had come from and saw Jess dangling where he had slipped over a precipice, clutching a spindly bush in both hands. With no little effort, he managed to pull himself to the safety of a narrow ledge and proceeded up the cliff, soon disappearing into the fog.

By now the full impact of the seriousness of my situation began to hit me. Still clutching my rifle, my left arm was out-stretched and pressed tightly to the rocks above me, helping maintain my balance. Near my left hand was a gnarled tree root that could help me in my ascent, but to grab it called for releasing my hold on the rifle. That would mean goodbye .270, faithful old companion of 30 years of hunting.

As I clung there trying to persuade myself to drop the rifle, the minutes ticked by, and the muscles of my leg supporting me began to tremble. Still, I couldn't bring myself to drop my rifle over that cliff.

Desperately looking about like a drowning man clutching at straws, I espied a root about 16 inches above my right hand that promised to be my only salvation. To reach it meant releasing my right hand from its hold and lurching upward toward the root. There would be no second chance if I failed in my initial attempt to grab it.

Finally summoning the courage, I released my grip and lunged upward, feeling a sense of profound relief sweep over me as my fingers found and tightened around the root, and a genuine thankfulness that the root held. Pressing my gun butt down against the root to my left, I pulled my body above the overhang and proceeded on my uncertain way up the cliff.

In a few minutes I found myself hanging onto some bushes directly under the dogs, who were barking up a 30 foot tree that grew out of a narrow ledge; a ledge that was completely occupied by Jess and the three hounds.

Loosening my grip, I dropped and slid to a wider ledge below the dogs.

From this safe vantage point, I was able to relax at last, and I began to search the fog-enshrouded treetop with my eyes for a glimpse of the bear. Look as I would, no bear was to be seen, despite the fact that his claw marks were found on the tree by Jess.

Looking about, I soon figured out the situation. A 2-foot diameter snag, rotted and freshly felled, lay shattered between the two ledges. Apparently the bear had scampered up the snag to escape the dogs, and the snag had broken off, falling against the upper ledge. As the snag toppled the bear leaped to the ledge and climbed the 30-foot tree. Growing out of the cliff above this tree was another, and above that, yet another; the bear had gone up the first, into the second and third, and escaped up the cliff through the clouds. Naturally, the dogs couldn't follow him, and they settled down treeing at the first tree they had seen the bear go up.

After sliding down to join me on my ledge, Jess called the dogs to us and leashed them to prevent their returning to the tree. I then informed Jess in no uncertain terms that I wasn't about to attempt returning the way we had come. He readily agreed that it was impossible, and we then admitted to each other how scared we had been during our climb.

Following the ledge on around the mountain, we found a sloping slide that led to a jumble of huge, automobile-size boulders far below. Holding the dogs, we slid, rolled, and tumbled downward, and soon reached the safety of the boulders. Two hours later, soaking wet, we reached the bottom of the mountain. My hat was gone, but I still had my old rifle. The sole and heel had come completely off one of Jess's shoes, leaving his stocking foot sticking out below the upper.

Wringing out our wet clothes at the truck, I remarked that I wished that I knew where there was a dance being held. When Jess asked why, I answered tiredly:

"So we could tell someone, and they could go."

The following month, wanting to settle the score with the "cliff bear", we returned for another hunt. The previous day had been a hot one, and this day promised to be even hotter. We left home at 5am and it was around 8am before we reached our hunting area on the Tolt. The sun rose with a vengeance and by 11:30 it was so hot we debated whether we should start a chase. The decision was made for us when the dogs struck bear scent, and we loosed them on the track. The chase split almost immediately and we now had dogs and bears going in two directions. I saw one of the bears, a blonde color-phase yearling, cross the road, but after only one hour in the scorching heat, all the dogs gave up the chase.

We now had dogs scattered all over the woods, and we spent the remainder of the day rounding them up. At 6pm, when the air had cooled a bit, the dogs struck the Proctor Creek bear. Jess's dog "Pete" hadn't been on the earlier chase, so we put her on the track by herself. The bear took the dog down the Tolt River, then returned and crossed various roads five times.

Once, just at dark, the bear walked into the old road, and Jess, seeing movement in the darkness, assumed it was his "Pete" dog. Unsnapping a leash from around his waist, he ran up the road in an attempt to catch her and end the chase. Imagine his surprise when he got close and realized it was the bear instead of the dog! The bear ran into the brush, and just as it did "Pete" dog came into the road behind it. The dog had quit barking because of the heat. After putting "Pete" back in the truck he released two fresh dogs on the bear's track, and at 10:30 p.m. they treed it in a stand of 60 year old timber.

Jess took his open-sighted rifle, I carried my revolver, and with flashlights lighting our path, we made our way to the tree, guided by the excited baying of the two hounds.

We found the bear ensconced in a big, bushy-topped hemlock, and it was necessary to stand directly under the tree to be able to shine our flashlight beam up through the limbs. Jess quickly tied the dogs back away from the tree while I probed the darkness with my light, trying to locate the bear. Finally, the bear looked in my direction, and I saw his eyes shining green, high up in the tree. I couldn't see his black body in the darkness, and he wouldn't stare at the light long enough for us to get a shot.

I decided to return to the truck and get my rifle and scope, hoping this would give us an advantage in the darkness. I ran through the timber, grabbed my gun and shells, and ran back to the bear tree, again guided by the hounds' voices. I arrived there very hot and very sweaty from the sultry heat that still hung in the air after the day's 91 degree temperature.

Once I stopped under the bear tree, my steamy body heat rose and fogged my glasses. I would wipe them, and by the time I located the bear's eyes they would be fogged up again. Finally, in desperation, I fired a shot where I thought the bear's body would be, and at the rifle's report, the bear made a great commotion among the limbs and started down the tree. My glasses were so steamed I could see nothing, and there was no time to clear them. Jess fired a shot at the bear's noise and hit it somewhere in the body. I was still standing directly under the tree, and I felt a gush of air as the bear fell from the tree, swished by my face in the darkness, and landed with a thump at my feet. The wounded bear immediately leaped up, and I pointed my rifle like a pistol and fired point-blank at his movement. This turned the bear and he crashed off into the dark underbrush and made his escape. I took after him and, using my flashlight, was able to locate lots of blood.

This was a predicament; wounded bears are nasty, and a wounded bear in the dark woods would be especially dangerous. We had crawled a short ways through a salmonberry thicket, following his blood trail, when Jess asked "Should I turn the dogs loose?"

"They are your dogs, Jess. You make the decision." I answered.

Jess ran back to the excited and bawling hounds and released them into the darkness. They had gone full-bore only 200 feet when they came upon the wounded bear laying in wait. We could hear one of the dogs screaming in pain when the bear bit it in the face, and again in a back leg. Before we could reach the fight, the bear moved out, with two dogs in pursuit. After a few hundred yards, the bear stopped again, and after a short, excited baying session, the hounds grew quiet.

We followed the bear's blood spore until we reached a dry, rocky creek bed at the base of a hill. Here the trail ended for us since we couldn't see the blood on the rocks with our flashlight. The two hounds returned to us and we reluctantly headed out of the woods in the direction of our trucks, reaching it at 1:05am.

We spent the night in our trucks, waiting for three hounds that were still missing from the morning hunt. At daylight we resumed our search for them, and by mid-morning had found all but one. Still thinking of the wounded bear, Jess and I returned to the scene of the bear fight, and in daylight were able to follow the bear's blood trail across the dry creek bed. The trail led us a quarter mile into a jumble of rotten logs, salmonberry bushes, and devilclubs. At one place we found where the bear had laid during the night. At this point we lost its trail and returned empty-handed to the trucks. The "cliff bear" had won again.

I can recall another hunt that lasted far into the night and gave us a little excitement. Bob Matthews, WFPA's director of forest management, and his son Mark had joined Jess and I for a hunt in the Promised Land. Crawling out of our warm nests at 5am, we rendezvoused with Jess and headed north to the hunting grounds. The day soon turned unbearably hot and humid, and although we started four "cold" tracks by 2pm, we couldn't get a chase going. We decided to change areas and wait until the cool of evening to continue our hunt. Driving up in the hills and arriving at the Camp 3 area, we rested in the shade and waited for the sun to drop behind the western hills. Finally growing weary of doing nothing, we resumed our hunt on the north side of Cougar Mountain.

We had traveled but a short distance on the old dirt logging road when the dogs struck a hot track and raced off into the canyons of the East Fork of the Humptulips River. The bear then ran down into the Furlough Creek area before heading down the East Fork. When darkness set in, the bear had slowed to a walk, and we could hear the chase fading off into the roadless distance. Driving down off the mountain, we drove many miles around to some ridges that lay between the East and West forks of the river. Driving down a spur road to its end on a high point in the timber, we cupped our hands to our ears and listenend. Away off in the darkness we could faintly hear the hounds and it sounded like they were barking "treed", but we couldn't be sure. It was now 11pm and it was at least a mile straight-line to the dogs from where we stood, much farther when you consider the ridges and canyons we would cross to get there.

Bob was definitely the wiser one of our bunch, for he opted to wait at the truck and man the C-B radio. Taking a hand-held radio with us, along with our flashlights, Jess, Mark, and I dived over the brink of the hill and headed towards the dogs. The night was moonless, and dark as a well, and we relied on our compass to keep us going in the right direction. Once down in the canyon, we could no longer hear the dogs, but after crossing many ridges, we again began to hear them. They were not far from us now, and we quickened our pace until we found ourselves in the middle of a huge, marshy swamp.

As we emerged from the far side of the swamp we entered an area of wiry bushes and tall swamp grass. The ground sloped gently up out of this thicket, for which we were glad. We could hear dogs all around us, racing back and forth, and baying. The bushes would swish around us and, in the darkness, it was impossible to tell if it was the dogs or the bear. To our left we could hear a great uproar from the dogs, and hurrying over there, we found them barking up a 30-inch diameter fir tree.

I looked at my watch; it was a little after midnight. Shining our lights up among the limbs, I spotted the bear by the brown on the side of his nose, but I couldn't see his body in the blackness. Jess and Mark tied some of the dogs and held the others, while I tried to find the bear's head in my scope. Holding my light alongside my rifle, I finally saw the little dot in my scope, but when I tried to find the bear's head, I would lose the dot. Finally, seeing the dot, I eased it down to the brown spot on the bear's nose, moved it a bit back to where his forehead should be, and squeezed the trigger.

When my rifle roared, the bear came crashing down through the limbs and hit the ground on off side of the tree with a great thump. We couldn't see any of this in the pitch blackness, but we ran toward where we had heard him hit the ground. We had a little trouble finding it in the dark, but finally located it, shot through the head, and very dead.

Releasing the dogs, we let them worry its carcass and then opened it up and fed the hounds all they could eat. What little remained we left for the coyotes.

We radioed Bob that the bear had been taken, and we were ready to head for the truck. I asked him to blow the horn so we could get a general direction, but we were too far away to hear it.

Leading three of the dogs, we started across the swamp, using our compass to guide us. Finally, after crossing a couple ridges, we could hear the truck's horn. When climbing the steeper hills, we would occasionally stop to rest, and the tired hounds would curl up and go to sleep. Before starting off again we had to locate each of them with our flashlight and wake them. Finally, at 3am, after a two-hour hike, we climbed the last hill to the truck. What a welcome sight it was! We made it home and to bed at 4:30 a.m., after a 23 1/2 hour day.

Shortly after this hunt, my brother Dale's son Wayne and his wife Vangie arrived from Michigan for a visit. Wayne and Vangie had just been married and were traveling across the country on their honey-moon. On August 10th, the day after their arrival, they joined Jess and I on a hound-hunt north of Elma. Around 11:15 the dogs "struck" and when I got out of my Blazer, I immediately saw the track of a big bear in the road-bank soil.

The hounds bailed down into the canyon and roared off on a "red-hot" track.

Within fifteen minutes we could hear the dogs barking "treed" off in the timber a couple canyons away.

Hurrying over there, we found the bear treed about twenty feet up a fourteen-inch diameter fir that stood on the brink of a steep hillside. Seeing our approach, the big bear shifted his position on the limb, just as I arrived under the tree. There was a loud "pop" as the dry limb broke, nearly dumping the bear on me. As he started to fall, he clutched the tree's trunk with his claws and whisked himself to the backside of the tree, intending to jump. At that moment, I found his head in my rifle scope, squeezed the trigger, and the big bear fell heavily to the ground, his weight carrying him over the canyon's edge until a tree stopped his descent. With no little effort, we dragged his heavy carcass to a point where I could use my truck's winch to pull him up the last hill.

Wayne and Vangie were enjoying their stay and spent their time fishing, "still" hunting and hound hunting for bears, and sight-seeing. Two weeks into their visit, on August 23rd, 1978, Jess and I took some Department of Wildlife personnel on a bear hunt at Aloha. The day started off ideally, and at 9:00am we had a bear chase started. At 9:15 the dogs went out of our hearing when they followed the bear into the Joe Creek "no man's land". At that point, the bear was jumped and the dogs were hot on his trail.

Then the rain started, and a north-west came up, making it impossible to hear the dogs. The rain poured all day long, and we heard the hounds only once around 2:30 in the afternoon. After that, the only sound was wind and rain, and we were forced to give up on the hunt at 7pm. Our wet companions were glad to call it a day, and while Jess remained in the woods to try and locate and round up his dogs, I hauled the game department fellows to my house, where their vehicle was parked.

We had just arrived when I saw Wayne walking hurriedly toward me, and as he neared, the expression on his face told me all was not well.

"What's happened?" I asked. And his two word reply hit me like a ton of bricks.

"Dad's dead," was his reply. "He was killed in a boat collision this evening on Williams Lake. His body sunk in 60-feet of water, and they can't find it."

Grabbing Wayne in a bear hug, I bade a hasty goodbye to my hunting companions. I tried to comfort him and get more details of the accident, the news of which had left me in unbelieving shock. After changing from my soaking wet clothes, I set about lining up airline tickets for Wayne and Vange, and the following morning I saw them off on an early flight to Michigan.

I remained to cancel meetings, appointments, and make arrangements for a flight to Maryland to be with my Mom and Dad. On the third day after the accident, divers recovered Dale's body, and on August 26th, Velma and I arrived at my folk's home in Maryland. Early the following morning I drove Velma, Mom, and Dad to Michigan where we attended Dale's funeral on the 28th.

He was only 51 years old, and well known in the Pontiac, Michigan area as a concrete construction contractor. A long line of cement trucks joined the funeral procession, and over 400 persons filled the chapel, a tribute to his integrity.

Life never ceases to amaze me. Events that begin as tragedies often evolve, through various circumstances, into pleasant experiences. And vice-versa. Today I am thinking of the former. While visiting with friends and family after my brother's funeral, I renewed my acquaintance, and kindled a warm friendship with a friend from my upper penninsula Michigan deer hunting days. He had, in recent years, became interested in moose hunting. He had made several successful hunts, and was planning another trip to northern Ontario, Canada that fall.

I was intrigued by Phil's description of the hunts, the apparent solitude of the location, and most of all by the fact that no guide was required. When he invited me to join his crew for the upcoming hunt, I agreed without a moments hesitation.

Mid-October found me, my duffle bag, and my old .270 Remington rifle squeezed in Phil's crew-cab pickup and beginning a 13-hour journey straight north from Grand Rapids. There were five of us, three of which I had hunted deer with before.

Our road ended at a lake-side dock in northern Ontario, where a sign informed us that this was the coldest spot in Canada; temperatures of -72 degrees had been reported there. We chartered an ancient "Otter" float plane, jammed it full of guns, provisions, and bodies, and began the 50-mile flight farther north to "our lake".

And for the season it was "ours". Since the season opener was yet a day off and we planned to stay 10 days - with freeze-up coming any time after that, and no one would be hunting the area before or after us.

I breathed a sigh of relief when the 40-year-old plane, burdened with a ton of gear, plus six bodies, cleared the treetops at the end of the lake and pointed it's nose north.

The flight was at low-level and the scenery was spectacular: lakes, marshes, and meandering rivers as far as the eye could see, nestled in a wilderness of yellow-pine, larch, poplar, cedar, willow, and birch. We soon left all vestiges of humanity behind, and not even a logging road could be seen.

Eventually, as the plane banked in preparation for landing, I could see our destination below us. The 2-mile long lake was narrow and kidney shaped, with smaller lakes located on the drainage within a half-mile of either end. Between the lakes were long marshes, the vegetation already yellowed by an early October snow that had come and gone.

I tried to imprint this quick aerial view of the terrain in my mind for future reference, noting rock-breaks, creeks, and other landmarks that would aid me, once on the ground.

In a few seconds we skimmed the treetops, dipped down sharply, and touched the water. Phil indicated a timbered point of land on the bend of the lake and the plane idled toward it. The pilot cut the engine as we neared the shore and we floated into shallow water within a few feet of our campsite.

After ferrying our gear ashore in two canoes and an aluminum boat that Phil had stashed in the woods from the preceding year, we waved goodbye to the pilot and instructed him to return to us in ten days. We watched as the plane roared off the lake and disappeared behind the hill, breaking the link between us and civilization. With no radio or other means of communication, we were now on our own. Better stay healthy and not get hurt!

Before the waves caused by his departure had ceased lapping the shore, we set about like a band of pirates, hauling boxes and trunks up the bank and into the woods, for the day was well spent.

While two of the fellows erected our sleeping tent, three of us set about constructing a kitchen. Selecting standing trees for corners, and framing our roof from pine poles, we enclosed our structure with heavy, clear plastic, using canvas for the roof. A small "air-tight" wood stove was set up for warmth, and a little propane camp stove was used for cooking.

The lake lay quiet in the darkness that night, and the air had turned cold. The notation in my diary that night reads as follows:

"Moose season opens tomorrow and I crawl into my sleeping bag with great anticipation. We have a good crew; three of them have killed moose before - Phil, Howard, and Lee. Don has never seen one in the wild and this is my first hunt. I have brought my faithful old .270 that I have carried for 30 years. Velma admonished me not to bring it, said it was too small for moose, but we shall see..."

I was glad that we had no thermometer when I crawled out of the tent at 5:45am that first bitter cold morning in our Ontario moose camp. I had no desire to know just how cold it was.

The plans for the days hunt having been agreed upon the previous evening, we hurriedly annihilated a hearty breakfast of pancakes and coffee, and made ready for the adventure.

Since we planned to spend most of the morning posted on moose crossings, heavy clothing was necessary. Encased in insulated underwear, wool pants and socks, a couple heavy shirts, insulated vests, rubber boots, heavy jackets and gloves, and with my pockets stuffed with shells and candy bars, I looked like an astronaut out for a space walk. After struggling into a life-vest, my arms stuck straight out from my body. Gathering up my rifle and flashlight, and wrapping a length of rope around my mid-section, I staggered off down the trail toward the lake.

Phil, Don, and I were to hunt the south end of the lake where we were camped; Howard and Lee would go to the north end.

Our canoe didn't have much freeboard when the three of us paddled off into the darkness, but by breathing in unison - or so it seemed - we managed to stay afloat. Dawn and our canoe arrived simultaneously at the south end of the lake, where we beached our craft, shed our life-vests, and followed a moose trail down the stream.

Separating, we posted ourselves on likely-looking crossings, and waited quietly in the biting cold. All was quiet until 9:20am, when a large, rather black wolf appeared at the edge of the woods, made its way into the marsh grass and disappeared. Moose tracks were plentiful, but none of our gang saw a moose that morning.

In the afternoon, we switched places, and our canoe went to the north end. I hiked upstream a half-mile to a small, deep lake with a rock cliff on its west side, and marsh around the balance of its perimeter.

I had just got settled on my post when I saw a moose moving among the trees at the edge of the marsh, nearly 600 yards upstream from me. I attempted climbing the cliff to get closer, but old "Banjo-nose" apparently spotted me and "va-moosed".

Just then, faintly, I heard three shots from the south end of the lake. When we canoed to camp at dusk, we learned that Howard had missed with three shots at a nice bull near the spot where I had spent the morning.

I lay awake a long time that night, reliving the evening's hunt, determined to do differently if the opportunity presented itself again.

And it did. During the night, the weather warmed and a south wind gave us a heavy rain that lasted into the following afternoon. Around 2pm, we canoed to the north end and I took the same post as on the preceding evening.

I had hardly made myself comfortable when, like a replay, the moose again appeared at the far end of the marsh, crossed the river, and walked briskly toward the end of the lake, where it stood looking toward the cliff.

This time I waited.

I must admit, after mentally digesting the huge proportions of the animal, I glanced doubtfully at my little .270, entertaining second thoughts about its capabilities of sending that monstrous creature to the great lily-pad swamp in the sky. The distance was too great to chance a shot until the moose did an about face and walked the perimeter of the lake, each step bringing it closer to me.

At 150 yards, it stopped, turned broadside, and once again eyed the cliff where it had seen me the day before.

This was my chance.

The dot in my 2 1/2 power Lyman-Alaskan scope rested just behind the moose's ear, and I squeezed the trigger. The 160-grain Nosler bullet sounded like a hammer blow when it hit. The moose collapsed, instantly dead.

Since the moose lay across the river from me, I had to climb the cliff and skirt the lake to reach it, a feat that, in my excitement, required only ten minutes. It was only when I stood over the fallen animal that I realized the true immensity of the beast.

Then the work began! With only a piece of rope and the 4-inch blade of my old "bear-skinner," I set to work, first tying one hind leg to a tussock clump to facilitate removing the entrails.

Before the process was finished, I had to step inside the body cavity in order to reach far enough into the rib section to sever the windpipe. With my knife, I removed the head, severed the legs at the knees, and cut the animal in half.

Shortly after dark, my companions arrived with the canoe and the aluminum boat. After quartering the moose with a chainsaw, we loaded it into our boats and made our precarious way in the inky blackness down the log-choked river to the lake, and camp.

Needless to say, my diary entry that night read thusly:

"I am happy tonight; the .270 performed well, we have meat on the pole…"

Chapter 5

A World of Mud

SPRINGTIME ARRIVED WITH A MIXED BAG OF WEATHER; SOME beautiful days in early April, followed by a couple weeks of cold rain and, at times, hail. Some bear tracks had already been noted, but the weather certainly wasn't conducive to much bear movement.

During the years of my bear control activities, my employer (Washington Forest Protection Assn.) encouraged me to allow members of the news media or other interested individuals to accompany me on bear hunting forays. This gave me an opportunity to explain our damage control program to them on site, where they could see the extent of the damage and better understand the need for "lethal" control, which, at that point in time, was our only alternative.

One instance occurred in mid-April, when Jess and I agreed to have a fellow whom I shall call "Buford" go along with us on a bear hunt. Neither of us knew the old gentleman or anything about him other than the information he had given us over the telephone regarding his qualifications as a rifleman and bear hunter.

Naturally, we looked forward with not a little apprehension to meeting him. Buford's arrival on the morning of the hunt left us with the unanimous feeling that it would be an interesting day.

He was a sizeable fellow, in his sixties, and sadly out of shape, a wonderful specimen for medical school students who wished to observe a heart attack waiting to happen. It was quite evident that he was no woodsman.

Nevertheless, what he lacked in fitness was offset by his infectious friendliness and polished politeness.

As Buford began loading his gear into our pickup, there was no doubt in our mind that he had made ample preparation for his safari. As he continued loading all manner of paraphernalia, including suitcases, gun cases, ammo, shoes, and an enormous lunch into the front seat, we began to wonder if he understood that this was to be but a one-day hunt.

Finally, utilizing two vehicles, we got all his gear stowed, loaded our hounds, and headed for the woods. Our destination was to be the Promised Land, northwest of Humptulips.

About halfway there, the April sky darkened and a cold rain lashed down. This was definitely not the kind of day to encourage bear movement, and so we stopped at a roadside establishment to wait out the storm and quaff a hot cup of coffee.

Although the morning was yet young, a few of the "good old boys" were already in residence, occupying their favorite stools and sipping an early beer. Our appearance in the doorway - or should I say, Buford's appearance - caused a chain reaction of elbow-nudging to ripple down the row of imbibers at the bar. And for good reason. Every eye in the room was fixed on him as Buford clanked over the threshold, weighted down with bandoliers of ammunition, hunting knives, mess kit and canteen, and a machete.

A big silver plated revolver protruding from a shoulder holster under his camouflage jacket was complimented by a huge cowboy hat, and this properly protected from soil and the elements by a plastic cover. A pair of very dark "shades" covered his eyes and a goodly portion of his face. Camouflage pants and a pair of high $150 boots made up the lower part of his outfit.

Oblivious to the wide-eyed attention, he sauntered over to a table, sat down with his back to the audience, and proceeded to remove his deerskin gloves. All the while, he was loudly expounding on the merits and values of the many guns in his collection, most of which I had never heard of. Once he got past the .30-.30 his exhortation was wasted on me.

Before we had finished our coffee, one of the boys at the bar had Buford all "sized" up and was attempting to sell him a $550 rifle. Luckily, Buford already had two just like it in his collection. The rain stopped and we hustled Buford out the door before they tried to sell him the establishment.

When we reached the hunting grounds, the day had warmed and the dogs rousted a bear from its nest just off the old logging road. After a short chase they soon had the bear up a tree. Eagerly pushing our way through a dense thicket of dripping wet salal, winter huckleberry and dog-hair hemlocks on our way to the treed bear, we noticed that Buford was no longer with us.

Stopping to listen, we could hear him puffing and thrashing in the brush somewhere behind us. Just then we heard an exceptionally loud crack in the bushes, followed by silence.

Quickly backtracking, I climbed atop a big log, pulled back the huckleberry bushes and saw a pair of $150 boots sticking up in the air. Buford had fallen off the log and landed upside down in the wet brush on top of his new Stetson. He was flailing around like a capsized beetle when I found him.

After getting him right side up again and retrieving his "shades", we proceeded on to the tree where we found the bear eyeing the dogs uneasily from his perch thirty feet up a small hemlock.

Admonishing Buford to make a clean kill by shooting the bear in the head, I received assurance from him that he was a good shot; he had been practicing on the range and he was ready to give us a little exhibition of his skill.

At the report of his rifle, the bear came clawing and raging down the tree, only creased by Buford's bullet. Almost as one my partner and I shot and the bear fell to the ground, dead.

Buford was so excited that, with the uproar from the hounds, he hadn't heard our shots and assumed that he had killed the bear. After the hounds had worried the carcass awhile it was hard to distinguish bullet holes from tooth holes, so we told him no differently.

Buford subsequently accompanied us on other hunts and we grew to be quite fond of the old fellow. Each hunt with him was a roar, but despite his eccentricities and ineptitude as a hunter or woodsman, we respected his desire to attain the attributes that would identify him as a seasoned woodsman.

About a month later, Buford accompanied us on another hunt, this time in Lewis County on the North Fork Newaukum River. On this hunt the dogs somehow managed to take the bear's backtrack and the chase petered out with dogs scattered out and no barking to guide us to them. One by one, we picked up the dogs as they made their way back to the road and by late afternoon had them all accounted for except two.

Finally, in the evening, we faintly heard the missing hounds, their voices rising from the very bottom of a huge and deep, timbered canyon, through which the reaches of the North Fork wound its way. The dogs were far from us and as near as we could determine, across the river. Driving down an old, overgrown spur road, we soon found ourselves at its dead end.

The hounds' voices were indistinct due to the distance but as near as we could ascertain continued to carry to us from the same spot. We assumed that they were barking "treed" and with no roads leading anywhere near them, we had no option except to descend down into the canyon in the general direction of their baying.

The only problem was Buford. He was out of the truck, ready and anxious to go with us, but did he realize what he was getting into? The hike down the mountain would be easy enough, but what about the return? Buford insisted that he was capable so off we went at a trot, down into the canyon.

As we neared the bottom we began to hear the dogs' voices more clearly and were able to pinpoint their location. They were definitely "treed" and Buford's face beamed in eager anticipation. When we finally reached the river, the sounds of the dogs were drowned out by the rushing waters. The river was knee-deep, swift and cold, and so we quickly pulled off our shoes, preparing to wade.

Buford's face was quite flushed by now and it seemed to take him forever to get his boots off. While I waited, I waded into bone-achy cold water and carried my rifle, my shoes and Buford's rifle across to the far bank. Wading back, I found Buford finally had his boots off. Taking his boots across the river, I sloshed back and, taking Buford by the arm, managed to get him across the river.

By now my legs and feet were nearly numb from the cold water and so I hurriedly pulled on my socks and shoes and had just finished lacing them up when Buford announced that he had forgotten his deerskin gloves on the other side of the river. At this point I felt like my patience was being tested like Job's (from the Bible) but I gritted my teeth, said nothing, pulled off my shoes and socks, waded the river yet again and retrieved his gloves. Buford finally being shod and properly gloved, we set off once again, heading upriver in quest of the dogs.

So far Buford's adrenaline was doing its job and his excitement really showed when we at last heard the dogs, loud and clear, just ahead of us. Reaching the dogs, who were barking up a hemlock tree, we searched the tree limbs with our eyes, looking for that spot of black that would reveal our bear. You can imagine our disappointment, after all this effort, to find not a bear, but a porcupine staring stupidly at us from a limb near the tree's trunk!

Buford's illusions were dissipated in an instant by this let down and his reaction was like the air being let out of a balloon, especially when he remembered the long, steep climb ahead of him to retrace his steps back up the mountain!

Leashing the dogs, we started our trek out, repeating the several trips across the river, and this time remembering Buford's gloves. About halfway up the mountain Buford began to give out on us and begged us to let him lie down and rest a while. I began to worry that he might have a heart attack but with darkness not far away

I also knew we must hurry if we hoped to find our truck while it was still light.

I asked Jess if he would stay with Buford while I hurried on ahead. Since we were parked at the end of the old road, I dared not get too far to the left or I would miss it and we would be in for a night in the woods.

Luckily, just at dark, I came out right at the road's end. I yelled to Jess and guided them out by flashlight. Poor Buford collapsed when he reached the road and not long after we got him in the truck he was fast asleep.

Surprisingly, this experience didn't sour him on bear hunting and before we reached Jess' house, Buford was asking about another hunt! Though it had nearly killed him, he had enjoyed the hunt.

By sensing the value and enjoyment that Buford received from every facet of a day in the woods, I was helped to develop a new awareness and appreciativeness of things I too often took for granted.

One beautiful spring day in mid-May, Jess and I drove up in the Skokomish River area to make a hunt for a tree-peeling bear. About halfway along the Deer Meadows road the dogs struck a "hot" bear track and off they went, headed north towards lower Lake Cushman. There were no roads to get us closer to the chase and after we determined that the bear had swum across the lower lake, we set off on foot in pursuit. Jess drove to the upper Cushman Lake dam, walked across it and hiked through the woods to the lower dam. I set out on foot from where the chase started and made my way through the hills to the south side of the lake.

For three and a half hours the hounds bayed the bear on the sheer hillsides above the lake while Jess and I ran up and down the cliffs trying to get a shot. I felt sure that the bear would tumble off the cliff into the lake if we killed him there but he refused to leave the cliffs. Finally, the bear climbed to the top and Jess got a good shot at him and ended the chase. To his dismay he saw the 250-pound bear tumble over the cliff's edge but breathed a sigh of relief when it lodged behind a tree, breaking its fall.

Leaving the bear where it fell, we hiked back to our trucks and drove an hour and fifteen minutes, and through a wet crossing on the river, to reach the bear. Using my truck's winch, we retrieved the animal and headed for home.

Two weeks later we hunted the area again in an effort to capture a bear that was peeling trees on McTaggert Creek. We hunted hard until 2 p.m. with no success and since the day had turned hot, we took a break in the shade. After an hour, we drove across the head of McTaggert Creek and struck the bear, red hot.

The dogs caught up with the bear almost immediately and "bayed it up" in the creek. Before we could reach the dogs, the bear broke and ran north across the main logging road and treed on a steep hill not far above it. When I reached the tree I was amazed at the bear's size and also by the fact that it had treed high up in a big cottonwood tree.

Jess tied the dogs back and I shot the bear from the tree. His huge carcass really thumped the rocks when it hit the earth; the bear weighed 325 pounds. Luckily it was a downhill drag and after taking the dogs and our guns to the truck, we soon had our prize loaded in my Blazer.

The next day Jess made a hunt by himself in the same general area and treed a 250-pound bear.

I had obtained several permits for sportsmen to hound-hunt a problem bear on the Snoqualmie tree farm. They had chased this bear many times but it refused to "tree". Consequently, on June 19th I took Jess and his hounds to the area to give it a try. Jess' friend Sasser also rode along for the hunt. A biologist with the Seattle game department region met us at Snoqualmie and accompanied us on the hunt. After an hour or so, the dogs "struck" the bear's scent on Proctor Creek and bayed it all the way down into the North Fork Tolt river canyon.

The bear and hounds swam the raging river and started up the opposite mountainside. Jess stayed put on the north side of the river canyon while the biologist and I drove around to the south side, reaching a point directly above the bayed bear.

Grabbing my rifle, I dived down over the steep, rocky canyon side but when I neared the dogs and bear, it scented me and headed up the hill towards my truck. It reached the road, right where the weaponless biologist was standing, and then crashed back down into the canyon with the hounds right at its heels. The chase went all the way to the river, crossed it, and started up the north side.

By this time I had reached the river, which was roaring so loudly that I lost track of the chase. Wading the swift, rocky river was no fun experience but I soon reached the far side, dripping wet, and headed up the hill through the timber. Once I left the river behind me I stopped to listen but could hear nothing of the dogs. The river still roared in the distance, making it hard to hear.

I kept climbing and eventually reached the logging road where I had last seen Jess. I couldn't hear a bark anywhere and so I started walking down the road. After a few minutes, Sasser drove up with Jess' truck and hauled me seven miles back to my truck.

Arriving there, I found Jess and the hounds waiting on the road. He had hiked down to the river from the north side, met up with the dogs and bear, apparently while I was wading the river, and had shot the bear. Due to the noisy river, I had heard nothing. Only one dog, Dan, had been hurt on the hunt and this was the third wound of the year for him. The bear was a large 250-pound bear that apparently had an aversion to climbing trees. Its stomach contained tree cambium and the remains of a fawn.

In late July of that year, I received a call from a Department of Wildlife game agent, asking if I would consider setting up a bear hunt for a contributing editor of a national hunting magazine. I arranged the hunt and at 5 a.m. on the following Sunday morning Jess and I and my daughter Sylvan met the game agent and sports writer in Aberdeen. Taking two vehicles, we drove up to old Camp Three at the head of the Wishkah River and struck a bear, red-hot, in a pre-commercially-thinned stand of Douglas fir on Parker Creek.

Jess dumped all nine of the hounds and the canyons rang with the sweet music of their varied voices. There was no problem to follow the chase with our ears and when the bear headed in the direction of Windy Pass, I fired up my Blazer and Sylvan and I headed over there. Jess opted to stay on Parker Creek in case, as often happens, the bear decided to circle back to where the chase started.

When we reached the end of the old road on Windy pass the dogs had the bear at bay directly below us. Their voices grew louder as they moved nearer to us and in a matter of minutes the bear decided to climb a tree only one hundred yards from where we were standing. What a noise the nine hounds made, for they could see the bear in the thinly limbed hemlock. I called Jess on my C-B radio and in a little while he and his passengers joined us.

In short order we, too, were standing under the tree, looking at the bear and the earsplitting uproar from the hounds made it necessary to yell to communicate.

After the dogs were tied safely back from the tree, our sportswriter shot the bear quite dead. To our disappointment, the bear hung up in the tree and when it was evident that it wasn't going to fall, Jess climbed the skinny tree like a native going for coconuts, and pushed the bear out.

After skinning the bear and feeding the hounds, we started out of the woods with our spoils. The writer wanted the hide and skull but refused to touch or carry any of it. My daughter carried the skull out for our citified sportswriter and we were soon loaded up and on our way off the mountain.

On the way out of the woods, the sportswriter commented that this was the first bear hunt he had ever been on. The game agent took notice of this and said, "But I read a story in your magazine about a successful bear hunt you had been on a while back."

"Oh," the writer responded. "The editor wanted a bear story so I just made that one up!"

Trust your mother, but cut the cards…

Freshly peeled trees were appearing on Berry Creek, not far from the Aberdeen city limits, so Jess and I began to concentrate our efforts in that area. On one hunt we started a bear chase at 6:30 p.m. that turned out to be two bears. Just before dark we heard the hounds and they had the bears bayed up behind Bel Aire hill. A few moments later the dogs moved on while one stayed and began barking, "treed". We could hear the pack baying the bear as it moved up Steward Creek and, eventually, out of our hearing.

Taking our flashlights, we hiked into the timbered canyon where the lone dog was treeing. This dog belonged to a friend of Jess' and was a very shy "one-man" dog type. When we were within one hundred yards of the bear tree, the dog heard us coming, stopped barking, and left the tree. We looked up a lot of trees but they were huge, with thick tops that our lights would not penetrate. Finally, a little disgusted, we were forced to give up and climb out of the canyon.

An hour or so later we located the rest of the hounds scattered out in the area of the original strike and not barking much. By 10 p.m., dogs began appearing on the roads and within another hour we had them all rounded up and left the woods, planning to return soon to even the score.

Two days later found us in the same area with the hounds roaring off on a red-hot track. Within a few seconds they had the bear "jumped" and after a short run down into Steward Creek, the bear treed. It had climbed a bushy-limbed hemlock and its body was nearly concealed by the thick branches. Getting a quick glimpse of its head, I shot and missed, causing the bear to change its position to the other side of the tree. Jess and I both shot at the same time and the bear crashed down through the limbs, landing with a thump near our feet. This bear was a small, adult female and our earlier chase had probably been her and her yearling.

Being such a short chase, all the dogs had made it to the tree, which makes for a happy ending to a hunt. After feeding the hounds the heart and liver, we hiked out to our vehicles, reaching them just as it started to rain.

After making some hunts in other areas, we returned to Berry Creek six days later around 4:30 on a warm Monday evening. Again, we started a bear immediately, had a good thirty-minute race, ending with the bear treed up a thirty-inch diameter fir. The bear was a yearling and when I shot it from the tree we found that my bullet had shattered its skull, followed along the neck and shoulder, backbone and into a hindquarter. Since there was very little edible meat left on the critter, we fed it to the hounds and were home by 6:45 p.m.

These hunts whetted our appetite for more so we returned two days later, on Wednesday evening, arriving at the hunting grounds around 6:45 p.m. Again, we started a hot track on Berry Creek that led to a good snappy chase, but this bear, unlike the others, made a long run down over the East Hoquiam side of the divide.

Then the chase headed south and, just as darkness fell, the bear treed far below us in the Woodlawn swamps.

Taking our guns and flashlights, we started hiking towards the hounds' voices that could but faintly be heard in the distance. After an hour, we finally reached the bear tree, which was a big, living cedar about four feet in diameter. After tying the dogs back away from the tree, lest we make a bad shot in the dark and the bear fell wounded among them, Jess located the bear with his flashlight and I put a bullet through its head. The bear hit the ground, very dead, for which we were glad. A wounded bear in the pitch-black darkness of this swamp would have created a problem.

The bear was an adult female and being in such a miserable place, we fed the dogs all they could eat of its flesh and left the remains for the coyotes. Now the challenge was to find our way out of the swamp and hit the right ridge to locate our vehicles. Each of us led a leashed dog, hoping to escape the swamp before the dogs struck another track in this "bear Heaven".

What a mess it was, leading a hound through the brushy swamp, carrying a rifle and a flashlight, and trying to keep oriented. The last part of the hike was up a near perpendicular hill that caused us to stop occasionally to rest and call the dogs together. At one point, Jess said, "Well, Ralph, if we make it up out of here, I guess we will never have to worry about a heart attack!"

The day before this last hunt, Kelly Lund (Game Department Agent) and I had gone to the Long Beach Peninsula in Pacific County to check out a reported bear problem. A sow bear and yearlings had been terrorizing a Methodist church camp and they wanted them removed. I set a snare for them and four days later received a phone call informing me that I had caught one of the three bears.

Kelly and I drove down and were met there by the local game agents. Our plan was to chemically immobilize the bear and move it to a new location. Since we had caught one of the yearlings, we hoped that this episode would convince mama bear to take the other yearling and vacate the premises.

Apparently the drug was old for it had no effect on the little bear so we had to use an aluminum "catch-pole" and noose to secure his neck and then manhandle him to get the snare off his foot. The cable had become so twisted that it was necessary for me to use a wrench to remove the cable clamps, which was no little chore. Even a small bear has tremendous strength.

Once the snare cable was removed from the bear's foot, we wrestled him into a barrel-live-trap and used it for a cage. Then we hauled the bear miles away and released it on the Palix River drainage in an excellent spot with lots of natural feed. We didn't want to kill the bear since it had done nothing except unnerve the church camp occupants, so moving the bear was our only recourse.

Moving a bear to a new location generally does not solve a problem. Either the bear will find its way "home" again, or it will find itself in another bear's home range and not welcomed by the resident female. It will be driven from that bear's area (or killed by it) and soon find itself in another bear's home range. If it does find an unoccupied piece of the woods it is often very nominal habitat, and the transient bear finds poor pickings.

While I am on the subject, I will relate an incident that occurred a couple years later and, again, in the Ilwaco-Long Beach area. It all started on Wednesday, December 29th, when game agent Kelly Lund and I responded to a couple of bear damage complaints from Ilwaco.

At the first complaint site a mother bear and her yearling offspring had been rummaging in garbage cans outside a log cabin in a wooded area at the end of a cul-de-sac. This caused the cabin's occupants no undue concern until the bears began exploring the front porch, showing a reluctance to leave even when the owner appeared.

Theoretically, by December 31, bears are supposed to be in bed. Apparently, some of them, like me, put off that chore as long as possible. These bears were still up and about only because a source of food—in this case, garbage—was available.

Personally, I hate to see a bear destroyed just because he has inconvenienced someone by upsetting a garbage can that was left tantalizing available to him. The first thing to consider if you plan to chop a clearing out of the woods and move your residence in among the bears is to keep your garbage inside where it is less apt to attract them. Thus, you will be doing both yourself and the bears a favor.

Our next stop was at the Ilwaco hospital parking lot where a bear had been making nightly raids on a pair of garbage dumpsters. Here, again, garbage was strewn from the dumpsters down over the bank and into the swamp. I shuddered as I imagined the type of "goodies" the bear was gleaning from the hospital's refuse!

Foot snares were set at both locations in an attempt to capture the marauders and instructions given that we be notified immediately upon the capture of a bear.

These instructions were religiously observed, the result being that I was extracted from my warm nest at 3:30 a.m. on Friday morning by a telephone call that sent me off into the frosty darkness on a "bring 'em back alive" mission.

Dawn found Kelly and I, flashlights in hand, wading into the swamp behind the hospital. The morning was a frosty cold twenty-five degrees, making me anxious to secure the bear as soon as possible and relieve him from his uncomfortable situation in the 10-inch deep ice water of the swamp.

The snare cable had been attached to a sturdy drag-pole and after locating the bear, which had tangled the pole in the swamp brush and settled himself on the only semi-dry spot in the marsh, we determined his size, returned to the truck and Kelly set about preparing the proper dosage of Ketamine needed to tranquilize our snared bruin.

Subsequently, using the capture gun, the bear was "darted" in the rump. After the elapse of ten minutes, the bear's tongue began to flick nervously in and out, his head nodding as the injection began to take its effect. At this point it was necessary for us to hold the bear's head up to prevent his nose from sinking into the water. A few moments more and I was able to remove the snare from his leg.

By this time, three more game department personnel had arrived to assist us and we carried the bear up the bank to the hospital's parking lot, where he was placed in a large iron cage.

And none too soon, for once inside he immediately sat up and groggily pondered his present predicament. His torpid attitude and bleary expression was probably not a little unlike the mirror reflection that greeted a lot of folks that New Year's morning.

This bear was transported to a location approximately twenty-five miles distant and released in an area of ideal habitat. With garbage not readily available, we hoped it would check its calendar and decide it was time for a long winter snooze.

But it was not to be. A week later this same bear was rummaging in garbage cans at Bay Center. The following week it was across the Nemah River and upsetting garbage cans at Lynn Point. When last seen, it was headed south along Shaolwater Bay in the direction of Ilwaco.

Yet another example was the ill-fated three-legged bear. A Seattle sportsman reported to me that he had shot and wounded a bear while "still"-hunting in a canyon just inland from the Sandpiper beach resort, just south of Pacific Beach. From his observations, his bullet had struck the bear in a front leg, apparently shattering the upper leg bone, and the animal had escaped.

His efforts to track the bear in the dense underbrush were obviously half-hearted and without consequences, and in most cases, the story would end here.

Not so with this bear.

On or about July 15 of the following year, a three-legged bear, thin and hungry-looking, showed up at the Iron Springs resort, about 3 miles south of the Sandpiper.

For one who was not "checking in", he certainly did a thorough job of checking the place out. His nose naturally fine-tuned for groceries, he immediately keyed in on the garbage shed, forced entry, and found all sorts of delectables among the refuse. With a wet spring and a slow berry crop, this sure beat the steady diet of salal blooms, ant eggs and grass that had sustained him in such poor condition since emerging from his winter den.

His belly now stuffed with assorted "junk" foods, plastic bags and other gourmet items, he proceeded to tour the resort, knocking over a few garbage cans en route. As could be expected, his presence was soon common knowledge and was met with mixed emotions by the clientele.

Being three-legged, he immediately gained their sympathy, but being a bear, he also won their fear and a certain amount of respect.

Some were delighted to have him around and encouraged his presence by throwing out food for him, while other guests packed up and left. As for the bear, he tolerated the presence of humans, devouring the goodies strewn about for him, and became increasingly "tame".

"Fearless" is a better word. A wild bear is never to be trusted as "tame".

At this point, the resort's owner contacted the Department of Wildlife and requested—in a tone that smacked of urgency—that they send their control agent and remove the bear from the premises. It was not desired that the bear should be harmed, for he had by now become quite an attraction. But his immediate removal was imperative lest someone suffer an injury from the bold freeloader.

A large live-trap, consisting of two fifty gallon steel drums welded together, end to end, and provided with a heavy iron trapdoor at one end, was set up by the agent behind a woodpile near one of the resort's cabins. Inside the trap, a string attached to an odorous bait led upwards to the trigger of a large wooden rattrap, securely mounted atop the barrel. A wire from the rattrap's spring led through a tube down the length of the barrels; its opposite end attached to a pin that held the trap door aloft.

Theoretically, it works like this: bear crawls in barrel, tugs on bait. String depresses rattrap trigger, spring flips forward, pulling wire through tube and withdrawing holding pin. Trap door falls, bear is captured.

Kind of reminded me of a Rube Goldberg invention. Although this type trap has captured hundreds of bears in Wisconsin, our Washington bears seem to have a peculiar aversion to it.

In the meantime, the bear had been seen on the deck of Waller's Iron Springs art gallery, his nose pressed to the window as he peered in at the paintings. An art critic, no less!

When, after three days, the live trap had netted only a squashed sparrow (that had accidentally stomped on the rat trap trigger), the agent asked me to accompany him to Iron Springs to assess the situation. While there, I placed a foot snare in one of the bear's trails.

The following morning, the bear made an appearance three miles away at the Sandpiper. That evening he reappeared, entered one of the resort's units and walked down the hall, startling a female guest whose husband proceeded to flail the bear with a broom.

By noon, the bear had returned to Iron Springs and was caught in my snare. The bear was then tranquilized and relocated thirty miles back from the beach in the Olympic foothills, far removed from garbage cans and people.

Less than a year later, on May 11th, I received a phone call informing me that the three-legged bear was—you guessed it—back at the Iron Springs resort and up to his old tricks again! He had made a touchdown at Camp 400 the day previous, scattering garbage (and people) in every direction and had then revisited Iron Springs before moving on down the beach to the Wind and Sea retreat just north of Copalis Beach.

The game agent and I drove out to access the situation and found the patience of the resort owners growing thin. The general consensus now was that the bear be destroyed.

In nine months, less four months lost in hibernation, this three-and-a-half year old bear had hobbled on three legs from the east fork of the Humptulips River, cross-country to Iron Springs. It is my theory that once he crossed the Humptulips River (probably in the Walker Bottom), the smell of salt air directed him toward the coast, and home.

After some discussion among ourselves, it was agreed that the three-legged bear deserved one more chance. Two foot-snares were set in an attempt to capture him, the plan being this time to haul him to an area at least 50 miles northeast of Iron Springs for release.

Two days later, before the snares could capture him, the three-legged bear was chased and killed by a local hound hunter, bringing this story, as well as the bear's antics, to an untimely and unequivocal end.

During early May 1980, I placed some bear foot-snares at some damage locations north of Shelton; some of these in a stand of predominantly large cedars near the Agate Road and a few on Deer Creek in a plantation of fifteen-year-old firs. The snares on Agate Road produced a two hundred pound boar bear within three days and fresh sign indicated that more bears were in the area. I also placed four snares on Swanson Hill near Morton, one hundred miles east of my home. This area was being hit hard by porcupine, mountain beavers and bears and the ravages of these three critters had left the mountainside speckled with red-needled, dying trees.

The mountain beaver, or sewellel, as the local Indians named him, carries the scientific name *aplodontia rufa*. It is a rodent or gnawer; one of the earliest forms of rodent known to have been on earth. It has not changed through thousands of years, remaining just the same as it was in prehistoric times.

The mountain beaver is a small animal, weighing approximately two-and-one-quarter pounds and measuring about twelve inches long. Its head is broad and triangular in shape, and its eyes are very small and bright. It has a short, stout, very muscular body with short legs and large feet. It is tailless, except for a short stub covered with a cluster of long hairs.

Its claws are long and good tools for digging. The front teeth are long and yellowish brown and are used to cut off ferns and other plants. It often climbs up small evergreen saplings, gnawing off the branches and the terminal stem.

Its body is covered with a course, shiny brownish hair with short under-fur. The Indians used the fur for their robes, but today it has no value.

The mountain beaver is a burrowing animal, digging its tunnels in the soft, rich soils of ravines and draws. It digs with its powerful claws and pushes the earth ahead of it like a miniature bulldozer, using its shoulders and broad head. The dirt is deposited in a soft pile in front of the entrance. One burrow may have as many as fifty exits. The roots of ten- to fifteen-year-old fir trees are often loosened by their burrowing, causing the tree to tip over and die. They also gnaw off and consume the bark of trees of this age, often girdling them much as a bear does. This damage occurs usually on the lower twelve inches of the young tree's trunk. The damage inflicted is often confused with bear damage but can easily be differentiated. The mountain beaver consumes the bark, leaving none on the ground while the bear leaves the bark strewn about and devours only the cambium, or new growth ring, from the tree trunk.

Our western Washington porcupines were relatively scarce prior to 1950, but now, although abundant only in localized areas, it occurs throughout the western portion of our state. They travel mostly at night and feed primarily on low-growing greens and woody plants, but hard frosts and snow will cause them to climb and feed on the needles and bark of coniferous trees, and on elderberry stems.

Tree damage attributed to porcupines generally occurs January through March. Unlike eastern porcupines, our western Washington porkies do not spend much time sleeping in trees, but prefer a sheltered den under logging debris or stumps. Like the mountain beaver, porcupines also consume the tree's bark but tend to damage much larger trees. Often, porky damage to trees is confused with bear damage, but the tooth pattern of the gnawer and absence of telltale bark on the ground make it easy to identify the porcupine as the culprit.

On my trips to Morton to check my snares, I had an excellent view of Mt. St. Helens from the top of Swanson Hill. There was some concern about the mountain since it had recently been spewing some smoke and ash from its summit. On Thursday, May 15, while checking my snares on Swanson Hill, I found that a bear had climbed a tree at one of my log sets and stolen the bait. The snare was also tripped so I reset, re-baited, and continued on up the mountain.

I had placed a trail set in a low saddle near the summit and when I reached it, I found a large male bear tied up and waiting for me. After taking care of the bear and loading it in my Blazer, I reset the snare and headed for home. The snares would be due to be checked again on Sunday, May 18. Nature had different plans.

At 8:31 on the morning of the 18th, Mt. St. Helens erupted with a terrible blast, disintegrating 1,200 feet of its summit and sending tons of volcanic ash eastward toward Morton and on across the state, past Yakima and as far as Spokane. Four inches of volcanic ash covered the highway, in fact all of the area around Morton. Huge clouds of dust created by vehicles reduced visibility to zero and traffic was being stopped near Morton. Needless to say, I cancelled my trip to Morton.

Here on the coast, due to a westerly wind, we had been spared from the ash and we enjoyed a beautiful spring day. The following day turned cloudy and cool and by evening it was raining. The rain persisted through the night and even though a misty rain continued into Tuesday, the Morton highway remained closed. When Wednesday dawned misty-rainy, I decided to try to get to Morton and check my snares, which were three days overdue. The highway was now greasy-slick from the rain-soaked ash that had acquired the consistency of sloppy sheet-rock "mud".

Near Morton, I found the road blocked by a sheriff's vehicle but when I explained my concern about the overdue snares that might be holding a hapless bear, he agreed to let me proceed.

When I left the highway and entered the woods on the Swanson Hill logging road, I found myself in an eerie, spooky-looking woods that looked like something out of a science-fiction movie. No one had traveled the road since the eruption and I had to use the four-wheel drive to negotiate the slippery hill. The trees had held an inch of ash on their boughs and this was now sticky-wet and heavy, causing the limbs to bend down over the road. My windshield was soon covered with gray mud from these limbs and in short order my windshield washer-fluid was used up. I now had to roll down my window and keep my head outside to be able to see the road. By the time I reached the first snare my face and glasses were splattered with mud.

Everything was coated with mud; trees, bushes, logs, weeds; the world had turned into a gray, muddy nightmare. There were hundreds of porcupine tracks in the mud, lots of deer and coyote tracks, as well as the tracks of a bear, but thank God my snares held no animals. As I checked each snare, I removed it for there was no guarantee when I might be able to return. There was no way to remove the gray mud from my shoes and clothing or hands. I, as well as my truck, was a muddy mess when I left the woods and headed for home.

It is hard to describe the feeling when I left the area of gray, muddy, ash-covered desolation and entered the green, beautiful and untouched area near my home. It was like awakening from a bad dream.

Four days later, at 3:45 a.m., Sunday, May 25th, the mountain blew its top again, sending volcanic ash and smoke 45,000 feet in the air. This time we were not so lucky here on the coast. A southeast wind aloft carried the ash cloud one hundred miles, bumping into rain clouds as it traveled. At 7:30 a.m. it was dark as night and raining mud. A drizzly rain had turned the ash to mud and it clung to everything as it fell; power lines, trees, bushes, roofs, driveways, lawns—everything was soon covered with a quarter inch of sticky, muddy gray. At 10:30 a.m., the mountain erupted again, sending us more muddy ash. I remember looking out of our window, feeling deeply depressed as I surveyed the world of mud that surrounded us. It was like being held prisoner in our own home; one step outside and you would be covered with mud that would be carried back inside with you. I felt trapped.

It continued to rain for the next three days which alleviated the mud situation a bit but when it turned sunny and warm on the fourth day, the mud turned to dust, great clouds of dust, as the wind moved the trees or vehicles passed by on the highway. To minimize the danger from poor visibility created by these swirling clouds of dust the speed limit was reduced to thirty-five miles per hour on the highways and fifteen miles per hour in town. This was the situation until late fall when the trees shed their dusty foliage and the winter rains scrubbed the woods.

Parts of western Washington had been spared the baptism of ash and I focused my bear control efforts in these areas for the remainder of the summer. One such area was on Deer Creek, near Shelton, where bears were ravaging plantations of fifteen-year-old firs. I set some snares there and on June 2nd caught an adult female bear in one of them. On a subsequent trip to that area I saw fresh bear tracks on the road bank about one quarter mile east of my snare. Just as I started walking into the plantation, I heard a pickup truck rattle by on the logging road behind me. A few minutes more and I heard a shot, then another, and another coming from the direction they had gone.

Realizing that they were target shooting and not shooting at game, I continued on to check my trail-set snare. Finding it undisturbed, I thought maybe the bear whose tracks I had seen by the road might be in the area between me and the shooters. I was carrying only my .357 magnum revolver and wished for my .270 that was in my truck. Walking quietly along an old cat' road that skirted a marshy area I watched closely for the bear's tracks and stopped often to listen for the sounds of his feeding. Freshly ripped rotten logs were everywhere and before long I heard the sounds of a log or stump being clawed apart as the bear searched for ant eggs and grubs. He was very close to me and so far had neither heard no smelled me. He was on a brush-covered bank just above me and I crept as quietly as I could to try to gain a vantage point where I might see him. When I was within thirty feet of him the noise of his feeding suddenly stopped. At that moment the bear reared up in the salal bushes, saw me and immediately turned to run. Firing quickly, my revolver went off prematurely and I knew I had shot three feet above his head. In a second the underbrush swallowed the bear so I ran to the top of the hill where I could watch for him in a more open stand of mature timber. A small draw lay between the timber and me and I immediately heard the bear moving through it. Another few seconds and I saw the bear on the opposite hillside, just entering the timber. I popped off another round with my revolver and the bear gave a great leap like he had been hit. I hurried over to where I had last seen the bear but could not find a drop of blood, even though I searched for an hour and a half.

When I shot at the bear as he entered the big timber, I noticed that his fur had a large, brown rubbed spot on his right side.

A couple of weeks later I found this same bear, an adult male, caught in my trail-set snare not far from where I had previously shot at him. He was easy to identify by the large brown rubbed spot in his fur. When I skinned him I found no bullet holes in his hide and realized I had earlier missed the bear with both shots.

Chapter 6

THE KING CREEK JINX

IN EARLY JUNE OF 1980 I RECEIVED REPORTS OF EXTENSIVE BEAR damage to young fir plantations in the White River drainage and also on the St. Regis tree farm near Orting. At 4:30 a.m. on the morning of June 12, Jess and I headed for the Weyerhaeuser forestry office at Enumclaw to be briefed on the exact location of this damage.

We finally arrived at the hunting grounds at 7:45 a.m. accompanied by a state wildlife agent and the local Weyerhaeuser forester. Lots of deer, elk and bear sign was in evidence on the tree farm and it wasn't long until the dogs struck a hot bear track. The bear led the dogs on a long chase through the hills, eventually circling back to the point of beginning where it sought refuge in a big cedar tree. We worked our way through the brush toward the sound of the baying hounds and just as we reached them, the bear bailed out of the cedar, ran 100 feet with the hounds hot on its tail, and skittered up a skinny alder with the agility of a squirrel. I shot the bear, a yearling female, but its carcass hung up in the tree's limbs. Since the tree was limbless at the bottom and of small diameter, we had to bring an axe from the truck and fell the tree to procure our bear.

After taking the bear to our truck and loading it, we set out to hunt some more but the day turned cold and rainy, bringing bear movement almost to a halt. After a couple hours and no strikes, we called it a day, planning to return the following morning.

The next day dawned cool and cloudy but the rain had stopped. It felt like a perfect morning for bears to move and it proved to be so for we had no more than entered the woods at 6 a.m. when the dogs struck a bear. This chase started at the same spot as the previous day's chase. Jess' dog "Dan" lined out on the bear at full speed and we got the other five hounds turned loose a little late. As they raced to catch up with "Dan" they bumped into another bear and we ended up with a split race. Within twenty minutes we heard three of the dogs barking treed and not far from an old road. Hiking in to the tree we found the dogs roaring at a good-sized female bear that was ensconced on a limb about thirty feet above them. After dispatching the bear and dragging it to the road, we loaded the hounds and set out to locate "Dan" and the other two hounds who were on the original track.

After quite a bit of searching, we finally heard them treeing in a roadless area of old-growth timber. The going was rough and to get there we had to wade the river twice. But soon the dogs voices became much clearer and a few minutes more found us standing under a big, limby spruce tree that hung out over the river. The bear, a large male, was about thirty-five feet up the tree, standing on the first heavy limb. My first thought was that the bear would tumble down the steep hill and into the fast-moving river when I shot him but luckily he didn't. This bear presented more of a problem to get him from the woods and we were more tired than the dogs when we reached the road and our truck.

Since there was still quite a bit of daylight left, we loaded the hounds, put "Dan" on the truck's hood as strike dog and drove up the road in search of another bear.

About a quarter mile past the point where our earlier chases had started, Dan's bark from the truck's hood alerted us that another bear was close. We dumped all the hounds and the chase headed toward the river, going full bore. Luckily, the bear chose not to cross the river but turned and headed back towards where Jess and I were standing in the old road. It was coming directly towards us and so we stood back to back, facing in opposite directions, in hope that one of us would get a shot at him as he crossed the road.

A few more seconds and the bear, a large, brown-colored one, bombed onto the road at full speed. I heard Jess' rifle roar but the bullet missed and the bear headed towards the high hills. The dogs were close behind him and the sounds of the chase soon became distant and indistinct. After a six and a half mile chase up into the steep hills the dogs began to tire and, one by one, drop out of the chase. We managed to round up all of the dogs and by 1 p.m. we were headed down the highway on our three-hour trip to home. This had been a good hunt; three bears bagged and no dogs injured or lost.

Our next hunt, five days later, was a different matter. It seemed that everything that could go wrong on a hunt did go wrong, with a few extra plagues thrown in.

This hunt took place on St. Regis' King Creek tree farm near Orting and commenced on June 18. Jess and I had arrived there at 6:30 a.m. and were met by a game department agent and a biologist, who intended to accompany us on the hunt. We had taken Jess' pickup and also my Chevy Blazer, and with the game agents riding with me, set off to hunt the Voight Creek portion of the tree farm. Heavy damage to young fir trees was in evidence everywhere you looked, the freshly girdled treetrunks shining wet and white in the early morning sun.

Almost immediately the dogs struck a bear track; red-hot. With the hounds bawling at his heels, the bear headed down into the Voight Creek Canyon, then slowed to a walk as the dogs closed in on him. There was quite an uproar of hound voices rising up from the canyon as the bear walked and fought the dogs on his way up the hill. Soon the bear reached a road on the far side of the canyon, crossed it, and lined out at full speed in the direction of Fox Creek. Though we searched all day, that was the last bark we heard from that chase. We found where the chase had crossed another road but we could hear nothing.

Now, as was usual for game agents that accompanied us on hunts, they never seemed to carry a lunch and by noon on this trip they had devoured all of mine. When we hadn't located the chase by 6 p.m., I took the game agents to the King Creek gate where they had left their vehicle and then I returned to the woods to help Jess hunt for the dogs. During the first part of the chase, Jess' truck had a tire go flat. Just before dark, he had another flat tire and had to park his rig and ride with me. Darkness fell, quiet and windless but although we searched until after midnight, we couldn't hear a bark. We felt sure the dogs were treed down in some deep canyon or we would have found some of them on a road.

By now we were dreaming of some food so we headed for the gate, intending to go to Puyallup for a late meal. But this wasn't to be either; when we reached the gate it was closed, securely locked, and all personnel were in bed. We spent the night in our sleeping bags on top of the dog hauling-crate, exhausted and hungry.

We were awake at 6:30 a.m. and finding the gate now open, we roared off into Orting for a much needed meal, taking Jess' two flat tires with us to be repaired. As soon as we had satisfied our hunger and had loaded the two tires, we headed back to the woods. Putting one tire on Jess' truck and loading the other, we separated to look for dogs.

We had hardly got started on our search when Jess radioed that a front wheel had fallen off his truck—the lug bolts had sheared off! I drove to where he was and once again we left his truck parked by the road. He had picked up one of his dogs that had come from across the Puyallup River which meant that the dogs had been "treed" all night near Ohop; miles from where the chase had started. We then crossed the river and spent the day searching but found no more dogs. Returning to Jess' truck we saw that it had another flat tire! Leaving the crippled truck, we drove my Blazer to the King Creek gate and forestry office where the forester called Camp Kopowsin and learned that Jess' dogs "Dan" and "Rosie" had been seen on the Ohop Road near Ohop. Dan had been picked up but Rosie was shy and escaped. The watchman said "Dan" had a face-full of porcupine quills and someone had taken him to the Tacoma Humane Society. Since the day was getting late, we fired off in that direction and rescued "Dan" from the dog pound at a cost of $13.00. Then we left him with a veterinarian to be cared for. The next stop was to buy lug bolts for Jess' truck before returning to the woods to look for dogs again.

Returning to the King Creek camp, we phoned home to see if our wives had received any calls regarding the dogs and learned that Jess' dog "Pardner" had been picked up walking down the top of the Electron flume on the cliffs over the Puyallup River. He also had a face-full of porcupine quills. We then drove to the power plant at Kapowsin, got the dog, and spent an hour in the dark pulling quills out of him.

By this time the King Creek gate was locked again and our sleeping bags were in Jess' truck. This necessitated another drive to Puyallup where we found a motel room, a much-needed shower, and some food. "Pardner" slept in my Blazer.

The next morning, after a good breakfast, we returned to Ohop to look for "Rosie", the last missing hound. Being unsuccessful, we decided to concentrate on repairing Jess' truck and with the King Creek mechanic helping, soon had the lug bolts installed, the flat tire fixed and the vehicle back on the road. After one more trip to Ohop and no sign of Rosie, I decided to head for home while Jess would remain another day to continue the search (which proved to be fruitful).

On my way home I drove north of Shelton and checked my snare on the Agate Road. I was a little more successful at this and found a large female bear tied up and waiting for me. After dressing her out, I reset the snare, dragged the bear to my Blazer and headed for home, still sixty miles away. After skinning the bear at the Game Department cooler, I called it a day and arrived home, half-starved, at 7:30 p.m. To top off our misfortunes, I found our hot water tank had gone kaput!

But we weren't done with the King Creek bear yet! At 6 a.m., four days later, we were once again headed up Voight Creek, hoping for a little better luck on this hunt. The dogs struck the bear at 11 a.m. and it started pouring rain immediately, almost as if by signal. Being the bear's mating season, the dogs had apparently struck a male and female traveling together and in a few minutes we realized we had a split race.

With the rain roaring on the foliage it was impossible to hear the dogs and once again we lost them. Finally, at 4 p.m., I heard four of the dogs in a huge canyon above the Puyallup River. Later when the chase came out of the canyon, the dogs quit and by 9:30 p.m. we had picked up all the dogs but two.

By this time the gate was locked again and we spent another night in our sleeping bags in a low compartment in the dog crate, just above the tired dogs. The rain hadn't ceased and it poured all night, slacking off a little just at daylight.

Reluctantly, we crawled out of our cramped sleeping space at 6:30 to be greeted by a cold, wet, gray morning. Once again, no food but we did make a pot of coffee on the truck's tailgate. At 7 a.m. we set out to look for the two lost dogs and found both of them. With Jess' strike dog on the hood we continued hunting but it was 3 p.m. before we got a strike, red hot, and at the same place as yesterday's strike.

And once again the clouds burst and it rained and hailed so hard I could hardly stand to be out in it. This drowned out the sound of the dogs completely but when the rain slacked we located them and kept track of them for three and a half hours. By now it was 6:30 p.m. and all the dogs played out and quit except two. We searched for dogs until 11:30 p.m. and once again slept in the dog crate. The weather remained atrocious, with cold rain, hail, wind and thunder.

The following morning greeted us, cold and rainy and we spent the entire day searching for the dogs. We gave up the search at 6 p.m., went to Orting for dinner, and thus refreshed, Jess returned to look for dogs while I headed for home.

So far, the bear was winning. Jess succeeded in rounding up his dogs and four days later, on July 1, we decided to give it another try. We drove through the King Creek gate at 6:30 a.m. that morning and had gone but a short distance when the dogs struck the bear, red hot, on the No. 6 road. The chase lasted three hours and covered nine miles, with the bear crossing the road six times as he traveled through five sections (square miles). It was a beautiful morning and we were able to keep in contact with the entire chase until the bear bounced onto the Fox Creek road right in front of Jess. One blast from Jess' rifle ended our three-week hunt. The bear was a large male and a tough old fighter. Jess' dog "Pete" got tore up pretty bad on this chase and his "Dan" dog also got bit.

We loaded our hard-earned bear, took "Pete" to the vet, delivered the bear to the cooler, skinned it and called it a day. Some bears are tougher than others!

Jess and I terminated our control activities at the end of July that year with a successful hound-hunt in the upper Wishkah's Parker Creek basin. Going in to the tree was easy, since we were guided by the far-off baying of the hounds. After crossing the creek on a beaver dam, we topped a timbered ridge and heard the dogs just below us.

We soon arrived at the bear tree which was a huge hemlock and located the bear high up among its upper limbs. After tying the hounds back away from the tree, lest they should be hurt by the falling bear, we knocked the critter from his lofty perch. After the dogs were allowed to "worry" the dead bear's carcass, we fed them all of the front half that they could eat. Then, severing the back half of the bear, I placed the hind-quarters astraddle of my neck and we started out of the woods. My cousin, Bernard Spade, who was visiting from Maryland, had accompanied us on this chase and he was awed by the wilderness that he now found himself in. With Bernard tight on my heels, we began to climb the ridge in front of us. Jess, ahead of us with the hounds, and unencumbered by any load, was soon over the ridge and gone.

Once we topped the ridge we found ourselves in an entanglement of devils club, salmonberry bushes, vine maples and huge rotting logs. As we worked our way down through this mess, the side hill branched into many side canyons and ridges. The canopy of mixed fir, hemlock and alder trees towering above us made it impossible to look ahead for any landmarks to keep us oriented and so we pushed our way down into the draws and up the side hills, hoping to reach the Windy Pass logging road where our vehicles were parked.

After nearly an hour of this we came to a small opening in the brush on top of a high ridge. Dropping my load of meat, I climbed up on a high wind fallen tree and was able to locate a line of alders growing among the hemlocks along the top of a far-away ridge. I knew the alders indicated the course of a road which had to be Windy Pass. I then realized that we had been traveling far to the left of the course we should have been on. I also knew that Bernard was getting a little apprehensive about the situation and his wild, roadless surroundings didn't look like the kind of place he would want to spend the night in. Having got my directions, I climbed off the windfall, shouldered the bear hams, and led the way down into another canyon. After another hour, I came upon an old skid road that led up the valley and after following it for a while I recognized it as one I had discovered on a previous hound-hunt in that area. I also remembered that it would eventually lead up to the top of Windy Pass and reach the road not far from my truck.

Finally, tired and sweaty, we reached our vehicle, three hours after we left the bear tree. Jess had also taken a wrong ridge and reached the road two miles west of his vehicle.

This was not only the last hunt of the control season but also my last hunt with Jess. Jess had decided to terminate his employment with WFPA and return to professional-guide hunting for bear and cougar in eastern Washington. I hated to see him go. We had developed a kinship like brothers in the five years that I had known and hunted with him. I was proud of him as a hunter and hound trainer and had spent many enjoyable days (and nights) in the woods with him. We parted as good friends and with good memories.

Chapter 7

Hungry Hunters
Spare the Cook

THE PREVIOUS YEAR (1980) SHOWED A SIGNIFICANT IMPROVEment in damage levels in most, but not all, of the spring bear hunt units and a continued reduction of affected acreage. Eleven hunt-units had been established for the 1980 spring bear hunt, encompassing 1,866 square miles. This was a 7% decrease from 1979.

At the January 1980 State Game Commission meeting, I had approached the Commission with the request that the spring bear season be extended through July in lieu of totally dropping that month from the bear season as recommended by the Game Department regions. My request was considered and granted and as a result, concentrated sport hunting was directed to the spring bear units for an additional month in 1980. This turned out to be a boon, especially after Mt. St. Helen's eruption brought hunting to a near stand-still in most units for nearly a month.

I had retained three professional hunters during 1980. Two of these, Jesse Caswell and Bernie Paque, worked four months (April-July). Jim Bryan, in our southwest area of operations, had a great part of his control area either annihilated by St. Helen's eruption or restricted by the consequential "Red Zone." Of necessity,

Bryan was terminated for the season on June 30.

Our three hunters took a total of 58 bear while I took 7 bears by snaring, for a combined total of 65 bear. The total take was a decrease of 30% (28 bear) from 93 bear taken in 1979.

My annual aerial survey conducted in July indicated damage at the lowest level since the beginning (1960) of our control program. The Skookumchuck unit, which had traditionally been one of our worst areas, showed only a few red trees. The Capitol Forest also looked very good with only a few red trees on Waddell Creek. Huffaker Mountain was clean. Only two units—Sekui River and Promised Land—showed damage in amounts significant enough to require continuing control efforts in 1981 to correct the problem. Because these two areas were relatively small—representing only 21% of the area open for spring bear hunting in 1980—I couldn't justify recommending to the Game Department a conventional spring bear damage control season for 1981. I, and the Game Department, agreed that it would result in over-crowding and a poor experience for both the hunter and the land owner alike.

Having arrived at this crossroad in our control program's journey, the problem arose of establishing a limited bear damage control effort to replace the comfortable and effective routine of the Spring Bear season. WFPA's Forest Management Committee was opposed to using our professional hunters in any situations where the sportsmen would not be offered equal opportunity. The Game Department favored WFPA administering control by snaring any and all damage locations, but withdrew their stand when it was met with emotional and near-violent opposition at the Washington State Hound Council meeting in December. A liberal permit system was then devised that would utilize the sport hound-hunter to hunt damage hot-spots in the spring damage period. I intended to maintain my professional hunters although my hunting staff would be reduced to two men working 1-4 months in 1981. These individuals would be hunting in harmony with the permit-holding sportsmen in the major damage areas, and snaring only in those localities where hound-hunting was not feasible. My WFPA hunters would "follow-up" on any unsuccessful sportsman permit-hunts.

The burden would now be upon the sport hound-hunter to demonstrate to the Department of Game and forest land owners that they can hunt under a hot-spot system with such a high degree of success that it would eliminate the need for us to rely on the assured expertise of our professional hunters. We couldn't become complacent and assume that our bear problems were over. There was the possibility that in a couple of years, damage would build up to a level that would call for re-establishing the spring bear hunting season. The Department of Game advised me that this tool would be available if needed in the future.

That same fall of 1980, remembering the fun moose hunt I had enjoyed the previous year with my Michigan friends in the wilds of Ontario, I found myself once again on a flight to join them in another adventure. I arrived in Grand Rapids on October 14 and the next morning at 5:45 found Phil, Howard, Lee and I crammed in a pickup and headed north to the land of the moose.

Twelve hours later we were ensconced in a small, unheated cabin at White River where we spent a frigid night in our sleeping bags. The foliage had been beautiful on our trip through Michigan but the farther north we got into Canada the more barren the trees became. An early snow had already come and gone and the temperature was now in the low teens.

The morning dawned clear and frosty and we were up to greet it at 6 a.m. As soon as the flight service opened its doors we made arrangements with them to fly us 50 miles northeast to the roadless area that we had hunted the previous year. Loading all our gear in two amphibious Beavers, and with our aluminum boat tied to a pontoon, we roared off the water and winged our way to our old campsite, arriving at our lake around 3 p.m.

After shuttling all our gear to shore and instructing our pilots to return for us in eight days, we bid them farewell and watched as they lifted off the lake and disappeared behind the hills. We immediately surveyed our lean-to and saw that a bear had torn a huge hole in its plastic-sheeted walls and had been rummaging through the gear we'd left behind. This time we left the tent at home, remembering that it wasn't much fun to crawl in and out of it when you awoke in the morning to find it covered in a foot of snow. Our plan was to improve our lean-to and we hurriedly set about the task for the day was drawing to a close.

Selecting some sizeable pine trees to serve as corners for our shack, we nailed some poles across them at head-height and then cut more long poles to serve as rafters. Once the roof framework was built, we cut more poles and used them for wall studs and a door frame. With this completed to our satisfaction, we wrapped clear, heavy plastic around the building in a double layer to form our "walls," tacking it to the studs. Howard, being a long-haul truck driver, had brought two huge tarps with him and these we used to cover our roof. After building a pole and plastic door we found ourselves with a weather-proof shack that gave the four of us lots of room to move around in. We had also brought with us an air-tight sheep-herder type wood stove and some pipe and a piece of tin to tack across the studs where the stove pipe went through the wall. At one end of the shack we laid some plastic on the ground and covered it with a thick layer of pine boughs to form our bedding area. The hardest part was using our lungs to inflate our air mattresses, but once this was accomplished and our sleeping bags lined up atop them, we had a fine boudoir. At dusk we had our toilet trench dug and enough plastic wrapped around and over it to keep the snow and cold wind from freezing any occupants.

After devouring a hastily prepared supper, we snuggled into our sleeping bags for a much needed snooze. The moon shone brightly through our plastic "picture-window" walls and our conversation soon grew quiet. We were snug in our nests with a good roof over our heads and luckily so, for at 10 p.m. it started pouring rain and continued to do so all night. Since the first day of moose season was still a day off, we slept in until 8 a.m., while it continued to rain until noon. The day remained dark and cloudy but around 2 p.m. I had to get out of the shack and explore our surroundings. Walking through the pine woods behind our camp I soon came upon fresh moose tracks leading around a small cove in the lake. Things were looking good!

All hands soon turned out and after cutting and carrying a supply of dead pine wood for our stove, we shoved the canoes into the lake and set out to capture some fish for our dinner. After an hour or so we returned with eight Northern Pike and filleted them for the evening meal, along with a huge pan full of fried potatoes. The wind had come up while we were fishing and was flowing briskly from the south. A south wind usually meant rain but in that part of Ontario the wind could shift on a moment's notice and a north wind meant frigid temperatures, snow and ice. After our dinner, Lee and I cut some poles and built a rustic bench, complete with arms and back, which we placed in front of our stove.

Just before dark it got black-cloudy and a thunder-lightning storm roared in with heavy rain. After cleaning our guns and assembling our gear for the next morning's hunt, we settled in our beds at 9 p.m. while the rain continued to pour down. We were cozy in our plastic "house" and the canvas roof did its job.

The rain continued all night and into the morning and the much-awaited first morning was partially slept away. By 10 a.m. the rain had stopped and a gentle north wind had come up. Phil and I headed to the north end of the lake where I had shot my moose the previous year, while Howard and Lee steered their course to the south end. Wanting to keep my cotton gloves dry, I didn't use them while paddling and my fingers soon became numb. The cold north wind was freezing the water on our paddles and anything the water splashed on. My fingers began to ache like crazy but I continued to paddle for it was tough going into the wind. It took us a half hour to cover the one mile to the lake's north end and the entrance of the slow-moving river.

Phil stayed on the cliff at the head of the lake where he had a good view across the lake and also for 400 yards up the river. I walked a half-mile through the timber until I reached the small upper lake and settled myself in a good vantage point on some high rocks. On the way to my stand I saw lots of moose tracks and I grew excited at our prospects of getting acquainted with the gentleman moose that made them.

All day I sat on those rocks while snow squalls blew past me going parallel with the ground and the cold wind made me glad for wool pants and insulated underwear! Around 3:30, the wind laid, for which I was thankful. It became so calm and quiet that I expected a moose to appear at any minute but when 6 p.m. arrived with darkness not far off, I decided I should leave my perch and hunt as I slowly made my way through the pines toward the head of the lake where Phil was posted.

Under the pines it was already becoming dusk but the world brightened a little when I entered the marsh near the lake. When I arrived at Phil's post I was surprised to find him gone, as well as the canoe. I stood there a few minutes wondering where he had gone, all the while watching the opposite shore for any movement of game. The light was fading fast when I heard a moose grunting in the pines on the opposite shore of the lake. My heartbeat quickened when he grunted again, followed by a big splash of water. Then, 200 yards away, I saw him appear in a little cove, standing up to his knees in the water. I could see his front half and a dandy set of horns. Shooting off-hand, I aimed at his neck, squeezed the trigger and missed him! As he wheeled to escape I fired again and hit his neck, but just below the spine. My third shot broke his back at the base of the neck. At this shot I heard a tremendous splash and the moose disappeared. I tried to make my way up the slippery rocks on the lake's edge to a point where I could see into the cove but it was impossible. Without the canoe, I was beat.

Just then, in the pines behind me, I heard another moose walking and figured it was the one "my" moose had been challenging. At the same moment I heard Phil coming down the river with the canoe, attracted by my shooting and probably wishing he had remained on his post!

Quickly crossing the lake, we found the moose lying in three feet of water and very dead. I was happy with him; a half-ton of animal with a 37-inch antler spread. Using a block and tackle, we were able to get him to the lake's edge and, after gutting him in the water, we managed to pull his huge body part way onto the shore. Most of this was done by flashlight and we were happy when around 9 p.m. we saw a light far up the lake and the sound of the aluminum boat's outboard motor. With Lee and Howard's help, we got the moose quartered and loaded into the boat, nearly swamping it. Lee and Howard got in our canoe and tying it to the bigger boat, we set off down the lake toward camp, but at a very slow pace to keep from taking on water.

Arriving at camp, we found some dry socks, enjoyed a feast of camp stew that Phil had left bubbling on the stove since morning, and then set about hanging and skinning the moose quarters. We finished our work at 1:30 a.m. and everyone retired to their nest elated; at least I was.

The night had turned cold, just right for cooling meat, and a light, powdery snow was drifting down through the pines when we finally blew out the lantern and drifted off to sleep.

Moose hunting is infectious and a subsequent hunt found us once again unloading gear on the lakeshore by our "plastic" shack. We removed the canvas tarps each year but left everything else covered with plastic inside the abandoned shack. Cooking utensils, stove, etc were in covered plywood boxes with the lids nailed down. Bears often investigated our shack but since we left no easily available food stuff, they seldom harmed anything but the "walls." After getting our camp in order, stacking some wood and catching some fish, we settled in for the night.

A light covering of snow accumulated overnight but the morning dawned clear and cold. After a quick breakfast, Howard and I paddled to the north end of the lake while Phil and Lee headed south. Howard posted at the head of the lake but since it was such a pretty day with a covering of "tracking" snow, I hiked north for two miles, hunting slowly and quietly as I went. I saw very little moose sign that day but I did hear a cow moose bellow around 1 p.m., on a hill above Elbow Lake. I hunted my way back to the canoe, arriving there at 6:30, and found Howard still on his post. He had seen no game either and we arrived at camp after dark.

The next morning was cold and some ice had frozen on the edges of the lake. That morning the four of us took the motorboat and putted slowly to the north end. The layer of ice would make beaching a canoe a little precarious and we felt safer in the bigger boat. Even so, we made a lot of racket getting ashore through the ice and we spooked a moose that was feeding a couple hundred yards upstream. Later, we saw its tracks, running across the trail in the snow, as we walked in. Phil and Howard posted by the river while Lee and I hunted our way one and a half miles upstream. Seeing nothing and hearing no shots from Phil and Howard's direction, we headed back down the river, keeping to the bluffs above the willow marshes, and arrived at the little lake just at dusk. Lee stopped there to watch awhile and I continued on down the moose trail through the pines to where the moose had crossed in the morning. On the way, I found fresh wolf tracks crossing my morning footprints in the snow.

I stopped to wait and listen and soon Phil arrived. As we stood in the semi-darkness under the pines, we heard a moose snort not far from us, then heard it break and run toward us, the limbs cracking on its antlers. Apparently it had been spooked by the wolves and was unaware of our presence for it turned before it came in sight and ran out into our trail about 75 feet from us, but hidden from our view. It then caught our scent and ran parallel to the trail toward the lake crossing where

Howard was posted.

When it came within thirty feet of Howard it scented him and turned back into the pines without showing itself. Nevertheless, the noise of his crashing through the pines gave us quite a thrill and high hopes for a hunt on the morrow. By now it was 7:40 p.m. and dark, but a full moon was just coming over the hill. We paddled the boat quietly until we were quite a distance down the lake before starting the motor and putting off to camp. Everyone was tired and Lee was catching a cold.

We must have been anxious for the next day's hunt for Phil set the alarm wrong and we were all "on deck" an hour early. Dawn broke to show us a fine, wet snow falling through the pines. Lee was not feeling well and so, after our breakfast, he stayed in camp while Phil, Howard, and I headed for the north end of the lake to try to capture the big bull, arriving there not long after daylight. We posted between the two lakes and although Phil heard the moose, no one got to see it. At 11:45 we headed back to camp for a quick lunch, returning to the head of the lake around 2:30. This time, Phil sat on the cliff above the lake where he could see the cove where I had shot a bull on a previous hunt.

He could also see upriver about 400 yards. Using the canoe, Howard and I paddled upriver and I went ashore on the off-side of the river at a point where I could still see Phil on the cliff. That meant we wouldn't have to shoot over 200 yards if a moose appeared between us and we could readily see each other. Howard went upriver another 400 yards and posted on a big rock at the edge of the pines, across the river from me. It was a beautiful, sunny afternoon, just a little overcast, and very cold. Some powdery snow still hung on the trees and covered the marsh grass, making the visibility perfect. I had no place to sit, so I leaned against a small pine and kept my eyes busy watching both upstream and down.

After three hours I had seen nothing but a mouse, a mink and a young beaver and I was starting to get cold, beginning at my rubber-booted feet that were resting in the snow. I also cast glances at my companions on their posts and I suddenly realized that Howard was no longer on his post. His red plaid jacket had showed up well, but I could no longer see it. Just then I heard a loud crack in the pines, across the river and not 50 yards from where Howard was supposed to be. Another few seconds and a huge bull moose stepped out of the pines, walked through the marsh to the river's edge and stood broadside, looking across the river. I expected any second to hear Howard's rifle roar but all remained quiet. Howard wasn't there, but had left his post and walked to the upper lake.

The bull was 350 yards from me and to get a shot I would have to shoot offhand. My .270 was loaded with 150 grain Nosler hand loads and had taken care of lots of elk over the years so I took aim at his rib section, held a little high, and squeezed the trigger. At the rifle's roar the moose made one step and was down the bank and into the river. This put him below my line of sight, which was also obstructed by dead windfall cedar snags and marsh grass. I could just see the tips of his antlers shining as he moved across the river and so I ran with all my strength upriver towards him. When I neared him I saw that he had come within six feet of the shore where a six-inch tree lying in the water had stopped him. The big fellow was dead, my bullet having passed between two ribs, rupturing his lungs, and exited between two ribs on the opposite side! A small piece of his lung still floated on the water nearby.

At the same moment Howard came running around the point and gave a victory yell that brought Phil and the aluminum boat in short order.

Now we really had a job on our hands for this bull weighed at least 1,200 pounds and had a 48 inch rack. After sizing up the situation, we tied a rope around the moose's antlers, attached the rope to the rear of the boat, and with me sitting in the bow to help hold it down, Phil revved the motor. The boat nearly stood on end but soon the moose began to move and we towed it like a giant log down the river, trying to locate a place were we could beach it. About 100 yards downstream a six-foot wide point of land jutted fifteen feet out into the river, its point tapering down to the water. Pulling the boat alongside the point of land, we maneuvered the moose until his head was on the end of the little peninsula. The swamp grass was covered with snow and the moose, being wet, slid up far enough that I could remove its entrails. Then we halved the animal and nearly sunk the boat when we rolled the halves into it. My companions were big, skookum farm boys, both of them, big enough to hunt bears with a switch and I was sure glad for it. A moose on the land is a big chore; one in the water is almost impossible.

At dark we headed for camp, again under a full moon. The evening was cold and ice was again forming on the lake. At camp we used a little chain saw to quarter the beast and after hanging and skinning it, we enjoyed a late dinner. By now the night had turned so cold that I was forced to stay up and cape out the moose's scalp, otherwise it would be frozen solid by morning. Finally, at 12:25 a.m., we settled down on our warm, pine bough beds and faded into dreamland while the temperatures outside dipped to near zero.

All moose hunts aren't productive, at least not meat-wise. Nevertheless, they are all productive memory-wise. Hunting success is usually dictated by the weather and my next moose hunt had lots of the wrong kind. That year I returned from my annual pilgrimage to Moose Mecca somewhat fuzzy of face, lean of wallet and definitely devoid of moose meat.

I began having second thoughts about the trip when I arrived in Grand Rapids,

1. *I often made a pack by tying the bear's opposing front and hind paws together.*

2. *Bears are alerted by the slightest noise or human scent.*

3. *My friend and mentor, the late Bill Hulet. A tough exterior but a tender heart.*

4. Ron Munro examines a cottonwood freshly peeled by a large bear.

5. Bears are evasive and secretive and seem to melt noiselessly into the dense cover.

6. Minutes old bear damage to hemlock. *(Photo credit—Tim Veenendaal)*

7. Bears have the advantage in our brushy coastal forests.

8. Jesse Caswell and I; a successful rainy day hunt. (Photo credit—Bob Matthews)

9. Seeing a flash of tawny fur through the foliage, I thought my snare held a coyote.

10. The 19-Creek peeler bear is captured.

11. Jesse Caswell, houndsman par-excellence.

12. Sylvan and I tracked the little band of elk 5 ½ hours before I got a shot.

13. Long Island, Washington bear den in late February. (Photo credit—Rollin Duane Morris)

14. Cubs are born in late January. (Photo credit—Rollin Duane Morris)

15. Carrying sedated "Little Bigfoot" to the cage.

16. It required six men to carry 300 pound "Buford" bear and 100 pound cage from the swamp.

17. *After completion of food preference tests, Big Buford leaps from my Blazer at release site.*

18. *Later that fall Big Buford is recaptured using hounds. After sedation and collecting a blood sera sample for analysis, I released him.*

19. I set up a pellet mill in my shop to produce bear feed.

20. A remote control flash camera was set up to determine what animals utilized the feeders. (Photo credit—Terry Domico)

21. *To reduce costs of maintaining the feeders, the 5-gallon buckets were replaced with large 50-gallon drums holding 200 pounds of pellets. (Photo credit—Jim Hackewitz)*

22. *Framing our Ontario Moose camp.*

23. Our snug camp was always a welcome sight at day's end.

24. After my shot, the moose plunged into the river, collapsing near the far shore.

25. Our moose camp shack was a cozy place. Lee Oxendale (L) and I share a laugh after a cold day's hunt.

26. Prime Ontario moose habitat.

27. Austrian roe deer, buck and doe, taken in December on banks of Danube River. Buck has already shed his antlers.

28. Trophy roe deer buck, taken on hunt with Franz in Austria.

Michigan on the first leg of my journey and discovered that my rifle and duffel bag had been mis-routed to Grand Forks, North Dakota. I should have suspected the airline did things backwards when they had us deplane through the tail section.

Twenty-four hours later I was joyously reunited with my thunderstick and duffel, the latter being crammed with enough of my earthly belongings that it would have caused a twenty-year postponement of my retirement should it have been irretrievably lost.

Being now behind schedule, we drove through the night and a blinding snowstorm, arriving at the little village of Manitowadge, Ontario at 3 p.m. the following day.

Strong winds and snow flurries caused us to wonder if the bush pilot would consider flying us to our isolated lake. But happily pocketing our American dollars, he stowed our gear in the back of his old Beaver float plane, crammed our four bodies, plus his, into the remaining space, and with no little effort the old craft roared off the lake.

Howard, Lee, and I languished in the back seat with a huge 100-pound duffel bag across our laps, a boat gas can under our feet and me clutching my rifle. Lee's leg was extended forward over the gas can, between the pilot and front passenger seat, making it necessary for Phil to pick up Lee's leg each time the pilot needed to adjust the controls.

As we banked over the village on take off, a strong side wind hit us and I realized with a little trepidation that we were flying more sideways than forward. But, as this writing attests, we arrived safely on our lake a half hour later.

While the plane idled slowly down the lake toward our old campsite, I experienced an euphoric, happy feeling like someone returning home after a long absence. I had been dreaming of this moment ever since our plane had snatched us off the same lake during a snowstorm last year. This was a place of wild and crazy weather, but I loved it.

After admonishing the pilot to return for us in eleven days, unless severe weather dictated otherwise, we hardly noticed his departure as we climbed up the snowy bank of the lake and started putting our old shelter in order.

The shack's polyethylene plastic walls had once again been shredded by marauding bears, leaving us practically nothing but a pine-pole framework to work with. Its pole rafters lay open to the sky and the shack's dirt floor was covered with snow.

The continuing snow flurries and darkening skies brought with them a sense of urgency and a portent of worsening weather, causing us to repair the damage in record time. By 6:30 p.m. we had a snug shack again, smoke was curling from our stovepipe and the remaining snow was melting on the floor.

While Phil peeled potatoes, Lee and I launched a canoe and paddled into the cove near our camp, returning a half hour later with two Northern Pike, the largest measuring 32 ½ inches. These were quickly filleted, rolled in fish shake and bake, and transported still twitching to the frying pan.

Later, groaning in satisfaction from our luscious repast, we sat by the fire and conspired against Bullwinkle until the warmth of our shack and the weariness from a 38-hour day caused us to nod.

Dousing the lantern, we settled into our sleeping bags and except for an occasional drip of water from the ice thawing on the rafters, the shack grew quiet. The breathing around me grew heavier and was punctuated by an occasional gurgle as, one by one, my three companions signed off.

I lay awake for awhile, thinking of how fortunate and blessed I was to be here enjoying this wilderness experience and then, breathing a prayer of thanks for an understanding wife, I slipped off to sleep.

The snow continued through the night and the cold 22-degree north wind blowing down from James Bay blasted us with the stuff for 36 hours. It was a driving snow that came in sideways, plastering the north side of the tree trunks and quickly turning our hunting shack into an igloo.

Visibility was limited to 100 feet and the lake soon disappeared from our view, melding itself into the gray-white blur of driven snow. The Ontario winter was setting in.

When the storm finally subsided, the snow lay thigh-deep in the open marshes, while 14 inches of the powdery stuff, that had filtered through the sheltering pines, surrounded our polyethylene plastic moose camp shelter. We were pretty much cabin bound and spent a lot of time drinking coffee and eating. I remarked that I once heard of a fellow who saved the lives of his entire group in a moose hunting camp; he shot the cook.

Have you ever noticed that the same fellow who finds a hair in his omelet and demands that the restaurant's cook be fired will endure horrendous atrocities at the hands of a hunting camp cook and never utter a whimper? At least not loud enough for the cook to hear.

Complain, and next day you find yourself doing the cooking.

But that might not be all bad; at least you'd know what you were eating. I usually have a pretty good idea of what I am eating by its taste, but the camp cook generally calls it something more suitably uttered in mixed company.

Culinary and hygienic abominations committed in moose camp would be cause for immediate divorce, or worse, if they occurred in the home. The fact that the cook neglects to wash before preparing a meal fades into insignificance when you discover that he has been secretly bathing in the dishpan and using the dish towel to dry himself.

Early morning mouse tracks in the hardened skillet grease I accepted as part of roughing it, but when the cook served up my bacon well peppered with mouse droppings, I bristled! That was it! It was time for a showdown. He couldn't do that to me and escape my wrath—I'd kill him!

The mouse, that is, not the cook.

I might be dumb but I'm not stupid enough to tackle that big fellow. He has muscles in places where other people don't even have places!

Each night the pesky mouse could be heard rummaging in the groceries, chewing on a roll of paper towels, or rattling a half-frozen caramel on the table. How a creature so small could create such a racket was beyond me. Even if he had tip-toed, I still would have known that he was there, immensely enjoying messing up our breakfast makings. But how to capture him?

That night I lay awake in my sleeping bag, listening to the mouse stomping through our provender, and devised a plan to trap him. It couldn't wait 'til morning, I'd rig it up right now!

Bounding out of my sleeping bag, I made a light, sending the mouse scurrying into a dark corner and silencing the chorus of lusty snoring that had been emanating from my companions. I was about to add another use to our already versatile dishpan.

Turning the pan upside down on the table, I propped up one edge with a four-inch long stick. Plopping a liberal dollop of peanut butter on the table, under the pan, for bait, I then tied a long length of nylon fishing line to the prop-stick. After leading the line to my sleeping bag, I tied a stick to the end of it for a pull handle. Dousing the light, I took my flashlight with me into my nest and lay awake, waiting.

I hadn't long to wait. When his pilferings on the table became suspiciously quiet, I sat up suddenly and shined the flashlight on my "trap." The sight that greeted me was as satisfying and exciting as seeing a bull moose after a long hunt. There he sat, under the pan, stuffing his jaws with peanut butter and staring at me with those two big eyes. Delirious at the thought of victory, I yanked the string and the pan clattered to the table. I couldn't believe my eyes when I saw the mouse leap to safety with but millimeters to spare before the pan fell.

Once again all hands were awake, the lantern was lit, and I reset my trap amid connotations from the sleeping area regarding my chances of ever reaching retirement age. All being in order, I hastily retreated to my roost, this time with the string in my hand, already drawn taut.

For a long time all was quiet. Then, gently at first, the snorers began to tune up. An almost inaudible rustling from the direction of the table prompted me to spot my light on the trap and there he sat again, his back to me this time, smacking his lips on the peanut butter. A quick jerk of the string, a clattering of the pan, and once again the shack came to life. When the lantern was lit, a quick peer under the edge of the pan revealed that Mr. Mouse had been captured!

"Now," asked Lee, "what are you going to do with your prisoner?"

"Destroy him," I answered. "No mouse is going to vilify my bacon! Besides, he is guilty of breaking and entering, malicious mischief, vandalism and disturbing the peace!"

The cook suggested that we canoe the mouse to the opposite shore of the lake and release it. Howard suggested setting it adrift on a piece of wood, while Lee sided with the mouse, averring that the mouse was there before us and therefore had inalienable rights to the premises. Put it in a box, he said, feed it and water it, and release it when we break camp.

Deciding to stay the sentencing until morning, we placed the mouse in a large plywood box with a tight fitting lid and enjoyed a sleep without further interruptions.

On the morrow, we again discussed the mouse's fate and decided to confer with the prisoner. Gathering around the box, we removed the lid, only to discover that the mouse had escaped in the night! A fugitive from justice! I knew he was a bad one.

And the cook wore a funny grin all that day. Come to think of it, the stew did have a strange taste to it ....

* * *

The night following the storm was clear, cold and silent without the slightest breeze to dislodge the snow that still clung precariously to the pines. It was midnight and the smoke rose lazily from the stovepipe as the four of us, encased in sleeping bags, slept soundly on the dirt floor of the shack.

Then it happened.

"Ralph! Wake up! Wolves!" Phil's urgent half-whispered call wasn't necessary for I had already been jolted from a deep sleep by the first notes of the wolf pack's serenade. My mouth was open to answer Phil but for a few seconds no words came.

It sounded like there were three or four wolves but the acoustics were unbelievable, somewhat like a pack of coyotes using amplifiers. The howling, which was uncomfortably close to our shack, grew louder and louder, their voices harmonizing into an eerie, primeval orchestration that literally raised the hackles on my neck.

I reminded myself that only a thin sheet of plastic separated us from those hungry boogers. The howling intensified to a fever pitch and then, as suddenly as it had started, it ended, punctuated by three deep, gruff "woofs" that I supposed had come from the alpha male.

"Wow!" I exclaimed. "This has been worth the whole trip!"

We lay there, talking in muted tones for quite awhile, imagining the wolves slinking noiselessly in the darkness around our camp. Finally, we dropped off to sleep.

Around 3 a.m. we were treated to an encore, and this time it was closer than before. Again, at the end of the serenade, came three gruff barks. Next morning showed wolf tracks in the snow only 100 feet from our shack. The largest track was four inches wide; comparable to the track of a yearling bear.

The eastern timber wolf is more plentiful in Ontario than any part of Canada, to the extent that an all year open season was in effect in that province at that time. (1982)

They come in various colors ranging from slate blue, chocolate brown, ocher, cinnamon, gray to blond. One of our group was privileged to see three of the wolves in daylight and they were of the brown color phase.

An adult male wolf will average around 95 pounds but they sometimes go well over 100 pounds. The largest on record weighed 175 pounds and was killed in 1939 by a government hunter on 70 Mile River in east central Alaska. An 172-pound wolf was killed in Jasper National Park in 1945.

The wolf is quite a hunter and kills even the largest animals, such as moose, by running alongside them and ripping at their flanks, hams, abdomen, nose and head and generally weakening the animal through loss of blood and torn muscles until it can be thrown to the ground.

The wolves then tear open the stomach area and begin eating, often before the animal is dead. A wolf has terrific stamina and often travels twenty miles in a day. They can turn their back to the wind and sleep soundly at minus 40 degrees. There are many frontier-days stories of wolves attacking humans. There is no reason why wolves wouldn't attack a human and it would be foolish to assume that they never have or never would, although attack stories nowadays are extremely rare.

It is known that healthy wolves have killed Eskimos and Indians. The editor of a Saulte St. Marie newspaper had a standing offer of $100 reward if anyone could substantiate a wolf attack on a human. He eventually died with the reward unclaimed.

Wolves, like their human counterparts, are not always successful at moose hunting. One study showed that of 96 moose, seven were attacked, six were killed and one was wounded and left. And that's better than our group did that fall; we didn't even see a moose.

The thigh-deep snow made walking in hip boots a chore and every tree you nudged in passing sent a cascade of dry snow down on your head. As a result, most of our hunting was done by posting ourselves on known crossings in the marshes. The icy-cold wind soon chilled us to the bone and by evening we could hardly navigate our chilled-stiff carcasses through the deep snow to the lake's edge and our canoes.

The moose tended to stay in the pine timbered areas, out of the wind, and on the worst stormy days we stayed in our shack, close to the stove, hoping for a break in the weather. With four guys confined to the small shack we were hard-pressed for entertainment and much time was spent story telling, drinking coffee and cooking.

After a couple more successful moose hunts, I began to look forward each fall with impetuous anticipation to my two-week sojourn in the land of the moose. Northern Ontario—wild, watery land of solitude and miserable weather; biting winds that send geese scampering south at the same time we moose hunters are winging north.

Usually, moose or no moose, I was rewarded primarily by the experience of being isolated in a wilderness camp, cut off by storms from our only means of escape—the bush pilot and his float plane.

On my last trip there the weather was no disappointment—lots of wind and rain—but our moose hunt was a fiasco; rather more like a bad dream. I should have been forewarned when things started to go bad from the first day of the expedition.

After flying to Grand Rapids, Michigan and rendezvousing with my three hunting companions, I set off with them on the 13-hour drive to White River, Ontario. Planning to make the money exchange in Canada, we found the banks closed, leaving us at the mercy of the merchants who could give us whatever rate of exchange they desired, which varied 5 to 15 per cent below the bank's rate. Although not sufficient to deter us from our mission, this was misfortune No. 1.

Arriving at Wawa, where we usually purchased our camp groceries, we found all the stores closed except a little convenience store. Misfortune No. 2. Time being of the essence, we were forced to shop there despite the outrageous prices. With items like a candy bar marked at $1.39, our $220 allotment for groceries was soon expended and the purchase packed in two apple boxes.

Obviously, this gave us little variety, with potatoes, eggs, pancake flour and bacon being a big part of our order. This didn't concern us much at the time, remembering that we had quite a few items of canned stuff stowed at our remote moose camp from previous fishing and hunting excursions.

After enjoying a good meal and phoning ahead to reserve a motel room, we hit the road for White River. The night had turned clear and cold and the desolate 60-mile stretch of road that lay before us was deserted except for an occasional bus or semi. About six miles from White River misfortune No. 3 struck us. A weird, popping, grinding noise in one of our front wheels soon brought us to a halt and a quick inspection showed a burned-out wheel bearing.

To shorten my narrative, the driver of a huge semi stopped, assessed our situation, and gave Howard and me a ride to White River. Making a beeline for the motel to confirm our room, we found misfortune No. 4 waiting for us.

Since we were so late in arriving he had sold our room and had no others available. Hurrying across the road where another motel showed a vacancy sign, we were dismayed to see it change to "no vacancy" before we even reached the door. Misfortune No. 5.

By now, the temperature had dropped to 20 degrees and frost sparkled all around us. With no beds available, the buttoned-down village of White River suddenly became cold and unfriendly. By chance, the motel owner also owned a restaurant, service station, garage and tow truck—all closed for the night. He did, however, roust out his boy and soon we were roaring down the highway in his old truck to rescue our crippled vehicle and shivering companions who were "waiting with the stuff."

Twenty dollars later we were back in White River, encased in sleeping bags amid the clutter of camp gear on the floor of the van where we put in a cold, miserable night. Misfortune No. 6.

The following morning we were able to purchase replacement parts and one of our crew being an expert mechanic, soon had our wheels turning as good as new. After a hot breakfast things began to look brighter. The day was beautiful and sunny and the misfortunes of the previous day now seemed insignificant.

Upon arriving at the outfitters seaplane base where we were to pick up our moose permits and our flight to camp, we were advised that our deposit had been received too late and, consequently, our moose hunting permits had been returned to the Ministry of Wildlife. This misfortune No. 7 stunned us all. A phone call to the ministry, however, eased the pain when they informed us that our permits were still at their White River office and available.

All being settled and our $200 licenses in hand, we chartered two float planes to take us and our gear fifty miles north to our remote lake. Things were looking up. Once on that lake we could set about rebuilding our bear-ravaged shack and get things in shape for the following morning and the opening of moose season.

As the old plane roared northward, ever nearer to our destination, I felt as excited as a kid halfway down the stairs on Christmas morning. With the roar of the float plane's motor making conversation impossible, I relaxed beside the pilot and drank in the beauty of Ontario's wilderness, still draped in bright fall colors, as it unfolded from the horizon and passed beneath our slow-moving craft. The day couldn't have been more exhilarating to my spirit—clear, sunny, and actually warm—and I began to watch anxiously for familiar landmarks that would signify the general location of our lake.

Although we had passed over hundreds of lakes in our flight, I recognized our lake the moment it appeared in the distance and pointed it out to our new pilot. The same old feeling of "coming home" swept over me as our ancient plane swooped low over the marsh of my first moose, touched the lake and taxied into the little cove. The pilot cut the engine and we floated quietly toward our old campsite of seven years.

We saw immediately that fate wasn't through with us yet; misfortune No. 8 was waiting to greet us. Even through the scratched window of the plane I could see that this had to be the grand finale of two days of misfortune. To our surprise we saw our boats, which had been stashed in the woods, now sitting on the lake. A second look showed a huge shelter, constructed from our canvas, erected next to the pole framework of our shack. The arrival of our plane soon brought some hunters, in one of our canoes, who made it apparent to us that an outfitter from Hornpayne had taken over our lake and camp, as well as our gear, and had set four Canadian hunters there to hunt moose.

Much agitated discussion and a couple more plane flights subsequently brought Mr. Outfitter himself to the lake where he loudly proclaimed, while standing safely on the pontoon of his plane a goodly distance out from shore, that our gear was, indeed, not ours but belonged to a trapper friend of his by the name of Wolfgang. Appropriate name, I thought. Furthermore, he roared, if we couldn't produce receipts from our pockets for our boats, motor and other equipment, then we had no claim to them and couldn't move them. Our pilot was caught in the middle, not knowing whom to believe, and refused to touch the stuff or fly it out for us until ownership was confirmed. Consequently, we were forced to return to White River and leave our gear in the hands of the outlaw outfitter. To add insult to injury, I spotted two huge moose from the plane, standing in the river below our camp, on our flight out.

In White River we contacted the Ontario Provincial Police and were advised to charge the outfitter with theft, but since our lake was in a different township it was out of his jurisdiction and it would be necessary to drive to Hearst—110 miles north on a graveled road—to file charges. Since it was Sunday and the following day was Canada's Thanksgiving holiday, nothing could be done until Tuesday.

Monday morning dawned bright and clear and with it arrived the opening of moose season. This did little to lift our spirits for we were now without a camp or sufficient gear to set up one. Finally, around 4 p.m., personnel of the White River Air Service either felt sorry for us or got tired of looking at us and offered to fly us in to their cabin on Dayohassarah Lake just for the cost of a transportation flight. The only problem, they said, was the fact there were no moose on the rocky-shored lake.

Studying a map, we noticed some marshes within two miles walking distance of the lake that promised a chance at a moose if we wanted to carry one that far. At this point any option looked good and within the hour we found ourselves ensconced in a mouse-infested log cabin on the shores of the six-mile-long by one and a half-mile-wide lake. This was to be our bailiwick for the next eight days.

After sweeping mouse droppings from the floor, cupboards and beds, we fired up our little chain saw and accumulated a huge stack of wood. With the stove roaring amicably, we lit the cabin's lantern and took stock of our situation. Our groceries leaned heavily to potatoes since we were depending on canned goods that were cached at our purloined camp. At our old camp, fish were plentiful and easily available. This new lake had no pike or walleyes but only lake trout which refused to bite. We were without axe, or plastic to cover any meat we might get. We had managed to "repossess" our boat motor from the outlaw when our pilot "wasn't looking," and this along with a battered aluminum boat provided by our flight service, was our means of transportation.

To sum it all up, it wasn't the type of hunt you read about in Outdoor Life. The weather turned bad immediately, with high winds and rain turning the huge lake into an ocean. This continued for six days and nights, with storms alternating north and south. I managed to hunt six of the eight days although the six-mile round-trip boat ride in three-foot swells wasn't to my liking.

From one to two and a half-mile hikes inland showed us some good-looking marshes but the freshest moose tracks were over a month old. My best hunting was done at night, in the cabin, where I captured a total of fourteen mice under a refrigerator-crisper pan deadfall.

Rather an expensive moose or mouse hunt; about $71.45 per mouse. Not exactly what I had in mind. Our stolen gear? We left it in the hands of the unscrupulous outfitter.

After we left Canada, the outfitter that had stolen our camp gear and boats informed the Ontario Ministry of Wildlife that some Americans (meaning us) had left two canoes and an aluminum boat in the bush without paying duty on them. Using this ploy, he hoped to gain legal possession of our boats.

When a flight to the lake revealed the boats stashed on the shore and a check on the aluminum boat's registration number determined its owner, my hunting companion Phil, in Michigan, received a letter from the Ministry agent. A two and a half hour series of phone calls eventually got the mess straightened out and revealed the following.

First, the outfitter hadn't purchased a land-lease on the lake and second, he won't be purchasing one because the Ministry has put a moratorium on leases for the time being. Third, no one has a trapping permit on the lake. Fourth, the outfitter had no right to use our gear or boats and the Ministry intends to have a little conference with him on that subject. The outfitter can set up a temporary hunting camp on the lake if he desires but cannot prevent us from setting up one as well. Fifth, if we pay the import duty on the boats, the affair will be settled and we can again hunt on our lake. The Ministry advised us to get on the lake at least three days before the moose season opener and get our camp established and occupied, thus discouraging a reoccurrence of the past year's incident.

Also, that year, Ontario's moose hunting policy had changed to make it necessary for non-residents wishing to hunt moose to be registered guests of and obtain validation tags from a tourist outfitter in the province. These outfitters would be allocated ten percent of the validation tags, right off the top, for their resident and non-resident clients. An "outfitted" hunt automatically increases the cost per person of an Ontario moose safari to $600-$1,200, depending on the length of your hunt.

Canada owes me nothing; they merely extend to me the privilege of hunting in their country and I appreciate it. When the time comes, and it probably will, when that privilege is no longer available or becomes too expensive, I will be glad that I took advantage of the opportunity while I could.

Meanwhile, our shack stands roofless and deserted. No doubt the red foxes and wolves are once again using the game trail that passes near it.

The raucous voices of the ravens that awakened us each morning go unheeded on the wind; likewise the lonesome cry of the loon echoing mournfully through the white wilderness will fall upon no human ear through the long, cruel winters.

Yet, as I write this, in the depths of my mind I can still hear its primeval cry. It stirs up an unexplainable lonesomeness of the spirit within me that will only be relieved when I once again steer my canoe quietly down a slow-moving Ontario river, heading for camp by the light of a full October moon.

Chapter 8

Snares, Bears, and Scares

THE SPRING OF 1981 STARTED OFF COLD AND WET WITH A seventeen-day stretch of rain, hail, and occasional snowflakes. Finally, on April 12th, a beautiful day dawned and warmed to 72°, causing me as well as the bears, to begin stirring vigorously. After a week of beautiful days, one of them reaching 80°, the woods really came alive with new growth and signs of increased bear activity became evident.

Since the general spring-damage bear season had been curtailed for 1981 in favor of a liberal damage-permit-hunt for the sport hounds men, I anticipated a busy schedule. Under the new system fresh tree damage would be reported to me by company foresters, I would tour the damage areas and document the extent of the damage, subsequently submitting a map of the area and a boundary description along with a permit-hunt application to the affected game department regional office. If and when the application was approved, the Department of Wildlife would conduct a drawing from hunters' names previously submitted, to determine who would hunt the area. When the permit expired, usually in a week or two, the sport hunter was required to report the results of his hunt to the Department of Wildlife.

If the hunt was unsuccessful, I had the option of renewing the permit for another sport hunt or dispatching one of my professional hunters to take care of the problem.

Some problem areas, such as city watersheds, areas near arterial highways, near national park boundaries or tribal lands would, by necessity, be handled by snaring.

It became evident early on that the new permit system would be an administrative nightmare. Often the permitees could hunt only on weekends and the hunt result reports were slow to come in, if they came in at all. Meanwhile, the bears continued to peel trees in the permit areas. Many times the hunters were unfamiliar with the areas covered by their permits and were unable to locate the damaged plantations.

One such location was on the Agate road. In mid-April heavy damage to cedar and hemlock was reported and a sport hound-hunt permit issued. After a hunt in that area, the irate permit holder phoned the Department of Wildlife and stated, "If that is a 'hot spot' area, I would hate to see a cold one." He reported there was no fresh damage in the area. I immediately drove to the area and discovered nearly one hundred more trees freshly damaged by bears and proceeded to set two foot-snares. On my third trip to check the snares I found a sub-adult female bear waiting for me in one of them. Freshly peeled fir trees evidenced her route to the snare. After eliminating this bear, the damage in that area ceased.

At the time, I had some snares set on a Port Blakely tree farm that bordered on the Bremerton city watershed lands. These produced three large male bears in short order, ranging in weight from 185 to over 300 pounds. For some reason the bears on Kitsap Peninsula tend to be much larger, generally, than the bears in Grays Harbor County.

On one of my trips to the Kitsap tree farm, I checked out a report of fresh bear damage near the village of Holly, situated on the east bank of Hood's canal. I found lots of damage to 50-year-old fir trees, some of them peeled high up among the branches and some completely girdled at their base. It appeared that I would be dealing with more than one bear, since the basal peeling (extending six feet above the ground) indicated a large boar while the high-up peeling was probably the work of a female or smaller bear. The large boars do not like to climb unless forced to.

The bear damage in that area was the worst I had seen in a long time and so I proceeded to place five foot-snares, scattering them throughout the ownership. On my return to check the snares three days later, I found a 2 ½-year-old male bear in one of them and an adult male bear in another. After dressing out the bears, I dragged them to my truck and them proceeded to reset the snares.

After three days, when I next checked these snares, I was accompanied by my pastor, Earl Johnson. The first snare to be checked was a quarter-mile walk down an old, overgrown cat 'road that cut through the stand of tall 50-year-old firs. Carrying my holstered .357 magnum revolver in my right hand and a sizeable chunk of beaver meat bait impaled on a hay hook in my left hand, I took the lead, pushing my way through the two-inch-diameter alder saplings that grew in the trail.

As we neared the snare location, the alders grew sparser and the sides of the trail opened up with occasional clumps of tall sword ferns, salal and winter-huckleberry bushes growing at its edges. The forest floor under the canopy of tall firs was fairly open with scattered thickets of salmonberry brush and an occasional large alder.

The snare setting was about twenty feet off to the left of our trail and when we had approached within thirty-five yards of it, I saw a huge bear walk from the direction of the snare, cross the trail in front of us, and enter the timber. The bear was unhurried and with the wind in our favor, was quite unaware of our presence. I immediately dropped the bait and grabbed my .357 from its holster, hoping to get a shot at that big fellow. Hearing the sound of the bait and hook falling to the ground, the bear stopped a few feet off the trail, behind a clump of salal bushes that hid all but his head. He was staring directly at us.

Gripping my revolver with both hands, I took aim between his eyes and squeezed the trigger. At the roar of my magnum, the bear was knocked flat but before I could find him in my sights for a second shot, he flopped back into the trail, regained his footing and thumped off around a bend in the trail like a racehorse.

Earl and I ran down the trail after him, following his blood trail into a tall thicket of salmonberry bushes. The blood on the brush was at a level with my pants pockets and tended to confirm that this was one big bear. Soon the bushes grew in so thickly that we were forced to crawl on hands and knees through the tunnel he had created in his escape. Earl told me later that he questioned his own sanity while following me, without a weapon, through this jungle with a wounded bear somewhere up ahead.

After another 50 yards, the bear's blood trail led out of the thicket and onto an open, grassy stretch of the old 'cat road. His bleeding had slowed to an occasional drop and our chances of trailing him ground to a halt when raindrops began to fall, washing away all sign of his passage through the sparse grass.

The rain came down in earnest now and although I made wide circles through the timber I saw nothing more of the bear. This bothered me and I worried that possibly I had shot him in the jaw. After a long search, I was forced to give it up as a bad deal.

Returning to the trail-set snare, I found that the bear had stolen both baits from the trees without stepping in the snare. After replenishing the bait, we hiked out to the road and continued on the snare route, but found bears in none of them.

Three days later I checked the snares again and found them undisturbed. On the third day after that, I returned, this time accompanied by Gene Tillet of the Aberdeen Department of Wildlife office. After checking four of the snares and finding them empty, we hiked down the grown-over trail to the snare where I had wounded the big bear six days previous. This snare was clamped securely to a large alder tree and out of sight of the trail and I could tell, even before we reached it, that we had caught a bear. He was raging and blowing as he fought the cable holding his foot and when I saw the size of him, I was relieved to see that his wrist was held firmly by the snare. When the bear saw us, he stood up on his hind legs, towering above us, and swatted the bark from the big alder tree that anchored the cable. Turning to face us, while still on his hind legs I was genuinely shocked at what I saw. Right smack between his eyes and just above them, was a big, round, blue bullet hole the size of a .357 slug! I thought I was seeing a ghost! This was the bear I had shot and wounded six days ago! But how could he be alive with a bullet hole between his eyes?

The bear then dropped to all fours before flopping onto his side on the ground. He then swayed his head back and forth, all the while groaning loudly. Then, in a flash he was back on his hind legs, swatting more bark from the alder. When he repeated his performance on the ground, I pulled my revolver and finished him off.

When I skinned him later, I found that when I shot him by the trail earlier, my bullet had entered just above his eyes, then followed around the skull, under the skin, passing under the base of his right ear, cracking the skull and had lodged three inches back in the neck, just shy of the neck bone. This definitely would affect his equilibrium and account for his flopping and groaning on the ground. It was a great relief to me to be able to capture him and put an end to his discomfort.

A bear's face is fairly "flat" and a bullet fired into it (while you are facing him) will often follow the path of least resistance, ricocheting under the hide around or over the top of the skull without penetrating the bone. Over the years I have had this happen several times, even when using my .270 Remington.

This was a huge bear, standing nearly eight feet tall on his hind legs and it posed a problem to get him from the woods. Returning to the truck, I used my cruiser's axe to chop a passage through the young alders wide enough to drive my truck through. When we finally reached the bear it was with no little effort that we were able to roll him over the tailgate and into the vehicle.

Continuing on the snare line, we arrived at the Agate Road snares late in the evening and at the last set found an adult female bear tied up and very unhappy about the situation.

After loading this bear on top of the big one already in the truck, I drove the sixty miles to my home, hung and skinned the bears and made it to my nest around

10:30 p.m.

That summer, during the period April 1 through July 15, 1981, a total of 163 individual permits, allowing 652 persons to hunt, were issued to sportsmen and a total of fifty-six bears were taken on these permits. In addition, my two WFPA "follow-up" hunters and I took thirty bears during the same April-July period, for a combined total of eight-six bears.

Although the special permit system worked well, it was, as predicted, generally an administrative nightmare for the three Game Department regional biologists issuing the permits. Consequently, when additional damage areas became evident during the summer, and also as a result of my aerial survey findings, it was agreed that a spring bear season, modified in area and duration, should be implemented for the 1982 season.

This system continued through the late 1980's with the spring damage unit boundaries mitigated and modulated annually as damage levels dictated.

Bear control activities were conducted quite differently during the 1980's than they were in the early years of the WFPA's program when bears were classified as predators in five counties and damage was rife.

Although bear damage to young timber stands certainly continued to exist, a general decrease in the scope of that damage allowed us to control it on a maintenance basis, using spring bear seasons and sport-hunter "hot-spot" permits instead of the large professional hunter staff employed in the past. Our control season had been curtailed from a year-round, no-limit basis to a two-month, designated-unit, spring hunt.

My professional hunting staff was now held at one man, Bernie Paque. He hunted with hounds only during the two-month spring season and also served as a damage-spotter. He was also used to "follow-up" on unsuccessful sport permit hunts where needed.

Snaring was held at a minimum and employed only in situations that could not be handled by hound hunting. I opted to do the snaring myself, enabling us to keep the cost of operation at a minimum. This involved a heavy work load for me along with my other duties since the snaring hot-spots were spread over five counties—Jefferson, Kitsap, Mason, Grays Harbor and Lewis. The sixty-two bears that I captured in the snares during the 1981-1986 seasons were brought out of the woods and distributed to the county jail, juvenile center and the Aberdeen Mission. The skins were sold at public auction by the Department of Wildlife at an average price of $29.30 per skin, the proceeds reverting to the state.

While snaring was not near as exciting as "still-hunting" or hound hunting, it was a very effective, as well as selective, method of removing bears from a damage area. More often than not, when placing a bear foot-snare in a trail or on a log, I would attach the snare's cable to a pole or "drag". This enabled the snared bear to vacate the area of the snare setting, leaving the trail or log undisturbed, and I could reset at the same location with very little labor expended. If the snare was anchored to a tree, the area would resemble a plowed garden spot from the bear's efforts to escape and the snare setting would have to be relocated if I wished to reset it.

In the jungle-y, brushy Promised Land area I could get by with a small drag since the bear usually did not get very far without becoming hopelessly entangled. In more open areas a larger drag was needed. Tracking a bear and the marks of his drag pole through the dark thickets tended to infuse a little life into the routine of snaring bears and often provided some stimulating experience.

I was doing some snaring in Kitsap County in the Bremerton Municipal Watershed where public hunting was not allowed. Bear damage to young timber stands was severe in that area and snaring was their only alternative for control. By mid-May of 1983, freshly peeled hemlock, fir and cedar trees were appearing all through the tree farm. When I checked my snares on May 14, I found one of them holding a large and very unhappy bobcat. Noticing that the cat had not put any kinks in the cable in his efforts to escape, I cut a long, slender pole and then sat down on a log, within reach of the cat, and waited for him to calm down. Once he did, I slowly moved the tip of my pole to the cat's snared leg to the angle-iron locking device on the snares cable. Slowly picking at the angle lock, I was finally able, after many tries, to loosen it and open the cable enough to allow it to loosen wider than the animal's foot. Then I stood up abruptly, causing the cat to back up, freeing his foot. The cat had scratched up a wide circle on the ground trying to escape and, not realizing that he was free, he stayed within the perimeter of that circle. I had to prod him several times with the pole before he found himself outside the circle and unrestrained. Looking a little indignant, he walked into the brush and disappeared.

When I arrived at my next snare, I found a large male bear waiting for me. This snare cable was anchored securely to a large tree and the bear had chewed and dug at everything within his reach. When I dressed him out, I found tree cambium in his stomach and his scat around the set consisted of nothing but cambium.

On May 17th, when I returned to check these snares I was accompanied by my friend Kelly Lund who was an Animal Damage Control agent for the Department of Wildlife. The first few snares were unproductive but when we walked across an old, rotting bridge trestle to a log set located above the creek, we found the snare and its drag pole missing.

The bear had thrashed through the brush and down a steep embankment to the creek. In the loosened dirt was the bear's track, a huge track that made us wonder what manner of bear I had caught. The mashed and torn underbrush showed the bear had climbed the opposite creek bank and finding himself in a thicket of downed trees and huckleberry bushes, turned abruptly to the right and ripped a wide path through the bushes as he headed downstream, parallel to the creek. When the undergrowth worsened, the bear then dropped down into the creek, crossed it and climbed the opposite steep bank about two hundred yards below the snare setting. Reaching the top of the creek bank, we followed his mangled trail straight uphill through the scattered alder and fir timber, expecting any moment to come upon him. Tall clumps of sword ferns four feet in height covered the forest floor, creating a perfect place for the bear to hide. Stopping occasionally to listen, we heard no sound. After following his sign another one hundred yards up the hill we found that he had turned abruptly to the right. We continued on his trail, which was easy to follow, for another two hundred fifty yards. This put us above the snare setting and fifty yards beyond it. At this point the bear had turned abruptly down the hill for fifty yards before turning to the right again and passing through the ferns just a short distance above the snare

About this time Kelly spoke up and said, "Ralph, I sure wish you would use bigger drag poles on your snares!"

After following him another one hundred fifty yards we heard a great commotion just ahead of us and presently came upon this humungous big bear, tangled around a small tree and raging like a big gorilla. One look at his foot showed that in the short time that he had been entangled he had been chewing on his now-numb foot and had it nearly severed. Wasting no time, I took careful aim at his head with my revolver and ended the chase.

After removing the snare from the bear's leg, Kelly offered to carry the drag pole back to the log set. I can still see the look of surprise on his face when he saw the size of the drag pole. It was heavier than he could carry and required the two of us to carry it.

After dressing out the bear, I drove my Blazer a mile or so around on a road that placed us across the creek and not very far downstream from the bear. Turning the big bear onto his back, I placed my hay hook in his lower jaw and with Kelly helping, attempted to drag him toward the truck. With both of us tugging, we could only move the bear twelve inches at a time. Finding a big wind-fallen tree in our way, I hiked out to the Blazer, ran all my winch line out into the woods and after adding another length of cable to it, attached it to the bear.

When the bear carcass finally reached the road bank I maneuvered the truck's tailgate against the hillside and after a hard tussle we managed to load our nearly four hundred pound bear.

Six days later, at the set where I had caught and released the bobcat, I found a coyote in my snare. I released him as well, and with much less effort. I have found that if you yell loudly at a snared coyote, he will cower down and allow you to do whatever you want with him. Three days after releasing the coyote I caught a bear in this same snare, which was obviously set on a main "artery" game travel route.

I had a couple of snares set on Deer Creek in Mason County, one of which was a trail set that produced a number of bears over the years. On May 23rd I checked the trail set and found a yearling bear in it. Freshly peeled trees were in evidence near the snare, so I re-baited and reset it in the same spot. All was quiet around the snare until a couple weeks later when I found a large, one hundred eighty pound female bear in it. She had taken the drag a short distance before becoming entangled in the brush and with very little disturbance at the snare site I was able to place it again in the same spot.

I checked the snare twice with no action but on my third trip I surprised a yearling bear that had been walking up the trail toward my set. He had located my bait hanging from a small tree along the path and was up on a limb devouring it when he sensed my approach.

Leaping from the tree he ran up the trail and stepped right in my snare loop. Running on up the trail with the small drag pole thrashing the brush behind him, he leaped onto the side of a large tree and scampered up among its limbs. After dispatching the bear with my revolver, I dragged him to my truck and once again reset my snare. This bear was a yearling, the mate to the one I had caught earlier and the offspring of the big female.

My snares on 19 Creek near Morton had produced two bears within as many weeks but fresh damage began to appear farther up the drainage on the upper parts of the mountain. Finding some fresh bear tracks along the old logging road, I dropped off the road, into the timber, and selected a three-foot-diameter log on which to place my snare. The hillside was very steep at this point and the log, lying parallel with the hill, seemed to be the only suitable spot to put it. After setting the snare to my satisfaction, I anchored the cable to a standing tree, knowing full well that if I clamped it to a drag, my bear would end up in the canyon far below where it would be next to impossible to salvage it.

Standing on the log, I wired a chunk of beaver meat to a limb at each end of it, making it necessary for a bear to climb up on the log to retrieve it and, hopefully, step in my foot-snare.

Returning a few days later, I worked my way down the hill through the roadside brush to check the snare. Before I reached the log, I could get glimpses of it through the bushes and could see that chunks of wood had been torn from it. Then I saw a flash of tawny fur on the downhill side of the log and my first reaction was, "Nuts! I've caught a coyote and he's torn up my set."

Pulling the bushes back for a better look, I found myself facing a large tom cougar that displayed quite a fine set of dentures when he snarled. Being tied solid to a tree, he had completely destroyed my set and by the way his ears were flattened against his head I could tell he was not the least bit happy to make my acquaintance. Legally, I could have shot him but I didn't want to.

Leaving the big cat to ponder his fate, I drove out of the woods and returned to Morton. There I contacted the local game agent, who in turn was able to acquire a tranquilizing gun and some Ketamine and finally, after four hours, returned to the woods. After darting and sedating the cougar, I removed the snare from his leg and we sat down to await his awakening. My fear was that the game agent had overestimated the cat's weight and had administered too much drug. It is hard to overdose a bear on Ketamine but cats are very sensitive and can easily be killed by too heavy a dose.

It was just getting dark when, after three hours, the cougar began to lift its head but it was still immobile when I left the woods at 9 p.m. It had been a long day and I still had an one hundred twenty mile drive before I reached home.

Two days later, after checking my Mason County snares and capturing another bear, I returned to 19 Creek to see if the sedated cougar had revived and left the scene. Arriving there I found everything quiet and the cougar nowhere to be seen. About ten feet downhill from where we'd left him, I found the soil and fir needles disturbed where he had thrashed about as he revived. From there he had headed down into the deep, timbered canyon and without a doubt, to water.

Tree damage had been reported in the Wishkah River drainage on Cedar Creek and a few snares that I had placed in the fifteen-year-old fir plantation had already produced two bears. When more damage appeared on the east side of Cedar Creek I decided to set another snare. At one time a make-shift logging bridge had spanned the creek but now all that remained was two stringer logs, devoid of planks. After crossing the creek on one of the logs, I located a dandy location for a trail set and soon had it installed and baited.

On the day designated to check the snare, I was accompanied by my oldest daughter, Sylvan, who was recovering from surgery. When we arrived at Cedar Creek, being optimistic, I took my revolver and hay hook (for dragging a bear) with me when I walked the log spanning the creek.

Sure enough, when I reached my snare I found an one hundred sixty pound boar bear raging on the cable. Sylvan, being incapacitated from her recent surgery, remained on the opposite side of the creek while I shot the bear, dressed it out and rebuilt the snare setting.

Dragging the bear to the creek was easy enough, using my hay hook, but crossing the stream was a different matter. The banks of the creek dropped straight off and it was twelve feet down to the rocky streambed. The banks remained steep for a great distance in either direction and the thought of dragging the bear up or down the creek to a better spot to cross did not appeal to me, especially with my truck sitting just yards away across the stream.

I eyeballed the foot log and wondered if I could maneuver the bear across it without losing it in the creek. The log was too narrow to lay the limber bear on; in fact you had to step nimbly just to walk across it. It was only fourteen feet to the other bank and the more I looked at it the more I thought I could do it. With Sylvan standing near the truck to watch the performance, I placed the hay hook through the bear's lower jaw, and with him lying on his back, I eased out onto the log. With my right arm stretched to its limit, I was able to almost reach the midpoint of the log before starting to inch the bear onto the log.

Teetering on the log, I pulled the bear onto my precarious perch with me and had taken one step backward when the bear slid off the log on the upstream side, taking me with it. I held on to the hook in an attempt to swing the animal to the far side of the creek and the next thing I knew the bear and I landed with a tremendous splash in the rocky creek bed.

Sylvan watched as I disappeared from the log, heard the splash and figured her dad had probably broken his neck or got himself killed. Making her way to the creek bank as quickly as her condition allowed, she looked over the edge and saw me sitting in the creek a little downstream from the bear while my cap floated around the bend and out of sight. I had landed on my butt, on the right side, directly on a round rock. Luckily, my wallet was in that hip pocket and absorbed some of the shock.

I stood up and was relieved that all my parts still worked after that twelve-foot fall. If I remember correctly, I used the truck's winch to pull the bear up from the creek; something I should have done in the first place.

For some reason, the upper Wishkah country has been the scene of some other accidents and misfortunes for me over the years, including being chewed on by a wounded bear, and having my truck side-swiped on a narrow road by a loaded logging truck. My closest call occurred at the Wishkah headworks reservoir many years ago while checking bear snares in that area. I had just come down from the Camp 3 area and was opening the city watershed gate near the caretaker's house when I heard someone target shooting with a .22 caliber rifle on the hill above me. Having heard my vehicle, the shooters, which turned out to be the caretaker and a visiting relative, came down off the hill to see if I had captured any bears.

After a short conversation I left them standing near the reservoir and drove across the dam to the east gate, directly across the water from them. Being a warm day I had my window rolled down. I stopped the truck and before I could get out to open the gate, I heard the caretaker's relative fire three shots from his rifle and at the same instant I felt a terrific blow to my neck. Instinctively, I put my fingers to the spot and drew them away with blood on them.

Stretching myself upwards to look in my rearview mirror, I felt a lump inside my shirt next to my belly. Quickly unbuttoning my shirt, I reached in and retrieved a .22 bullet! The fellow had fired three shots into the water, one of which had ricocheted through my open truck window and hit me in the trachea before dropping down inside my shirtfront.

What possessed him to do this when he could plainly see me on the other side of the reservoir was beyond me. Had the bullet entered my windpipe and dropped down to my lungs, it would have meant a one-hour drive to reach the hospital. Luckily, the flattened bullet had merely broken the skin. I won't record here the conversation I held with the guy before continuing on my way.

One day in May I found an adult female bear in one of my snares in Kitsap County. She had taken the drag about fifty feet before getting it tangled up in some bushes. The area around her was clawed and dug up in every direction that she could reach and I observed the tracks of another bear, a very large one, in the bare dirt. I reset the snare, which was a trail set, and loaded the bear into my Blazer. I had gone about a third of a mile down the old logging trail when I espied a big cottonwood tree that had just been peeled by a bear. The base of the tree had been completely girdled and teeth marks on the shining trunk reached higher than my head.

Suspecting that this was the big fellow that had left his tracks by the sow, I looked about for a good spot to place another snare. I finally settled on a big rotting log just down the hill from the peeled tree. When you think of dragging bears, it is always best to place your snares on the uphill side of the road but in this case I had to settle for the downhill side.

When I returned to check my snares, I found that I had caught a bear in the log set for the snare and drag were missing. Following the bears' departure route was like following a bulldozer and I soon came upon him tangled up in a pile of windfallen trees. He was a monster of a bear, a boar, and raging on the cable until his hide and hair fairly rippled. I always had visions of a bear this size slipping the cable through the clamps and so I wasted no time putting a .357 bullet through his head. He was too big to drag by hand and so I dragged my Blazer's winch cable down over the hill, secured it around his huge neck and yarded him out with very little effort.

I reset the snare on the same log and when I checked it three days later it was like an "instant replay." Again, the snare and big drag were gone and tangled up in the wind-fallen trees was a huge boar bear that could have been a twin to the one I had caught just previously. And who knows? Maybe he was. I was accompanied on this trip by a couple of good friends—Ron Munro and Pete Schoening—and their help was sure appreciated in getting this big fellow loaded.

Ron and I had been friends for several years but I had only recently become acquainted with Pete. Pete Schoening is a mountain climber, par excellence. In 1953, at age 27, Pete was chosen to be one of a party of eight mountaineers who would attempt climbing the as yet unconquered 28,250-foot peak of K2.

K2, the second highest mountain in the world, is located in the Karakoram (black rock) Range in Central Asia. This range of mountains lies north and slightly west of the Himalayas, with K2 rising five miles higher than all the oceans.

On this particular climb, the expedition reached an altitude of 26,000 feet, just 2,250 feet shy of the summit, where they were halted by a ten-day storm. Suffering from dehydration, they persevered day after day, hoping for a break in the weather that would allow them to gain the top.

Then one of the team, Art Gilkey, developed thrombophlebitis, making it necessary to abandon all hope of a push on the peak and to try to evacuate him in an effort to save his life.

Lowering Gilkey, on a stretcher, over a precipice, Pete took up a position on the cliff as belayer. Anchoring his rope around a rock, he held it tight while the remaining six men worked their way downward. Suddenly, one of the fellows slipped and was blown from the wall by the frigid, gusting wind. As he plunged downward he entangled in the lines of the others, pulling them from the face of the ice cliff. Down they went, five of them, until their fall ended in a jolt as the ropes fouled in Pete's belaying line.

Miraculously, Pete held the strain of the five falling men, plus Gilkey on the stretcher, without himself being pulled off the precipice. Virtually the entire crew was injured in the fall; some were hanging upside down and another was unconscious. Some lost gloves, packs, and ice axes.

Slowly and carefully they extricated themselves from the tangle of ropes and regained footing on the cliff while Pete doggedly struggled, with freezing hands, to maintain his grip on the belaying line.

Amazingly, the sick man had not fallen, and he lay suspended against the ice wall, as he had been at the time of the accident. One of the men, who had not been involved in the fall, made his way to the stretcher and anchored it securely with the sick man's ice ax. This allowed Pete Schoening to release his grip—which had held six men for thirty minutes!—and begin to warm his freezing hands.

The howling, freezing wind forced the crippled team to leave their sick companion on the cliff and seek a spot to pitch the two remaining bivouac tents. This done, two of the men returned to the precipice, only one hundred fifty feet away to aid the sick man.

The swirling snow cleared for a moment, allowing them to look into the icy gully where Gilkey had been left suspended. To their dismay, the whole slope was bare of life; Gilkey was gone!

An ice avalanche had swept him off the slope, over the precipice, to death in the storm far below. His body was never found.

Since that fateful day, Schoening had been on many expeditions all over the world, but at age 56, when I first met him, he had never experienced a bear hunt. Thus it was, in late September 1983, I found myself being rousted from my warm nest at Ron's Crystal Lake home at 2:20 a.m.

Now, there are only two things that would cause a person to leave his bed at that hour—insanity or a bear hunt. In my case it must have been a little bit of both, for I remember sitting on the edge of the bed thinking, "I must be nuts."

Nevertheless, I extricated myself from the warm blankets that had afforded me three-and-one-half hours of comfort, rubbed the scratchiness from my eyes and followed my friend Ron out into the darkness. The night air was clear, with a full moon hanging above the western horizon, giving promise of another hot September day.

In a few minutes we were joined by Pete Schoening the mountaineer. This was to be Pete's first bear hunt and his enthusiasm, even at this early hour, was contagious.

Eventually, we found ourselves high above the town of Skykomish, at the end of a logging road on Tonga Ridge. Far below us in a cleft in the mountains, the lights of the town twinkled, while at our elevation the moon shone almost bright as day.

Donning our pack boards and guided by flashlight, we struck out on a trail through the timber, headed for a hunt in the high elevation huckleberry meadows. After about a mile on the trail, I was dropped off with instructions for my morning hunt while my companions moved to points along the trail ahead of me.

I watched as the sky brightened in the east, paling the low-hanging moon, and bringing shadowy outlines into clear focus until that magic moment when darkness is gone and a new day was born.

This being my first hunt in the area, I stood in awe at the view that daylight had unveiled.

Standing at timberline, I looked down a heavily timbered canyon and across to stone cliffs rising to snowy peaks with glaciers nestled between. Above the trail were open hillsides covered with low-growing huckleberry bushes whose leaves, pinched by an earlier snow, now painted the mountain with brilliant hues of red, orange and yellow.

These colorful meadows, sprinkled with a scattering of evergreen trees, extended farther than I could see, finally winding around a third mountain and out of my view.

It was a fun morning, for the area was open for three-point and better deer as well as bear hunting.

At noon, the three of us assembled on a pre-determined promontory and shared lunch as well as our observatories of the morning. All had seen deer and both Ron and Pete had seen a bear go over the mountain just around a point from me and out of the range of their rifles.

Later that afternoon, after hiking out and driving to the end of the road under Sawyer Mountain, we sat glassing a meadow on the mountaintop nearly a mile above us. It was by now 2:30 p.m. and scorching hot, time for all sensible bears to be snoozing in the shade and making huckleberry burps.

Suddenly a bear appeared from behind a rock-break and ambled out into the wide-open berry meadow. Through the glasses I could tell immediately that it was a bear of heroic size; his humped shoulders and measured stride displaying all the characteristics of a real trophy bear.

If we were surprised to see the bear strolling along in the uncomfortable sun, we were doubly amazed when the big fellow began rollicking around the meadow; changing directions at a stiff lope, apparently chasing a ground squirrel until it escaped into a rock escarpment.

Pete's countenance lit up like a slot machine that had just been hit for a jackpot.

"Shall we go get him?" he asked excitedly, to which I answered, "Let's go!"

I must admit that mile-high climb in the hot sun didn't look near as inviting as it would have ten years earlier, while to Pete, the Himalayas conqueror, it probably looked like a piece of cake. Ron, with open-heart surgery one year behind him, liked the looks of it even less and advised us to strike out ahead.

Shouldering our pack boards, we hit the timber and climbed steadily upward for nearly one and a half hours.

Pete took the lead and set the pace, which was about one notch short of a trot. After a half hour of this the thin air and hot sun had me panting like a steam donkey and when we stopped (at my request) to rest, I realized that Pete wasn't even breathing hard.

As we rested on a weathered log, I studied the four stumps of fingers remaining on his left hand; fingers lost to a mountain climbing ordeal; and the fact that a man six months my senior could out-walk and out-climb me brought me no embarrassment.

At any rate, we reached the mountaintop to find our bear gone and a quiet wait until near dark showed us nothing but some breathtaking scenery and a covey of grouse.

Hiking out in the dark, we were glad that the rollicking Tonga bear had escaped us. We had enjoyed the stalk, the anticipation, the scenery and above all, each other's company.

In one respect, bears and fish are alike; the one that gets away leaves a more vivid memory than the many that didn't. The rollicking Tonga bear was no exception. He would live to again thrill some lucky woods traveler!

One morning that same summer, Kelly Lund and I were preparing to leave for the Long Beach Peninsula to take care of a bear problem when a telephone call changed out plans. It seemed that an elk was causing some apprehensive moments for motorists in Olympia. Not only an elk, mind you, but to make the story more preposterous, a big bull elk. Naturally, this shoved the Long Beach bear to the back burner and the troops assembled for an advance on Olympia. With our battle plan laid and armament assembled, which included two tranquilizer guns, a backhoe, flatbed truck and a set of heavy rollers for loading our anesthetized renegade, we fired up our convoy and roared off toward Olympia.

The plan was to anesthetize and tranquilize the critter and move it to a new location where, hopefully, the only traffic jams it would effectuate would be on opening day of elk season. Providing, of course, that we could locate and stalk it within the forty-yard range of our dart guns.

Exiting the freeway at the Lacey off-ramp, we headed west on Pacific Avenue for a couple blocks to our rendezvous point in a vacant lot beside that busy street and directly across from Puget Power. It wasn't hard to locate the spot, which, after our arrival, was crammed with ten vehicles including those of the Olympia city police and newspaper reporters.

The lot, which encompassed about half a city block, was swampy and overgrown with horsetail and dense willow thickets. On the lot adjoining the swamp, carpenters were busy banging a new house together. Homes surrounded the willow thicket and traffic roared by on Martin Way and Pacific. Nevertheless, fresh elk tracks near the swamp indicated that an elk had entered it and as far as we could guess, was quietly hiding there.

When all was in readiness, Kelly Lund and Jeff Skriletz, both Department of Wildlife control agents, were posted with tranquilizer guns while the "beaters", wearing hip boots, moved through the willows in an effort to rout the elk. The first drive was fruitless and subsequently a second push was made from North Martin Way. The strip of willows was narrow on that side, seemingly offering little cover and when the beaters came into view it seemed as if the elk wasn't in the swamp after all.

Suddenly there was a great thrashing among the tall horsetail weeds and a big bull elk with a magnificent rack of antlers materialized almost from nowhere, fought his way through the mire and raced across the busy street. A lady driver screeched to a halt and sat wide-eyed as the bull streaked in front of her vehicle and disappeared among the houses.

All of this happened within seconds and beyond the limited range of the tranquilizer guns. "Where are TV's Marlin Perkins and his helicopter?" I wondered.

Police cars and motorcycles roared into action, halting traffic and following the elk's progress by radio. As Jeff and I raced down Martin Way on foot with the tranquilizer gun amid flashing lights and police barricades, I assumed that the motorists were imagining an escaped fugitive chase rather than an elk hunt!

After a long foot race that took us through the storage yards of a gas company, private driveways and a small grove of trees, the elk escaped into the timbered area behind St. Peter Hospital. Since this wooded area encompassed several square miles, much of it a swampy area that drains into Woodward Creek and flows into Henderson Inlet, we ended our chase hoping the elk would be content to stay there.

Evidence in the area indicated that the bull was not alone. His appearance on Pacific Avenue was probably the result of being chased by dogs.

A week or so after this chase, the renegade bull again made an appearance on Pacific Avenue, crossed Interstate 5 at Lacey, and ignoring a thirty-foot breach in the fence provided by the highway department, sailed over the barrier and headed south to freedom.

Shortly after the elk episode, I received a report of bear damage in a young fir plantation near Leland Lake. After securing the necessary permits from the Department of Wildlife, I made arrangements for my professional hound-hunter, Bernie Paque, to meet me at Quilcene for an attempt to chase down the tree-peelers.

Arriving at the hunting ground we found tracks in the soft road bank dirt that indicated there were at least three bears using the area. From the sign, it appeared we were dealing with a sow and at least one yearling and an older track, much larger, was evidence that an adult male had traveled through the plantation earlier.

A single, mile-long logging road dissected our permit area, which took in the fifteen-year-old fir plantation and a tract of mature timber at its far end. To be certain of pursuing only the damage causing bears, we were restricted to this one-mile of road in our effort to start a chase. After a bear was "started", we could pursue him wherever the chase took us.

Bernie had a carpeted strike board on the hood of his pickup and with two strike dogs chained to it, we drove slowly through the plantation. It didn't take long to reach the road's end in the stand of big timber and the dogs having picked up no bear scent, we turned the truck around and waited an hour before retracing our route through the tree farm. We continued to do this and at 11 a.m. on our third pass through the plantation, the dogs struck, red-hot.

Bernie released the hounds and the chase was on, with the bear running circles through a two-square-mile area and showing no indication of wanting to "tree". The young firs and salmonberry bushes were crowding the road so tightly that it was next to impossible to get a shot at the bear, even though he crossed the road several times during the chase. Locating his track at one crossing, we determined that the bear was a yearling.

Finally, at 6 p.m., after a seven-hour chase, we pulled the tired dogs off the track and headed for home.

Two days later we returned and had a chase going by 8:30 a.m. Twice during the chase, Bernie saw the bear cross the trail, got one quick shot at it and missed. It was the same fifty-pound yearling and once again it won, when after a six-and-a-half hour chase, the hounds played out and quit.

Three days later, being determined to capture this critter, I crawled from my nest at 4:30 a.m., and made the two-hour drive to Lake Leland, where I was met by Bernie and his load of eager hounds. This time we were both armed with shotguns and #2 shot, which made more suitable weapons for the quick-shooting opportunities along the brushy trail. We got a hot strike immediately on the little runner bear and after a one-and-a-half hour chase he succumbed to a load of #2's from Bernie's shotgun at a range of forty feet.

Three days later, we returned to the area in an attempt to remove the old female bear. We hunted until 2 p.m., when the temperature reached 83°, and having seen no fresh tracks nor getting any "strikes" from the hounds, we quit for the day. During the following week we made three more hunts in that area, the first two producing no chases due to heavy rain one day and roaring wind on the other. We did, however, see the track of another yearling. The day following the windstorm dawned calm and clear with promise of a beautiful day. We returned to the tree plantation and though we traveled back and forth through it all day, we didn't get a bark.

At 3 p.m. we pretty much gave it up for the day. We had stopped the truck in the middle of the plantation and still had the strike dogs on the hood while we stood, debating what we should do. Suddenly the dogs became alert and with their heads raised high, began sniffing the air. The scent was faint but it definitely was a bear. Grabbing my rifle, I walked out into the mature timber, which was pretty much devoid of underbrush, while Bernie took the two strike dogs and walked through the dense plantation brush in the direction of the scent.

He had gone about three hundred yards into the thicket when the dogs struck the bear, red-hot. Running back to the truck, he released the other four dogs who quickly joined the chase. As we had expected, the bear ran from the plantation and entered the mature timber stand where I was waiting. The dogs had the bear stopped on the ground and were baying it not far from me. As I ran towards the scuffle, I saw Bernie enter the timber and we separated in an effort to get a shot at the bear.

Sensing our presence, the bear broke and ran, streaking by Bernie, who missed it with two shots from his .44 magnum revolver. With the dogs hot on its tail, the bear ran another five minutes before taking refuge about thirty feet up an old-growth fir tree. Bernie and I arrived at the tree at the same time and noticing that the bear, an old female, was hanging on the side of the tree and nervously eyeing the ground, he grabbed two of the hounds and started to tie them back away from the tree.

A large cedar grew next to the fir and its bushy limbs obscured my vision of the fir's trunk below the bear. All of a sudden the sow decided to leave the tree and started clawing her way backwards down the tree. All I could see through my riflescope was cedar boughs and black fur. Bernie had his hands full with the dogs and so I chanced a quick shot that hit the bear in the throat and firing again as quickly as I could jack a shell into the chamber, I knocked the bear from the tree.

The bear hit the ground, still alive, and the dogs that were yet untied piled onto her. The bear got up and was snapping at the dogs when I found an opening, stuck my gun barrel against the bear, pulled the trigger and killed her.

We skinned the bear and fed the entire carcass to the six hounds. Carrying the hide and followed by the hounds, we reached the truck around 5 p.m. and headed for home. By now the peeling season was over and we terminated out bear hunts for that summer. According to my diary, this was my 1,076th bear.

Chapter 9

JAPAN

MY ANNUAL AERIAL SURVEYS SHOWED NEW DAMAGE situations cropping up in some of the defunct spring hunt units due to young stands of fir reaching the prime peeling age. Damage levels within the now much smaller spring hunt units continued to be comparable with the previous year's damage, even though bear populations in these units had decreased dramatically, with the average age of the bears taken being four years or less. A bear's age is determined by extracting a pre-molar, slicing it longitudinally and counting the cementum rings, much like the growth rings on a tree.

Since the female black bear generally reaches reproductive maturity at age 3 ½-4 ½, and produces cubs every other year, this meant that reproduction potential was at a critically low level, causing the Department of Wildlife to voice its concern. Nevertheless, even with the much reduced bear population, bear damage continued to occur to young timber stands in levels that could not be tolerated.

That year, 1981, the Washington Forest Protection Association (my employer) and the U.S. Fish and Wildlife Service co-funded a three-year black bear research program, under the auspices of the Utah Cooperative Wildlife Research Unit, Utah State University, to evaluate the relationship between logging and the black bear as affecting the habitat and changes in bear populations. This was to add to our understanding of the bear timber damage problem, and perhaps suggest methods, other than killing bears, of minimizing its occurrence.

Clear-cut logging was modifying thousands of acres of timbered habitats in the Northwest annually. The size, configuration, juxtaposition and age of these clear-cuts definitely affected their use by black bears.

Black bears tend to avoid new clear-cuts, feeding only on the edges until the clear-cut is about six years old and contains enough vegetation to provide good cover. The bear is a secretive animal and generally will not be found far from a bushy escape route or standing timber.

Naturally then, a large clear-cut will tend to bring about temporary changes in a bears home range and travel routes, often forcing him to travel through wooded areas that he formerly spent little time in.

If this new travel route should lead through a ten- to twenty-five-year old fir plantation, tree damage could be expected to occur there, generally at an insidious rate, with additional trees damaged each year.

Long Island, situated in Pacific County between the mainland and the Long Beach Peninsula, was chosen as the study site because of its long history of logging, a continuing occurrence of bear damage to its timber stands, and because of its known population of bears.

Bears had been radio-collared and monitored on Long Island since 1973 and the number of bears present on the island in the spring of 1981 was estimated at twenty-five to twenty-eight bears over one year old. The population in 1980 was estimated at thirty-three to thirty-six bears, the decrease in 1981 resulting primarily from hunting mortality and dispersal to the mainland.

The traditional fall bow-hunting season was closed on the island during 1981 for the sake of the study, making it a unique laboratory for the ongoing research. Even so, two of the radio-collared bears were killed on the mainland by hunters and a third, a two-year-old male, was found dead near its den.

Long Island, comprising eight square miles, had an exceptionally high bear population at approximately four bears per square mile. Each of these bears, with the exception of the young still with their mothers, had their own individual range on the island that remained very similar from year to year.

Because of the high population, many of these ranges overlapped. Female bears often sub-divide their ranges with their female yearlings. Ranges left vacant due to the death of a bear are quickly utilized by bears in adjacent ranges. Quite a few of the adult male bears leave the island after the June-July mating season, returning in the fall to den.

In my mind, the large number of bears on the island resulted in a high utilization of its habitat, causing the low reproduction rate of bears living there and the high mortality rate of the cubs that are born. In 1981, only three or four cubs out of a potential twenty-seven were alive at ten months of age and entered dens with their mothers.

About forty percent of the females do not give birth, or if they do, lose their cubs soon after birth; half of them dying in the den or soon after emergence and half dying in late spring or summer.

The eight breeding-age female bears were examined in their dens in late February 1981. Four of these females had two cubs each and the fifth had three. The other three females had no cubs. By May of 1981 only three of the original five females still had cubs; one had only one cub and two still had two cubs. In November of 1981 only two females still had cubs; one had two cubs, the other one cub. Thus, only three cubs out of eleven survived their first summer on the island.

In late February 1982, I traveled to the island to help examine the denning mother bears and assess the year's cub production. As a rule, bears have cubs every other year, unless they lose their cubs before the summer breeding season, in which case they will produce cubs again the following winter. By coincidence, due to the loss of cubs, eight bears were again due to have cubs. Of these, five had not given birth in 1981, while three had given birth and lost their cubs.

I spent two days on the island with Kim Barber, Master of Science candidate, Utah State University, assisting him in assessing the 1982 cub production. The cubs are usually born during the last week in January through the first ten days in February while the mothers are in hibernation. Our job of counting cubs entailed locating the den sites of the females and exploring them by flashlight to determine if they had borne cubs and if so, how many.

Since the twenty-five adult bears on the island were equipped with radio-collars, the general area of their dens was easily determined by using a hand-held receiver and directional antenna.

We moved quietly through the woods, stopping often to monitor the signal and adjusting our course accordingly. As the intensity of the radio signal increased, indicating that we were nearing our goal, we watched closely for possible den locations.

Most of the dens were located below ground level, either under huge logs, rootwads or beneath the roots of living trees. Some were found in hollow stumps or standing snags. Often the den was located in a dense salal thicket and the sound of the cubs crying and whining was the only clue to warn us that it was nearby.

Once the den was spotted, the final approach to its entrance was made quite exciting by not knowing exactly what to expect of the occupant. We carried no weapons, for our purpose was to study, not to destroy.

We found the females in all degrees of dormancy, ranging from quiescent immobility to high-speed activity.

At one den, situated in a hole under a root-wad, the mother bear boiled out of the nest when we were only three feet away from its entrance. This particular den was hidden in a thicket of salal that reached eight feet in height and made quick movement on our part impossible. We felt like we were caged. Luckily for us, the bear chose not to make our acquaintance, but bombed off through the dense thicket with the agility of a snake.

A quick peek into her den revealed three squalling cubs about a foot long. Their eyes were closed, they were finely haired, and two of them sported a blaze of white on their chests. This was the same bear that had produced three cubs the previous winter and lost them all.

It was growing dark in the woods and we didn't linger long when our radio monitor revealed the mother bear to be circling us and drawing near.

At two other dens, one with cubs and one without, the mother bears raised their heads to give us a slow look, then closed their eyes and continued, quite audibly, to snore. One female licked her cubs as they nursed but made no effort to rise or leave the den.

The baby bears were as cute as a bug's ear and the temptation to hold them was great, however we handled none of them for fear that the mother would reject them. Quickly making our count, we moved away from the den in the direction that we had come.

Each of the bears on the island had been given pet names by the study team; names like Blaze, Gopher, Brenda and Mrs. Jones.

Mrs. Jones had a unique den insomuch as it was located inside the hollow shell of a huge old-growth hemlock stump. The top of the den was open to the elements but she had found a dry spot where the base of the stump swelled into the roots. Here she had attempted excavating a nest hole but solid portions of the stump prevented her from making it big enough to lie down in.

When I peeked into Mrs. Jones den, she was asleep, sitting upright in her nest with her head resting on a shelf of wood debris, looking not unlike an inebriated man sleeping it off with his head on the table. After a few minutes, she roused stiffly from her bed, crawled through an exit hole under a root and disappeared into the salal. Mrs. Jones had no cubs.

All of the dens had nests lined with ferns, salal leaves and hemlock boughs. This material is brought into the den green but is tinder dry and cozy by the time the cubs are born.

We entered eight dens and found a total of eleven cubs. Three of the females had no cubs. This compared with the previous year's production.

By radio monitoring on the day following our den census, we found all the females that had been disturbed had returned to their young. We also picked up a signal from the largest male bear on the island—a 300-plus pound bruiser—and were surprised to find him out of his den and moving about in February.

The objective of his mid-winter wanderings became apparent the following spring when it was determined that he had been roving the island, searching out denned females with cubs. At one den he killed and partially devoured the mother bear and also made breakfast of her two cubs. At the den containing three cubs, he had killed and devoured them all although the mother bear escaped.

Once again, only three cubs lived to emerge from their dens and only one of these survived its first summer.

The results of this study tended to verify our suspicions and observations of bear activity regarding feeding habits and preferences, home ranges and cub mortality. After studying a diagram depicting the home-range boundaries of adult female bears on the island, and realizing that they lived their entire lifetime, which could span thirty years, within these boundaries, I was struck with the realization that these mother bears and their yearling and sub-adult offspring were the culprits creating the heavy concentrations of tree damage. Their home ranges were smaller on the island than on the mainland, where a female's territory generally encompassed three to seven square miles, depending on the quality of the habitat. Adult males, on the other hand, had huge ranges, often covering one hundred fifty or more square miles. These bears also created tree damage, more scattered in nature, and over a vast area.

Then I had a brainstorm, one that promised to revolutionize the way we controlled bear damage to young timber stands—if I could make it work. Over the years many theories had been developed and expressed as to why bears peeled trees. I had always contended that bears consumed the cambium of trees, not just as an emergency food source, but primarily as a source of sugar. During peeling season—April, May, and June—very few berries were available and the bear's main source of sugar at that time was false dandelions, the tender shoots of salmonberry bushes and tree cambium

Why not, I reasoned, develop a supplemental food that met the bear's nutritional needs, as well as satisfying his craving for sugar, and feed the bears during the April-June period. The feed could be placed in traditional areas of heavy damage, which more often than not denoted an adult female's home range.

Considering these things, in 1984 I proposed as experimental program of supplemental feeding that was subsequently approved by the WFPA and the Department of Wildlife. Now it was up to me to put actions to my words.

Some years previous I had attended the 4th International Bear Conference at Kalispell, Montana. The conference, set up to publish and share the results of bear research, was attended by bear managers, biologists and university students from all over the globe. Sixty scientific papers were presented, among them four from Japan.

These latter four were especially interesting to me, since they dealt with subjects that I had been concerned with during a great part of my life—damage to conifers by black bears and the impact of human activities on survival of the black bear.

It seems that the Japanese black bear (Selenarctos Thibetanus Japonicus Schlegal) on Honshu and Shikoku islands have acquired the same taste for tree sapwood (cambium) that has caused our Washington black bear population to be vigorously controlled, particularly in the areas of extensive tree damage.

The Japanese black bear is a subspecies of the Himalayan black bear. As the forests in the warm-temperate zone were exploited and natural forests disappeared, the bears became confined to mountainous areas in the cool-temperate zone at medium to high elevations.

Around 1950 these forests were destroyed. By 1970, when forest regeneration in this area approached twenty years of age, bear damage to the young stands increased to the point that the Japanese black bear was classified as vermin and trapping and killing was encouraged by the government.

Since very poor records have been kept on the number of bears killed annually in each prefecture, meager information is available for them to critically evaluate changing population status, and they know little of the consequence of these actions. It is apparent that the number of black bears killed in Japan increased between 1950 and 1972 from one thousand animals annually to over two thousand.

Seventeen conifer species are attacked by Japanese bears with the most frequently and severely damaged species being the Japanese cedar and cypress. These are the most useful tree species in Japan and are planted extensively.

Sharing common interests, I made myself acquainted with the Japanese envoy at the conference, particularly Shigeru Azuma, who was from Kyoto University at Inuyama, Japan, and during our discussions found our bear problems to be quite similar.

After the conference ended, I remained in contact with Dr. Azuma and in 1983 received word that an intimate friend of his, a Mr. Norio Yamamoto, was planning a visit to Seattle and would like to spend a couple days with me "in the forest of the Olympia Peninsula".

Plans were laid and a few weeks later Mr. Yamamoto arrived. A Japanese-

American friend accompanied him to our appointed meeting place, where I quickly learned that neither Yamamoto or the two photographers with him could speak English.

Through the interpretation of his American friend, I was quickly filled in and learned that Yamamoto was a ranger for the Joshinetsu Highland National Park in Japan. For many years he had been a government hunter and had killed a grand total of twenty-three bears. As such, he was highly respected in Japan. He was an older man, (one year older than me!), extremely fit for his age and possessed a personality that made me ache to be able to communicate with him.

In recent years Yamamoto had given up bear hunting and was now devoted to the conservation movement in the Shiga Plateau, which was his old hunting field and which was now under the pressure of development as a winter ski resort. He lived in a rustic log cabin in the mountains, used an oil lamp for light and cooked on a Russian type wood stove.

To my dismay, I learned that the interpreter would be unable to accompany us on the tour! So I set off with Mr. Yamamoto and his two photographers amid a clicking of camera shutters, heading for the Morton area. Yamamoto carried a tablet with many English nouns pertaining to forestry written on it and our conversation was conducted very laboriously by pointing to keywords.

Nevertheless, it was a fun time in the woods for we captured a large bear in one of my snares and he got to see a "passel" of tree damage that probably made him feel right at home.

He must have enjoyed the day, including the ride back to his Seattle hotel with a big, stinky bear carcass in the back of the Blazer, for he was all smiles when I dropped him off.

Subsequent correspondence from Japan indicated that Mr. Yamamoto had indeed enjoyed the outing and wished to return again for seven days of "walking and talking in the Olympic Peninsula". I invited him to come, the only prerequisite being that he bring an interpreter.

On May 24, 1984 they arrived; Mr. Yamamoto, his twenty-two-year-old son Naoki, and Makio Okabi, who was to act as interpreter. Once settled before the fireplace in my trophy room, we sipped coffee and became acquainted. I found him to be a very interesting and amiable man and we became close friends immediately. His son, Naoki, a very polite young man, was attending a university in Tokyo. Mr. Okabi, our patient interpreter, identified himself as a freelance writer in Natural History.

They accompanied me to the woods on my job each day and were amazed at the vastness of our forests, the size of our timber and the immensity of the equipment used in harvesting it. And to my surprise they knew the local names of most of our wild vegetation.

Tree damage had been reported on Coulter Creek north of Shelton and I took the fellows with me when I went to check it out. Finding lots of trees freshly peeled by bears, I began searching about for a good snare location. I chose a big, rotting log at the timber's edge, next to a swampy area and set about placing my snare on it. After hanging baits on tree limbs at each end of the log and "touching up" the set to my satisfaction, I stood back while my Japanese friends snapped pictures of my handiwork. Rain had been pouring and continued to do so all day and my entourage was soaked to the skin before we made our way out of the woods.

Three days later, when we returned to check the snare, the weather was beautiful; a hot, humid 87° day in late May, the kind of day when you can almost hear things growing.

As we walked down through a mature timber stand towards the snare setting we began to hear cracking and brush-thrashing noises ahead of us. When we reached the snare we found it holding a large, adult female bear that had apparently been in the snare for only a short while for she was full of energy and very angry. She raged and snorted as we approached, lunging at us until the cable holding her leg brought her to an abrupt halt. Noticing that my companions had begun to fade back into the forest, I found the bear's head in my revolver's sights and ended the commotion.

Since the bear had destroyed the old log, ruining the snare site, I located another log a little farther up the creek in the same stand of timber and placed a snare on it. This log set soon produced another adult female bear and a few days subsequent I caught an adult male there. After this kill, I removed the snare from the woods.

During Mr. Yamamoto's visit, I told him of my aspiration and urge to develop a supplemental food for bears that might prove to be a solution to the tree-peeling problem, enabling us to grow trees without killing bears. I wanted to share these thoughts with the Japanese researchers at both Tokyo and Kyoto Universities to get their opinions and, hopefully, interest them in some research along this line. Mr. Yamamoto was very sympathetic with my plan and invited me to spend two weeks as his guest in Japan. Once I reached Japan, he added, all my expenses would be his responsibility. He would arrange meetings for me with any bear researchers that I wished to contact and provide transportation. It was an offer I couldn't refuse.

Since my travels would take me into remote areas and subject me to strange customs, my wife (wisely) was reluctant to accompany me on this foray. But most experiences are more memorable when they can be shared with another and in short order I had convinced a 39-year-old friend, Gene Tillet, who was employed in habitat management by the Department of Wildlife, to be my traveling companion. I had no idea what we would encounter in Japan as far as food, lodging, communal baths or other mysterious unknowns, but I knew Gene, like myself, would be game for anything.

Our plans were laid and on August 11 we flew out of Seattle on our 9½ hour, non-stop flight to Tokyo. About halfway there we crossed the International Date Line, which transported us magically from Saturday to Sunday and into the land of tomorrow.

After spending an hour in two customs inspection lines at Narita International Airport, we shouldered our packs, grasped our luggage and escaped through an automated door to curbside. Instantly, the heavy 90° heat pressed its weight upon us stopping us in our tracks to survey hundreds of Japanese faces amassed before us, waiting for arriving friends or relatives. I had been instructed that Tsutom Miyata—a companion of Mr. Yamamoto's on his 1983 visit with me—would meet us at the customs exit and I anxiously scanned the sea of faces in a desperate attempt to recognize him.

Ten minutes had passed without a hint of recognition from anyone in the crowd when a man suddenly emerged from the throng and asked hesitantly, "Are you Mr. Flowers?"

I can only say at that moment Miyata-san was the most beautiful creature in the world; I had arrived a stranger in a land of a hundred million souls and had heard my name called!

In short order we were crammed, along with our luggage, in Miyata-san's little car and headed down the expressway on the sixty-mile drive to Tokyo. After two hours in atrocious traffic our chauffeur pulled off the street and up a spacious drive, stopping in front of the new Akasaka Prince Hotel in Tokyo.

"You are to stay here tonight, lodging and meals, all Mr. Yamamoto's treat. I will pick you up at 9:30 in the morning and drive you to Mr. Okabe's house, 110 miles inland at Fujimi. You will spend two days with him and, finally, on Wednesday, he will take you to Shiga Kogen to Mr. Yamamoto's hut."

Uniformed attendants surrounded us immediately, helping us from the car and ushering us into the expansive lobby. Once ensconced in our plush room on the 34th floor with a fabulous view of Tokyo and the Imperial Gardens, Gene and I looked at each other in disbelief. We had been transported from the airport without charge and likewise settled in one of Tokyo's newest western hotels. It was apparent that Mr. Yamamoto had planned every aspect of our sojourn in Japan.

After receiving phone calls from Mr. Yamamoto, his son, Naoki, and Mr. Okabe, all welcoming us to Japan, we faded off to sleep, anxious to see what the new day would hold.

The next morning Miyata-san arrived right on schedule, loaded our gear into and onto his little car and with Gene and me folded neatly within the limited space that remained, roared fearlessly off into the onrush of Tokyo traffic.

A 115-mile journey that was to consume five hours lay ahead of us before we would reach Makio Okabe's house. August, we soon discovered, was a poor month to visit Japan because most Japanese take their annual vacation at this time, crowding the expressways with traffic and reducing traveling speed to an average of 25 to 30 miles per hour. August is also Japan's hottest month with both temperature and humidity soaring in the 90s.

Nevertheless, the scenery was beautiful and fascinating and despite the heat the hours sped painlessly by.

Eventually we left the expressway for a narrow country road that threaded through tiny villages with streets so slender and winding that it was often necessary to back up in order to negotiate a corner. Open drain sewers on either side of the street made driving more precarious while maneuvering among motorbikes, pedestrians and oncoming vehicles.

Large polished-metal mirrors atop tall posts had been strategically placed at blind curves, corners, and road intersections to serve as a periscope of sorts to observe oncoming traffic. Since steering wheels are on the right side of Japanese vehicles, the passenger rides in the left front seat while traveling on the "wrong" side of the road, a combination that caused me not a little paranoia during our first day's travel.

The traffic gradually became sporadic as we wound our way through lush rice-paddied river valleys and upward into foothills embellished with acres of fruited grape plantations. Toward evening we reached Fujimi, where we left the paved road for a one-lane graveled trail.

After a few wrong turns we threaded our way downhill through a jungle-like growth of trees and vegetation, following an apparently little-used road, defined only be a single set of tire tracks.

At the end of this track and at the edge of a large garden sat an older-model, white Japanese station wagon. With Miyata-san assuring us that this was the place, we unwound ourselves from the innards of his little car and followed him down the bushy garden path through a grove of hardwood trees.

About two hundred feet down the path Okabe's house appeared, nestled in a small clearing barely large enough to accommodate it, completely surrounded by tall oaks and lush ground vegetation. Brilliant-hued butterflies of all sizes fluttered from plant to plant and the air was filled with the raspy voices of locusts, boom-boom and me-ming bugs. The setting was perfect, befitting my friend Okabe who was a naturalist and a journalist.

His house, large by Japanese standards, was an ancient unpainted wooden two-story farmhouse that showed signs of some recent renovations. The sounds of our approach alerted the three tots playing before the house and in a moment Makio Okabe's tall, lanky form appeared in the doorway to greet us.

Removing our shoes, we were barely seated in his tiny 10 x 10 foot living room when a motorbike carrying a diminutive helmeted figure putted into the yard. Wearing baggy jeans, secured around her tiny waist by a wide leather belt, the cyclist dismounted and hurried into the room. Extending her hand and flashing a beautiful smile as big as herself, she greeted us.

"Kinichi-wa! I am Makiko, Makio's wife. Welcome to Japan and to our house."

Both Makio and his wife Makiko spoke English, Makio slowly and with much thought while Makiko spoke freely and with a fluency that amazed us.

After a tour of their house and garden, Makiko kindled a small fire in their water heater—a five-gallon-can-sized open top stove with a built-in water jacket that stood in the entryway of their house. Poking small sticks on end into the top of the burner, the entryway soon was filled with smoke that added its contribution to the blackened oak timbers in the ceiling.

Water pipes led from the burner, through the wall to the bath, whose water was heated by convection.

In due course, Makiko informed Gene and me that the bath was ready. Bidding us follow her, she led us into the bathroom, a tiny, door-less room adjacent to the entryway and separated from the living room only by a flimsy draw-curtain. Against the wall was the tub, covered with boards to retain the heat of the steaming water within.

The floor of the bath was wooden and slatted to allow the escape of water. A large window, open and curtain-less, provided an unimpaired view from inside to outside and vice versa. On the floor was a stool about eight inches high, a large plastic basin and some soap.

Pointing to these, Makiko then instructed us how to take a bath.

"First," she said, "sit on this stool, dip water from the tub and wash well with soap in this basin. Then dip more water from the tub and rinse yourself well before you get into the tub to soak. Since we must all soak in the same water you can see that this is necessary."

I immediately began counting heads. Seven of us including the three tots. Needless to say, I was gratified, as guest, to be offered the "first water".

After we had all soaked in the communal tub, a process that consumed not a little time, Makio summoned us to gather around his thick chestnut-slab table for dinner. Since our meals at the Tokyo hotel had been western style, this was to be our first experience with authentic Japanese fare.

Earlier in the day when I had remarked on the beauty of a large bed of chrysanthemums that bloomed in Makio's garden, I was told that we would have some for dinner. That evening, as I surveyed the many small dishes of various foods surrounding my place at the table—pickled cucumbers, sliced raw cucumbers, steaming cucumber soup, okra sprouts, eggplant, plus a hamburger-creamed potato salad—I espied the chrysanthemum blooms, nicely fried and little resembling the lavender flowers I had sniffed in the garden.

To say you have eaten chrysanthemum blooms is only to say you have eaten chrysanthemum blooms. Filling, but not much to titillate the taste buds. The cucumber soup, however, drunk directly from the bowl was superb.

After our meal we retired to the little living room for more tea and to be entertained by the children with riddles, games and an amazing demonstration of Japanese paper-folding art. The children were summer visitors with the Okabes.

Later, we climbed a steep, rail-less ladder-like stair to reach our sleeping room. This room was long and narrow, devoid of furniture, and stifling hot. The sleeping platform, elevated about eight inches above the floor, was covered with a woven tatami mat. The bedding consisted of a thirty-inch wide, two-inch thick sleeping pad covered with a narrow sheet.

The top sheet resembled a fitted sheet placed upside down with a small quilt tucked within it. At home I use a feather pillow and the moment my head settled on my little Japanese pillow I knew I was in trouble. The pillow was neither feather nor foam—it was filled with small beans!

I did, however, become used to them before my trip was over because I found them in every home and inn that I slept in while in Japan.

The next morning Makio and Makiko led us on a four-hour hike through the little village and up into the foothills for a picnic. Shouldering daypacks filled with sandwiches, tea canteens and tiny teacups, we set off on our foray. The little girls, fresh and spanking clean in dresses and lacy bonnets, also carried tiny backpacks.

The tour wound through a community of tiny farms, each inch of immaculately groomed soil busy growing cabbage, rice, corn, okra, eggplant, potatoes and other crops in such lush profusion that it boggled the mind. There were no lawns; this space was filled with rice paddies or vegetables that grew right up to the door.

Squash and pumpkin vines were trained to climb a pole framework leaning against a building, allowing the vine to spread out over them and the roof, thus saving the ground space under the poles for other plantings.

Leaving the farmland, we entered a forest of mixed conifers and hardwoods. After climbing steadily uphill for half an hour through a lush growth of ground vegetation, white birches, oaks, firs and cypress, we broke out into a beautiful grove of old-growth cedars and firs that gave me the feeling of being back in western Washington.

A clear, cold stream originated there, gushing from a pile of rocks against the hill. This spot was revered by the villagers who had placed two tiny shrines near the spring for the "water gods". Here we enjoyed our picnic, slaking our thirst with cold spring water and green tea.

Returning, we followed a winding, graveled trail that led among thatch-roofed houses in another part of the village. Stopping at the store, a huge, unpretentious affair with bamboo rafters groaning under a two-foot-thick layer of thatch, Makiko purchased flour for the next morning's breakfast rolls.

Negotiating a circuitous route, we arrived once more at Makio's house where we again shared the tub, conversation, and finally, fireworks with the children before climbing the ladder to our nest and our last night in Makio's house.

Soko, Toko and Fuyuhiko were unusually quiet little tots on this, our last morning at Makio's house. Gene and I had grown to love these little kids and from the sad look in their eyes at this hour of departure, I could tell that the feeling was mutual.

After final picture taking I hugged each of the kids close to me and assured them that I would always remember them. Shaking hands with Makiko and thanking her for sharing her home with us, Gene and I followed Makio up the trail to where his little white station wagon was waiting to transport us far up into the mountains to Shiga Plateau where our host, Norio Yamamoto, waited for us at his hut.

After a slow, seven-hour drive through fantastic fairy-land scenery and heavy traffic we wound our way along a graveled mountain road, eventually arriving in early evening at Yamamoto-san's hut. It was everything I had envisioned it to be; a rustic jumble of architecture with partial upper-stories and a collage of roof angles. Built of logs, the entryway sported a large carved wooden bear head on its door while another stared down from the gable above.

At our approach the heavy door swung open and Yamamoto emerged, all smiles, to welcome us. As I've mentioned before, in his younger years he had been a professional bear hunter, serving in this capacity for twenty years to remove problem bears that invaded gardens, orchards and aviaries or damaged timber crops.

As years went by, he saw his traditional hunting grounds being developed for ski resorts and many mountain streams polluted by the sewage effluent that they produced. Consequently, he became very active in the conservation movement and now, at age 57, was holding a position as park ranger in the Joshinetsu Highland National Park. Shiga Kogen and Yamamoto's hut are within the confines of that park.

His hut at Shiga plateau was a gathering place for college students and graduates alike who looked upon Mr. Yamamoto as a teacher or sage. Having a great love for young people he savored these relationships and spent many snowy winter nights with them around his Russian-type stove conversing and sharing knowledge by lamplight. His closest friends knew him by his nickname "Oyaji"—brown bear—and I shall refer to him by that cognomen henceforth in these writings.

Once inside his hut, my eyes swept the dark interior, noting the heavy, smoke-blackened oak beams that supported the ceiling, the three kerosene lamps suspended from these beams by chains; the massive foot-thick, nine-foot-long table made from a single crosscut of a 700-year-old oak, this supported by two tree stumps; the black-iron chain suspended "chandelier" of six long candles that hung over the table; the Russian-type stove surrounded by a long padded seat on the window side, chairs on the other side and fronted by Oyaji's personal chair. Heavy planks flanked either side of the stove to accommodate tea or coffee cups. The floor was concrete in this portion of the house, which meant we could keep our shoes on.

Oyaji's son, Naoki, was on hand to greet us, along with Hitoshi, a 25-year-old graduate student; Masara, a lady friend of the Yamamoto's who had arrived from Yokohama to be our cook; Isogai Kunio from Tokyo who would serve as chef and houseboy during our stay; and several other friends of Oyaji's.

Darkness fell and kerosene lamps and candles were lit, these dropping cozy circles of orange light to brighten the area directly below them but fading before reaching the dark recesses and far corners of the room. Summoning us to the table, Oyaji took his place at the end of it, seating me on his immediate right, with Gene on my right. Makio, as interpreter, was seated at Oyaji's left, with the remaining five guests assembling themselves around the perimeter of the massive table. In the table's center, a huge wok rested atop a portable propane burner whose blue flames already had the contents of the utensil a-bubbling.

All grew silent around the table as Oyaji turned to me, his eyes sparkling and his brown face shining with an inner glow of happiness that exceeded the light from the lamp.

"It is like a dream," he said, "that you are actually here, that you have come so far from America to visit me in my house. I am honored, but it is not only an honor for me and my house; it is an honor for this whole region that you have come. And it is so appropriate that you would be here on this day—August 14—which is the 39th anniversary of the end of the hostilities between the United States and Japan in

World War II."

He went on to state that at age fourteen he was one of the youngest in Japan to participate in the attack on Pearl Harbor.

"It is always governments that instigate wars, not the populace," he added. "The people go to war because the government orders them to. Once you and I were enemies but now we can gather around the same table to feast as friends and brothers!"

With that, glasses were raised in a toast to friendship and the feast began. Oyaji insisted that Gene and I use chopsticks, which we soon were wielding with an adeptness that amazed the natives. Grabbing handfuls of beef, tofu and vegetables from various platters on the table, Isogai plunged them into the wok where they burbled in hot sake and water to produce delicious sukiyaki.

Following the lead of my host, I broke a raw egg, dropped its contents into my bowl and swished it a couple times with my chopsticks. Isogai them filled my bowl with steaming sukiyaki, covering the egg. I attacked the stuff with gusto, discovering after my third bowl that the egg was no longer there. Rice, salads and soup were also served, until, eventually, everyone was groaning in happy misery.

As more guests arrived, including Oyaji's wife Shizuko (who lived in Yamamoto's regular home in Yamanouchi), everyone migrated from the table to the area around the stove. Exchanges of conversation were animated and laborious since we were relying primarily on Makio to interpret but this was no great impediment and the evening progressed quite amicably with a festive atmosphere prevailing.

Presently Oyaji beckoned to Isogai who quickly produced three harmonicas from a side cupboard. Selecting one to his liking, Oyaji leaned back in his chair, crossed his left leg over his right and began to play the harmonica, and to play it very capably. Imagine my surprise when his first selection was "Red River Valley" and my greater surprise when everyone in the room joined in singing it in Japanese! This was followed by a German song, which was also sung with a Japanese accent.

Finally, around midnight, Makio began having trouble interpreting and announced that his "computer" had suddenly broken down, something we all recognized as the result of too much rejoicing and sake.

As guests departed and others headed for their nests I was inwardly very thankful for this evening of fun and fellowship that I had enjoyed. And these were the very people that I had hated with a passion during the war years. I marveled at what time and forgiveness could do…

By 9 a.m. the sun had topped the ridge across the river from the hut, fired its rays directly at the open window of our sleeping room and roused me from a delicious slumber. My bean-filled pillow scrunched audibly as I turned my head to seek relief from the glare.

Hearing voices in the kitchen area, I forced my carcass from its comfortable nest and waddled sleepily to the obenjo (bathroom). There I shocked myself wide-awake with a shave in the icy-cold water that flowed through a hose from the creek.

After enjoying some coffee with Oyaji, we again gathered around the big oak-slab table for a breakfast of steamed rice, broth, green salad, and strips of boiled beef, all devoured with chopsticks except the broth, of course, which we drank directly from the bowl.

The day was spent bouncing over forest roads in Oyaji's four-wheel-drive vehicle, observing Japanese forest practices, timber types and bear damage. Hardwood-forested mountains lay around us as far as the eye could see, finally fading against the snowy slopes of the north Japan Alps. In such a small country, populated by 140 million people, I was surprised to learn that fifty-two percent of the land was forested and basically unpopulated.

These forests, I learned, were the habitat of the Japanese black bear, troops of snow monkeys, serows (strange looking mountain goat types of animal), raccoons and hares. Logging is carried on in their national parks and as the natural hardwood stands are cut for pulpwood or saw logs the areas are reforested with conifers, primarily Japanese cypress.

The cutting of any old hardwood forest puts an end to the mast crop (acorns, beechnuts) in that area, wiping out a very important bear food. Then, as man-made conifer reforestation matures, the drastically changed habitat supports fewer and fewer animals, these often damaging the trees to consume the sapwood.

In late afternoon we returned to Oyaji's hut to find sashimi (raw fish) waiting for us outside, atop a big cable-spool "table". An entire, fresh yellow-fin tuna had been filleted and sliced diagonally into two-inch long strips. These were arranged artistically on a platter along with some raw squid. Using chopsticks, you snatched up a strip of fish, gave it a fleeting swipe through your little saucer of soy sauce–hot green radish paste mixture, and popped it in to your mouth.

I was a little apprehensive about that first bite but I found the stuff to be delicious! In fact, within minutes the six of us had devoured the entire fish, plus the squid! This, I assumed, was our dinner, but I was wrong. After a hot soak in the communal tub (I got the fifth water this time), Oyaji announced that we would have Japanese beefsteak for dinner.

Most beef animals in Japan are kept and fed in pens and hand-massaged daily to produce very tender (if not so flavorful) and very expensive meat. There were eight of us around Oyaji's table that night and we consumed ten pounds of steak along with rice, salad, vegetable soup, sweet-ripe pineapple slices, bananas and tea.

I still don't see how we did it after that big sashimi feed other than out of respect to our host who had furnished such an expensive repast.

The next evening, after Gene and I had followed young Hitoshi and Naoki on a fast-paced, five hour hike over the mile high mountains of Shiga in 90-degree heat and matching humidity, we staggered up to Oyaji's hut to a treat of creek-chilled watermelon and an ear of sweet corn, followed by a sumptuous tempura dinner by lamplight around the big oak table. This consisted of deep-fried mushrooms, onions, pumpkin, ginger stalks, various leaves and blooms and other delicacies that, in the dim light, I could not identify but devoured without question.

As usual, conversation lasted far into the night, during the course of which Oyaji informed me that the mayor of Yamanouchi had requested that I meet with him at the city hall. Apparently the local newspaper had written to Weyerhaeuser Company for some data regarding bear damage to timber and in subsequent correspondence my name had been mentioned. Somehow the mayor had learned that I was visiting with Oyaji and had arranged the meeting. I felt honored to oblige.

The next morning found five of us—myself, Gene, Oyaji, Naoki and Hitoshi—assembled in the mayor's meeting room at Yamanouchi city hall awaiting his appearance. In a few moments Mayor Tomono arrived, together with Yamanouchi's chief manager Kodama and the photographer and editor of the local paper.

Bidding us be seated on the soft divans surrounding three sides of the tea table, Mayor Tomono then sat down on a large chair, facing us. Oyaji made a pompous introduction, displaying a copy of my book and some of my map and artwork. Heaven only knows what he told the man for it was not interpreted. I then presented the mayor and Yamanouchi city a large print of one of my scratchboard bear drawings in behalf of friendship and brotherhood. As cameras flashed we shook hands and bowed.

The mayor nodded at a lady in the doorway who stepped forward with a shopping bag containing gifts for me. Reaching into the bag, Mayor Tomono produced a colorful jacket-type ceremonial costume and proceeded to help me into the thing, tying a sash around my waist and another diagonally over one shoulder. Finishing it off with a headband he stepped back with a big grin to survey his handiwork. Again we bowed and shook hands and again cameras flashed.

After dressing Gene in a similar costume, the mayor's secretary sat between us and served tea, and once again the cameras flashed. I caught Oyaji's eye and he was beaming; this was a proud moment for him.

Soon the combination of hot tea, the 90-degree temperature and the lack of air-conditioning brought the formalities and the discussion to a welcomed close. After more bowing and handshakes, we took our leave. It had been an interesting morning.

Our schedule while at Shiga Plateau was a full one; Oyaji had seen to that. The greater portion of each day was spent driving or hiking in the forests of Joshinetsu but time was always allotted for interesting side trips.

On one such occasion we hiked a mile up "Hell's Valley", followed a river to an area of hot springs inhabited by a troop of 140 Japanese snow monkeys (Macaca fuscata). These furry monkeys survive the harsh, snowy winters of the highlands by feeding on the bark and winter buds and as studies show, by engaging in lots of huddling. The monkeys utilize the hot springs, winter and summer, indulging in these natural "hot-tubs" with as much satisfaction as their human neighbors.

On our last evening at Yamanouchi town, we dined with Shizuko (Oyaji's wife), who had prepared for us a huge platter of sushi. This consisted of thumb-sized rolls of rice, flavored with a vinegar mixture, each topped with a single raw slice of either fish, squid, abalone, salmon eggs or octopus. After we scarfed up the entire contents of the platter, along with chicken broth soup, crisp green salad and tea, Shizuko led Gene and me to the living room. There she dressed us in kimonos, instructing us how to properly wear the gift kimonos she was in the process of sewing for us and our ladies.

Only half a sun appeared above the mountains of Shiga when we said goodbye to this gracious lady, after which Oyaji loaded us into his Jeep and roared over the winding mountain road toward the highland plateau. After a five-mile drive and just at dusk we arrived at a ski resort hotel in whose parking lot an ancient 14th century No drama was being performed. This type of Japanese drama was brought to a level of great art in Japan by dramatists Kanami and Zeami Kiyotsugu (father and son) in 1374.

As Gene and I sat cross-legged on the matted pavement, the only Americans among an audience of hundreds of rapt Japanese, the atmosphere carried us magically back in time. As darkness fell and thunder rolled among the darker clouds on the mountain horizon, a warm breeze moved lazily through the leaves of silvery birches that flanked the outdoor stage, while flames leaped upward from fires that had been lit in five large urns directly in front of it. Richly costumed actors and musicians performed as if in slow motion and I watched, completely absorbed in the presentation, even though I understood not a word.

Suddenly a floodlight was trained on Gene and me and we looked up to discover that we had been sought out by the TV cameramen who were filming the event! As the only Americans attending, I suppose we were newsworthy. It was interesting to note that we saw no other Americans in all our travels across Japan, except in Tokyo.

The following morning found us packing our gear in Oyaji's Jeep in preparation for the trip to the little town of Tsurugi. Here I would meet Dr. Eikichi Nozaki who was conducting bear research in the Hakusan National Park. Oyaji could not accompany us on this trip but in his stead sent Hitoshi and Naoki to be our chauffeurs, guides and interpreters. Informing us that he would meet us in Tokyo on Friday, now six days distant, we bid goodbye to Shiga Kogen and headed west to the Sea of Japan.

After following the coast to Takaoka, we again headed inland, arriving at Tsunugi and Nozaki's tiny house after a six-hour drive. There we were treated to iced tea and corn on the cob before Eikichi guided us twenty-five miles farther up into the mountains to the little village of Ichirino where we were quartered at a mountain inn, the San Ryoku So.

Once inside the inn we shed our shoes and climbed the stairs to inspect our room. It was actually one long, tatami-matted room, divided by sliding doors in the middle and devoid of furniture with the exception of two low tea tables and a television set. Sleeping pads and bedding were stored in closets at either end of the room. Large, open windows provided a view of the street and the hills beyond. There were no locks or latches on any of the doors. A communal toilet, also without locks and shared by both sexes, was located across the hall. Our room, including dinner and breakfast, use of laundry facilities, and tea served in the room, would cost us $17.64 (American) per night. We brought in our gear.

Hardly were we settled than it was announced that the bath was ready. This was located downstairs in a little room near the inn's entrance and here the four of us shucked down, lined up on little stools facing long mirrors on the wall and proceeded to lather up and slosh down our carcasses with basins of hot water. This done, we all clambered into a big sunken tub and sat facing each other, up to our chins in hot water.

Not much was being said until Hitoshi spoke up. "In America," he said, "you visit around the dinner table but in Japan we visit in the bath."

And so we visited. After toweling we padded up to our room and were just starting to dress when the lady innkeeper entered, bowing, and placed four yukatas (kimono-type garments) on the tea table. Hitoshi informed us that these were to be worn after the evening bath as well as to dinner and so, donning them, we sauntered down the hall to the dining room where another feast awaited us.

The furniture in the long, airy dining room consisted of four, eight-inch-high tables resting on the tatami-matted floor. Between them, in the center of the room, sat a huge rice steamer. At one end of the room two mounted bears cavorted stiffly on polished tree trunks while a TV set in the corner voiced warnings of an approaching typhoon.

Our table was set and waiting; at least fifty small dishes of various foods surrounded our four places and so, sitting cross-legged on the floor, we picked up our chopsticks and attacked it.

Along with many varieties of plants, stems and bulbs, we were served grilled rainbow trout and char—complete with heads, tails and entrails. After devouring these delicacies right down to the gill covers, I espied four slices of purplish-red, raw meat resting on a saucer by my place. This looks like raw bear meat, thinks I. My suspicions were confirmed when Hitoshi announced that this was, indeed, raw bear meat and a special treat from the master of the inn who had killed the bear. The inn master had learned that I, too, was a bear hunter and had supplied these dubious dainties for my benefit. To put it lightly, I was a long way from going through withdrawal from lack of raw bear meat but I devoured the stuff anyway. It was a rare treat. Very rare.

Although Shiga Kogen, Oyaji's bailiwick, was a beautiful place, the wild, near perpendicular mountains of Hakusan surpassed it in scenic beauty. Forested with natural stands of beech, oak, cherry, chestnut, walnut, birch and maple the imposing heights are home to black bears, serows and monkeys.

Here as in Shiga Kogen coniferous species are planted after hardwoods are harvested and these trees, especially Japanese cypress, are attacked by hungry bears that consume the sapwood. I had been anxiously awaiting my meeting with Dr. Nozaki and Tanaka, intending to present my research plans for their opinion and to "pick their brains" for any information that might prove helpful in solving the mystery of what bears are seeking when they consume sapwood.

The following two days were spent with Nozaki, scaling mountains to observe bear damage and habitat, and discussing the findings and objectives of their current research. I soon realized that even though their work revealed parallels in the habits of Japanese and American tree-peeling bears I would learn nothing new from these researchers; their bear study was merely a repetition of so many that have already been carried out in this country—radio-collar a few bears and study their travel patterns on home ranges. The thought of supplemental feeding to prevent tree damage by bears had never crossed their minds. I would have to seek elsewhere and I set my sights on Kyoto University and my friends, Drs. Wada and Azuma.

In the meantime I would enjoy my stay with Nozaki at Ichirino. One evening Dr. Nozaki's boss, Kinichi, who had for ten years been in charge of the Hakusan National Park conservancy, met with me at the inn for a two-hour discussion regarding bear problems and other conservation measures. He was a frustrated man, charged with the responsibility of managing the park's resources, yet having his efforts and recommendations for environmental preservation thwarted and superseded by commercial and economic interests.

"If they want to build a hydro-electric dam in the park, they do it," he said. "Stands of old-growth hardwoods are cut against my wishes. If a bear frightens a tourist, the animal is destroyed. How can I manage anything without respected authority?"

I could understand his plight. Japan, with an abundance of water, had strangled every main river on Honshu, save one—the Nagara—with hydroelectric dams to produce power economically. Fish runs have been annihilated by these dams as well as by the numerous small barrier dams obstructing rivers in stair-step succession, built to control floodwaters from typhoon rains and snowmelt.

In one of these rivers we measured a huge boulder—thirty feet wide, forty feet high and sixty feet long—that had been tumbled downstream for three miles during a typhoon flood before the river had been stabilized with barrier dams. But it was a tradeoff; to produce hydroelectric power and protect the fertile valleys from flood damage Japan sacrificed its salmon runs.

Returning late one afternoon from a field trip in the mountains that had been cut short by the onset of typhoon rains, we stopped at the country home of a local bear hunter and logger to observe a couple Japanese black bears (Crescent bears) he kept caged in front of his house. These animals were comparable in size to our western Washington bears except their heads seemed large and their legs short for the size of their body. Their ears were also large and rounded.

As we were standing in the rain, the owner first brought us some large black umbrellas and then some ears of cold, boiled sweet corn. Although the stench from the messy bear cage did little to enhance our appetite we somehow managed to polish off the corn. The fellow then invited us to come inside for a snack. Up to this point I had not recognized the unimpressive building as anything but a residence but once inside and out of the rain I found myself in a very cozy and interesting inn.

The room was divided in two parts by a stone passageway, one side consisting of a kitchen and a short counter with stools, the other side a tatami-matted platform raised two feet above the floor. In the center of this platform was a cooking pit with charcoal still smoldering among the ashes. Seating the four of us on the mat around the pit, the proprietor placed a small grill over the coals and in a trice produced a platter of pork slices, onions, cabbage leaves, tofu and sprouts, along with a dish of seasoned sprouts and a soft drink.

The little grill performed beautifully and we enjoyed an excellent meal and a good visit, all as a treat from the bear hunter-logger-innkeeper.

That night the typhoon struck with a fury of high winds and lashing, warm rain. The next morning the rain continued to pour as we loaded our luggage in the Jeep in preparation for our trip to Inuyama City. Always courteous, the innkeeper's wife stood in the doorway waiting to say goodbye. Shaking her hand and thanking her, I hurried through the rain to the Jeep and climbed aboard. As we pulled away from the inn, Gene pointed and said, "Look!" Upstairs, all the guests of the inn were leaning out of their windows and waving goodbye!

After a rainy, six-hour drive we arrived at Kyoto University in Inuyama City where we found Dr. Wada waiting. After greetings and introductions he announced, "You will stay with me at my home tonight."

A tour of the research institute was followed by a walk through the primate park and the drive to Dr. Wada's home. His home was more western than any we had seen in Japan and had been designed by our mutual friend, Oyaji.

A few minutes after being introduced to his wife it was announced that the bath was ready and I found myself on the opposite side of a curtain from her, sloshing myself with basins of water while she prepared dinner a fabrics-thickness away.

At 6:30 Dr. Azuma arrived and we gathered around the table to partake of a feast that lasted until 11:30! Mrs. Azuma had prepared sushi, along with various semi-western foods, cold sliced meats, fruit, cake—and kept replenishing the platters as the seven of us depleted them.

I was seated beside Dr. Azuma, whom I had met some years at a Montana conference. Azuma, fluent in English and Korean, is an extremely interesting and knowledgeable individual who has conducted bear research in the past. He was very interested in the research plan that I was proposing and felt that it was well worth pursuing. He volunteered some findings from an earlier study that I might incorporate in my venture and agreed to share any subsequent data that might be pertinent. I lay down on my mat that night feeling that the evening's dinner meeting had been fruitious.

Early the next morning we bade goodbye to the Wadas and also to Hitoshi who returned to Shiga Kogen with Oyaji's Jeep. Gene, Naoki and I then boarded the bullet train for Tokyo, arriving there by midday. Here we found a petite little lady, a friend of the Yamamoto's, waiting to take us shopping.

And, again, on our last night in Japan, we were treated to a night at the Akasaka Prince Hotel by Oyaji, who had come by train to Tokyo to be with us. After being treated to dinner in the Blue Gardenia restaurant atop the hotel, Gene and I hit the sack at midnight, first promising to meet Oyaji and his friend Yamura in the lobby at 6:30 in the morning for a tour of the Tokyo fisherman's warehouse and a 7 a.m. breakfast of sushi.

What a way to end our visit in Japan! The days had passed as if I were in a dream and now Yamura was parked in front of the hotel, loading our gear for the trip to Narita airport. It was time to say goodbye to Naoki and my friend Oyaji.

How do you say goodbye or truly express your gratitude to such a gracious host? A handshake did not seem sufficient to convey my inner feelings to this man so I embraced him in a bear hug, then held him by the shoulders at arm's length, looked him in the eye and said, "Goodbye, Oyaji. You are a good brother."

As Yamura's little car melded with the Tokyo traffic, I looked back to see Oyaji leaning on his walking stick, his hand held high in a final goodbye. Oyaji, brown bear, the bear man of Japan. My friend.

Chapter 10

AUSTRIA

Some folks are born with a Roman nose but I was born with a roamin' foot. It certainly wasn't inherited from my parents for they had been content to live out their lives within a few miles of their birthplace. Nevertheless, when opportunity beckons me to visit some remote, exciting or romantic place I somehow manage to make a way to bring it to reality. This gallivanting mannerism may not allow me to be the richest man in the cemetery at the end of life's journey but at that point a coffin-full of gold would afford little comfort anyway.

And so it was that just three weeks returned from Japan I was introduced by Max Zahn of the Department of Wildlife to his colleague Franz D. who lives in Austria. A subsequent letter from Franz carried the invitation for Velma and me to visit him on his farm near Vienna and as he put it, "stay as long as you want."

He went on to say that his village was on the river Danube and close to the borders of Hungary and Czechoslovakia. As I read his description of the area I became more and more intrigued until I reached the closing lines of his letter that invited me to join him on a hunt for roe deer, ducks, and hare. Here was an opportunity that might never present itself again; my feet were itching already and I knew I was hooked! We would go.

Two young friends of ours, German-born Marlin Carlson and her husband

Randy, were also planning a trip to Europe to visit Marlin's mom near Hamburg. Putting our plans together, we decided to fly with them as far as Frankfurt, Germany and then go our separate ways.

On learning of our plans, a friend remarked that we wouldn't find the German people as hospitable and gracious as I found the people of Japan to be. "You'll be lucky if they offer you a cup of coffee," he added. But I am happy to report that we were treated with openheartedness and warmth by the peoples of both Germany and Austria; well-coffeed, sausaged and quartered by folks we had never met before. Friendships were developed in that short span of time that made our visit most pleasant and our parting difficult.

At the Frankfurt airport we were met by the Ott family, friends of Marlin and Randy, who transported us to their home in Wolfersheim. Alfred and Anna Ott had migrated there from Czechoslovakia after the war and through hard work and perseverance established a now-thriving butchering business. Family operated by the Otts and three of their sons—Josef, Hubert, and Freddy—their stables, slaughterhouse, sausage factory, butcher shop and houses covered nearly a city block in the center of the little village.

Using the Otts' residence as home base, we spent four days making side trips to Frankfurt, Rudesheim on the Rhine and romantic Rothenburg, and four evenings scarfing up great quantities of sausage, smoked ham, pork steaks, kraut, and potato dumplings at Anna's table. Each evening was a roar, literally, as the entire close-knit family gathered around the long table to quaff vintage wine and fat bottles of warm beer, each member vying to out shout the other in order to be heard. With my knowledge of the German language limited to "danke schoen," "guten-morgen," and "was ist los," I could only lean back, grin, and half-know the content of the conversation.

On the fifth morning of our stay, Vel and I boarded a train in Friedburg for the eight-hour ride to Vienna, Austria where we would make contact with our known-by-correspondence-only friend, Franz. With the American dollar very strong (3.17 German marks to the U. S. dollar) the fare was extremely reasonable—$39.43 each for the trip across Germany and Austria.

As the train glided away from the station we waved goodbye to Marlin and our last link with the English language. Two train changes—one at Frankfurt and one at Nurnberg—lay ahead of us. With only four minutes to make each change and no knowledge of the language, it would prove to be an interesting trip.

Since we had been preadvised of the gleis (platform) from which we would catch the connecting train to Nurnberg, the train change at Frankfurt was executed without incident in the allotted four minutes. Struggling down the train's narrow side-aisle with our bulky luggage, we located a six-seat compartment with a couple of unoccupied seats. Stowing our gear on an overhead rack, we squeezed into the two remaining seats, facing each other and with just time enough for our eyes to meet in a smile of relief before the train oozed silently away from the platform. In seconds the electric train reached top speed, turning the near landscape into an indefinable blur.

As we glided along I studied our traveling companions and finally, opting for the oldest gentleman who sat on my left, I offered conversation. When I inquired if he was going to Vienna he responded in broken English that he wasn't. However, the man in the far corner indicated that his destination was Wein (Vienna) and I determined we would stay close to this fellow's coattail at the Nurnberg train change.

And this we did, again making the change by the skin of our teeth. This last train was crowded and we stood in the busy, narrow side-aisle for an hour and through many stops before we found a seat.

This time our compartment company was made up of a jovial crew; an ex-prisoner of war and his wife headed for a holiday in Austria and an Austrian lad returning to his university studies in Vienna. Henry, who had spent two years as a war prisoner in England, spoke English fluently, as did Freddy the student and the hours slipped by in pleasant confabulation until around 9:30 p.m. when the train eased to a stop in the big Vienna station.

With Freddy's help, I placed a phone call to Franz's home, breathing a sigh when I heard his voice on the line. "Where are you?" he asked, using very understandable English. "At the Vienna terminal," sez I. "Then I shall come and fetch you," he said. "I'll be there in forty-five minutes."

You must remember that I had never before seen Franz; I had been introduced to him only by his letter of invitation and mine of acceptance. Now Vel and I watched the street-level door of the station, wondering if our host would recognize us and what he would be like. We hadn't long to wait.

An American must stand out like a sore thumb in a foreign crowd for when Franz entered the station he walked without hesitation directly to me and asked, "Are you Mr. Flowers from America?"

"Franz!" I exclaimed, squeezing his hand, and before our introductions were over I knew that I like this man.

The night was warm and glowing under a full moon as we left Vienna in Franz's VW van and drove toward his farm twenty-two miles distant. On the way, we learned that Franz was thirty-six years old, an unmarried farmer and sportsman, living with his aged mom and dad in a tiny, red-tile-roofed village snuggled on the banks of the river Danube.

Arriving at Franz's home, we drove through a wide double-gated entry into a vast two-acre courtyard, the perimeter of which was completely enclosed by buildings with high stone walls between. Directly in front of us, as we entered and at the far side of the courtyard, stood the long, impressive, gold-colored farmhouse. A light from one of its windows sent welcoming rays through the lacy fronds of a great weeping willow growing in front. In the bright moonlight I could see two big barns flanking the main gate while the two ends of the courtyard were occupied by a tall, white, three-story building on the one flank and a long machinery shed on the other.

We learned that the Regelsbrunn family castle had stood on this site from the year 1025 until it was destroyed by the Turks in the 1600's. Franz's home and barns as we now saw them were rebuilt 300 years ago in the year 1684.

Although the hour was late, we found Franz's mother waiting up for us, her table spread with platters of fresh bread, butter, sliced ham and sausages. She was a gracious lady, as genuinely happy to see us as if we were long-lost friends. We both fell in love with her almost immediately and began to see where Franz had acquired his gentle mannerisms. Franz's hardworking father was an early riser and had long since gone to bed.

I looked about the room with its contrasts of dark, rich woods and stark white walls, these filled with the mounted antlers of huge red-deer stags and those of the little roe deer buck. Paintings and drawings of hunting scenes filled any empty wall space while a chandelier constructed from an arrangement of stag antlers hung from the ceiling. A tour of the house on the following day revealed a veritable museum of antlers and trophies in each of the seven rooms that we were shown.

After our meal, Franz drove us to the far side of the courtyard and carried our luggage into the tall three-story stone building that, as Franz put it, would be our home in Austria for as long as we liked. Entering through massive doors, we found ourselves in a large, two-room flat, dominated by a huge brass bed dressed in linen. Great feather pillows and thick feather comforters with linen covers formed a high, airy mound on the bed that certainly looked inviting to a couple of weary travelers. In the center of one room an immense, round timber supported the 14-foot ceilings. Three smaller beds, a table and chairs, wardrobes and a sink completed the furnishings of the two rooms. The bathroom, newly installed the previous year, was at the end of the entry hall.

Bidding us come to the house at nine in the morning for breakfast, Franz left us in our new "home."

That night, as the moonlight filtered into our medieval sleeping quarters, we lay awake in our feathery nest, marveling that we could be treated with such unselfish hospitality by persons who two hours previous had been strangers. Meanwhile, the

Danube flowed silently along, oblivious to our thoughts or to the distinction and atmosphere that its nearness added to this particular night.

In due course the comfortable bed first quieted our conversation, then our thoughts, until finally we drifted off like the quiet-flowing river on our magic carpet of feathers. It seemed like I had hardly closed my eyes before I was roused from my slumber by the soft cooing of pigeons just outside our window. Opening one eye, I peeked out from under the fluffy feather comforter to discover the floor brightened by sunbeams where only a few hours ago moonbeams lay.

Anxious to see our surroundings by daylight, we extricated ourselves from the warm nest, made ready and walked to the main house. There we found breakfast waiting; thin-sliced ham, salami, soft-boiled eggs, rolls, butter and coffee, the typical continental breakfast of Germany and Austria.

Franz was excited. "We must hurry and finish our breakfast for I have a very interesting day planned for us," he said. "I have just this morning received a phone call and we must be in another province to meet a man by eleven o'clock. We must be on time for he will not wait. I can't tell you what the surprise is but you have hunted bears and I know you won't be afraid."

By now all sorts of imaginings were going through my mind as to what adventure the day would hold and needless to say, breakfast was downed in record time. While Vel went to fetch her coat, Franz relented and enlightened me on his plan. It seemed that a pilot friend of Franz regularly flew officials on low altitude inspection tours of the Siberian pipeline's Austrian section. This day Franz and I had been invited to accompany them on the flight, a superb opportunity to view Austria and the Danube from the air for the weather was perfect.

After a forty-five minute drive, we dropped Vel in Rust, a tiny picture-book village with stork nests atop its many chimneys. Situated on a large lake whose waters extended into Czechoslovakia, the surrounding heavily-reeded marshes were important nesting areas for waterfowl and superb hiding places for wild boar. Leaving Vel to sight-see and assuring her that we would return in two hours (which ended up being four), Franz and I drove to the next village and its tiny, rock-rumpled airstrip.

Here we found our pilot, dressed in a short-sleeved khaki shirt, knicker-type baggy knee pants and long woolen socks, waiting for us along with the pipeline official. Pushing the little Piper Cherokee onto the grassy runway, we were soon airborne and cruising over Vienna.

Heading south, our course took us over the hilly Vienna forest, the largest piece of privately owned real estate in Europe. The vast hardwood forest, that I now saw draped in its fall colors, had been owned by the same family for many years.

Increased taxes, however, had jeopardized the estate's future and may force it to be divided by sale.

Skimming along at 600-700 feet altitude, we generally followed the course of the Danube, passing over clusters of red-tile-roofed villages with ancient castles and churches jutting up from them. It was interesting to note that very few homes were scattered about the landscape; everyone, including the farmers, lived in the villages, traveling from there on their tractors to work the fields. There were two types of villages—those that formed at tight, round cluster and those whose buildings joined each other in a solid line on either side of a road—a system persisting from the middle ages when this was necessary to protect the village from attackers. By continuing this custom, the surrounding lands were conserved for farming, woodlands, and wildlife. Sugar beets, corn, and rye seemed to be the important crops and many dairy herds were in evidence.

At the end of the inspection tour, Franz informed me that the pilot had a spectacular round-trip planned for me—a flight through the Austrian Alps! Pointing the plane's nose toward those distant mountains, we eventually found ourselves surrounded by high, wooded hills and alpine meadows.

Flying up the deep canyons between mountains afforded us with an excellent view of green grazing lands that wound their way up side valleys through hills covered with hardwoods until they ended abruptly against sheer rock cliffs and talus slopes.

Deeper into the Alps, we found ourselves pressed on all sides by steep, rocky mountains with hardwoods clinging tenaciously to any slope that would accommodate them. This was the home of the chamois and the few remaining European brown bear in Austria. A little farther and the trees disappeared, giving way to snowy peaks and inhospitable rock faces. This was the habitat of the Austrian ibex, a large member of the goat family with old rams sometimes reaching 300 pounds.

Incidentally, this game species suffered from extreme hunting pressure during the middle ages when its body parts were prized items of medieval medicine. As early as 1493 the Austrian ibex was becoming rare, forcing the emperor to enact strict law to protect it. The people, however, were greedy to obtain the supposed magical power of the ibex, just as parts of the bear and rhinoceros are sought after today for the same reason, and many battles ensued between poachers and game wardens. After many lives were lost, the duke-archbishops ordered their wardens to kill off all the remaining ibex and settle the issue. A few survived, thank goodness, and the ibex was re-introduced into Austria in the early 1900's as animals bred in captivity in zoos. The Austrian Alpine ibex population numbered more than 2,000 animals in 1984.

After our flight, we found Vel patiently waiting for us in the little village of Rust. There we joined her at an outdoor café for a late lunch of roast goose, kraut, and dumplings. I could envision myself leaving Austria weighing about 400 pounds!

When it comes to hunting privileges, we are indeed fortunate here in the United States. If we wish to hunt, all we have to do is buy the appropriate licenses or tags and by observing the various seasons available to us, enjoy hunting of some sort year around.

But not so in Austria! There hunting is enjoyed by a select few and at great cost. Austrian landowners lease their forestland hunting rights to the highest bidder and with these leases selling for fantastic prices; the ordinary citizen is usually eliminated from the running.

Three miles from Franz's home stands a great hardwood forest on which his family had for years held the hunting rights. The year that I visited there the lease had expired and was sold at a price so high that they couldn't afford to renew their lease. It was from this particular forest that the many stag antlers adorning their farmhouse walls had come. The Austrian red deer (cerfus elaphus) stag is a handsome animal which stands over four feet tall at the shoulders and resembles our western Washington elk. Its coat is dark red brown in summer and becomes somewhat grayish in winter. The antlers are long and beautifully branched, comparing in size to some of our best Washington elk racks, but with a "royal" stay having twelve, if not more, branches. It has long been a favorite quarry for huntsmen in many of the temperate regions of Europe.

This particular forest is also inhabited by huge wild boars. Averaging 200 pounds and sporting long, razor sharp tusks, they are a formidable quarry on any terms; much more so when hunted by moonlight as it is often done in Austria.

Hare, fox and pheasant also are found in the woodland, as are an abundance of roe deer. Roe deer is the common name applied to the smallest Eurasian deer, Capreolus capreolus. An adult roe deer buck stands 27 inches at the shoulders and weighs about sixty pounds. Its handsome antlers are short and upright; they are forked but do not have a brow tine. Their coat is reddish brown above and white below in summer and in winter it is grayish brown with a noticeable white patch on the rump. Although they spend most of their time in the forest, they venture out into open terrain in the summer, often bedding in corn fields during the day. These deer are so small that, with their heads down and feeding, they can be concealed by the upright leaves in a sugar beet field.

The roe deer mates in the summer time and at this time the bucks fight savagely with each other. In Austria the hunting season for roe deer begins in mid-May. Bag limits for red deer and roe deer are established according to the size of the hunting lease, with bucks, does and fawns included in the kill.

In addition to the hunting leases, each village's farmlands are hunted cooperatively (and exclusively) by the farmer-owners, provided their combined contiguous acreage amounts to at least 400 acres. For the sake of safety, no permit is issued for a smaller acreage. These farmlands also provide good hunting for roe deer and small game, with liberal bag limits. No "guests" are allowed to hunt the farmlands but on the "paid lease" woodland it is the lessee's option whether he wishes to share his allotted game with his guests.

After losing their prime hunting grounds, Franz and his dad leased a long, narrow strip of hardwood forest that extended one and one-half miles with cultivated fields bounding it on one side and the Danube River on the other. One-quarter mile across at its widest, the strip narrowed to 150 yards at its east end. It was to this area that Franz offered to take me for a roe deer hunt.

Their quota of roe deer per season on this newly acquired hunting area consisted of three animals—one buck, one doe and one fawn. Franz explained their system of game management thusly: "In Austria," he said, "we are trophy hunters, not meat hunters. We try to manage our deer to provide the largest healthiest animals with the most impressive antlers. To accomplish this, we must harvest does and fawns as well as bucks."

He went on to explain that on this newly-leased hunting area they were allowed to kill three deer. The buck was always taken first, usually in August during the rut. Then, if a doe and fawn were seen together, the fawn was killed before the doe; if she had two fawns both were killed and the doe spared.

Since the full moonlit October nights were apt to produce foggy and chilly mornings along the Danube and my hunt would be restricted to two and a half hours of standing on a game crossing, I rose early and climbed into my insulated long-johns, flannel shirt, nylon vest, blue jeans and red-plaid shirt-jacket. Topping this with my "Hendershot's Sporting Goods" bill-cap, I was ready for Broadway. A few minutes later and a half-hour before daylight Franz arrived at my door, bringing a 56x50R Magnum Blaser/20 gauge over and under for me to use, along with three cartridges for the rifle and two for the shotgun barrel. Not much margin for error!

We probably surprised one another with our contrasting hunting garb; one look at Franz and I knew I was out of uniform for an Austrian deer hunt. He was natty in his jaunty wool hunting hat and wool vest, pants tucked into shiny green boots and wearing a long, black, wool coat that reached his boot tops.

Reaching into his van, he produced another long wool coat which I donned, all the while thinking how quickly I would be mistaken for a bear were I to wear it in our Washington woods.

A short drive across a field and we were at the hunting grounds. Providing me with a wooden folding-tripod seat, he directed me to a spot in the hardwoods where I was to sit, stating that he would return for me about 9 a.m. My "stand" was on a steep hillside and as daylight crept under the oaks and beeches I strained my eyes to familiarize myself with my surroundings. As the haze of morning fog dissipated, I found myself in a beautiful spot with a good view under the trees that extended to the Danube.

The time slipped quietly by while I sat motionless and waiting; but no deer came past my post. A white heron strutted stiffly through the shallows of the river, spearing his breakfast. Presently he was joined by a blue heron and some ducks. Birds rattled the leaves of the hardwoods and occasionally a yellow leaf fluttered to the ground. I kept both eyes and ears busy but I saw no deer and heard only one on the two mornings and one evening hunts that I made while with Franz. I did, however, see ten deer in the fields that were off-limits to me.

Nevertheless, it was a memorable experience to sit in the Austrian woods watching a fresh new day break over the timeless Danube. Capturing a roe deer somehow seemed secondary in priority to being alone with my thoughts and in close communion with nature and the One who created it.

How time flits when one would have it tarry! Before we realized it the four days we had allotted for Austria had drawn to a close and we were saying goodbye to Franz's family before loading our gear for the short drive to the Regelsbrunn train station.

As we drove through the farmhouse gateway, we questioned Franz regarding a shrine that was built into the massive outer wall of the courtyard. This, we learned, was a memorial to his brother, a 7-year-old lad who had survived the terrors of World War II only to be killed a couple of years later while playing with a hand grenade he had found in the field just outside the gate. The memorial was near the site of the accident.

We were on the 11:39 when it pulled out of Regelsbrunn, glided quietly past Herr D. standing and waving by his gate, and pointed its nose toward Vienna. Eighteen hours later, tired and thirsty, we arrived at Luneburg, Germany where we were reunited with our young friends Marlin and Randy.

In a few days our vacation was ending. A drive in a rental car from Luneburg to Wolfersheim, a night with the Ott family, a 95-mile-per-hour ride to the Frankfurt airport with Josef, and it was all over. All but the memories and these, like wine, get better with the years.

Now it was time to settle down and get serious about my supplemental feeding research if I hoped to implement my bear-feeding field work by early spring.

My first project would be to develop a pelletized food that would be palatable to a bear as well as meeting all of his nutritional needs and his craving for sugar. During an earlier experiment liquid molasses had been placed in a bear-damaged tree farm in Oregon and despite the fact that bears consumed the stuff, tree damage continued. My hypothesis was that while molasses supplied sugar, the bear also needed bulk or fiber to mix with this liquid food and to obtain it he foraged on forbs and tree cambium.

After much deliberation I hit on the idea of using sugar beet meal in my pellet formula along with a high ratio of sugar. The sugar would cause the bear to thirst and when he drank water the sugar beet meal would absorb the liquid and expand in volume at least three times, causing the bear to feel full and happy. Adding a balance of vitamins and trace elements would keep the bear healthy.

Since all the micro-organisms in the body are found in the blood, I planned to capture bears in tree-damaged areas during April, May, and June, take blood samples and have the serum analyzed for trace element deficiencies. Then, in the fall when the bears were fat and sassy from gorging on the berry crop, capture more bears in the same areas and analyze their blood for comparison. If I could find any one trace element that all the bears lacked in the spring months but had it in sufficient amounts in the fall, it could prove to be a valuable element to include in my formula..

After much time was spent consulting nutritionists and locating materials, I arrived at a basic formula and commenced producing food pellets in April 1985. The use of a small, hand-fed pellet-making machine was provided without charge by the USFWS-DNR research center near Olympia. Some bear pens that had been used in a 1963 Department of Wildlife-WFPA bear study and a small building situated next to them were also placed at my disposal.

Once the little pellet mill was set up in the shed and a tub placed under its die to collect the pellets, I measured and weighed the ingredients and proceeded to mix them in twenty-pound batches in a restaurant-type cake mixer. The pellets were about ½ inch in diameter and were soft and moist. I had no assurance that the bears would eat them but since they tasted pretty good to me, I held high hopes. My plan was to capture two adult male bears, place them in the holding pens and use them in my food (supplemental food-pellet formula variation) preference tests. Since the bears were to be confined in adjoining holding pens it was necessary to opt for male bears in this test to prevent distraction that would be obvious if estrus females were present. If bears in the wild refused my basic pellet, these captive bears would help me arrive at and produce a pellet that was acceptable.

The selection of a study area for the supplemental-feed-station field work was restricted by the necessity to have a site far-removed from the 1985 Spring Bear Hunt units, yet showing significant bear damage and an abundance of bear. It was also important that the area be in a location that would be unattractive to illegal hound-hunting during the spring months and less apt to be sport-hunted during the summer bear season, thus lessening the chances of my research target-bear being eliminated during the study.

The study area that I selected for my research during 1985 encompassed parts of Clallam, Jefferson, Kitsap, Mason, Grays Harbor, Wahkiakum and Lewis Counties. These areas met the requirements for field work with bear damage having occurred there in amounts requiring control work during the previous 5-10 years and was expected to recur in 1985. Snaring and hound-hunting for the collection of biological samples was restricted to bear-damaged plantations of Douglas fir in the 15-20 year old class.

The supplemental-feed station field work site met all the criteria for the study inasmuch as it had experienced heavy damage over the past five years in 10-22 year old plantations of Douglas fir, both pre-commercially thinned and unthinned stands. The twenty-one square mile area, located in Jefferson County, was roughly a seven-mile long, three-mile wide contiguous rectangle of plantations, clearcuts and mature timber, bounded on the west by the Olympic National Park coastal strip, U. S. Highway 101 and the Pacific Ocean and bounded on the south by Quinault Tribal lands. Bear density was high in this area due to the safety from hunting pressure afforded them simply by fleeing into the sanctuary of the O. N. P. or Tribal lands.

Wildlife other than bear was abundant in the feeding-station study area and sign or sightings were noted of elk, deer, mountain lion, bobcat, coyote and raccoon.

It was necessary to devise a feeding-station unit for use in the field that not only would protect the food-pellets from the invariably rainy weather, but also one that would stand up to rough usage by bear. It needed to be small enough to carry into the woods, yet large enough to hold an ample amount of pellets, eliminating the need for daily trips to refill the feeder. It needed to be stationary to prevent upsets and wastage.

This criteria was met by fashioning the feeder in two parts: feeder and roof, and was designed by my friend, Ken Flodstrom. Utilizing a five-gallon metal bucket, some angle and flat iron, small chains and binders and a two foot by two foot piece of ½ inch plywood, the feeders were constructed and served excellently.

Feed-station locations were selected in or near plantations that had experienced damage from bears during at least the previous two years. The stations were set up on obvious travel routes of bear, evidenced by trails through areas of damaged trees, tracks, or other bear sign both new and old. Care was taken to locate them off and out of sight of traveled forest roads. As an initial attractant, five-pound pieces of beaver meat were tied with wire and suspended from tree limbs near the feeding station. The immediate area of the unit was cleaned to bare soil to enable me to determine the size (or species) of animal utilizing the feeder.

Seven feeding stations were used to cover the twenty-one square miles and these were monitored at three to five day intervals. A known-amount/weight of pellets was carried to the feeding station in a pail. After replenishing the feeder, the pail was again weighed to determine the amount used. Only the basic formula was used in the seven feeding stations.

Five two-acre test plots of tree damage, either surrounding or adjacent to the feeding stations, were established before any initial feeding was noted at the buckets. All tree damage from previous years in the plots was counted and segregated by year of occurrence and species. At the conclusion of the May-June 1985 feeding test the plots would be rerun and all 1985 damage, if any, documented to see if damage levels improved or got worse.

The feeders were in place by mid-April but the weather turned raw and rainy, with hail at times, and there was no action at the feeding sites until May 3rd. On that date I saw the tracks of a large bear heading down the trail toward the feeder. Arriving at the site, I noticed that the beaver meat was gone and two and a half gallons of pellets had been eaten. This was good news; now I knew that the bears would eat my concoction.

By mid-May three of the stations had been visited by at least five bears. Although they were eating the pellets they weren't consuming the quantity that I had hoped and that spurred me to intensify my efforts to capture a couple of bears and begin testing new feed formulas.

I had some snares set at freshly-damaged areas in Mason and Kitsap Counties and although I was capturing bears, none of them were the adult males that I desired for my study. I had obtained blood vials, syringes and so forth from my friend, Bill Foreyt, professor of veterinary science and micro-biology at Washington State University, and using these I drew blood samples from the femoral arteries of the bears I captured. Five bears were released (with ear tags) for possible recapture in the fall. Bear not destined to be released were killed on site and an immediate effort made to obtain blood samples from the femoral artery. If this failed, the bear was opened and an attempt made at collecting blood directly from the aorta. If this failed, hair samples were obtained for analysis. Tissue samples (kidney or liver) were collected from each bear killed. Blood and tissue samples were kept on ice during transit from field to home, and centrifuging to harvest serum was accomplished within twelve hours. As a safety precaution, bear immobilized with Ketamine hydrochloride were deemed unsafe for human or animal consumption for thirty days after injection. To prevent wastage, bear that were to be killed could not be first immobilized.

Consequently, in my quest for two adult male bears, I hauled the game departments' bear cage with me each time I checked my snares. Kelly Lund, my game agent friend, accompanied me on these trips, providing his tranquilizer gun and expertise. On one trip to the Quilcene area I found a yearling bear in my snare and being desperate to obtain a bear for my holding pens, I decided to "bring him back alive." After darting him and obtaining a blood sample, we loaded the drugged bear in our cage and continued on our route. As we drove, I noticed the little bear beginning to stir in the cage which was just behind my seat in the Blazer. Soon he was on his feet and growing more alert by the minute as he took in his new surroundings. Nearing Hadlock, I espied a veterinary clinic and decided to stop there and have the bear's blood sample centrifuged. Just as we were parking in front of the place, an older couple walked by carrying their cat. Our bear eyed them critically and the lady remarked, "Oh, look at that dog! He looks just like a bear!"

As we headed down the highway, we opened our lunches and started to eat. I offered the little bear a piece of my banana and when he devoured it, I gave him part of a sandwich. Before we reached Belfair, the critter had eaten most of my lunch! It was growing late when we reached Deer Creek just north of Shelton and I hurried up the logging road to check the last snare of the day.

When we arrived at the snare, which was set in a trail, we found it to be missing and a great commotion just yards away let us know we had captured a bear. The bear, an adult, brown-color-phase bear, had apparently stepped in the snare just moments before our arrival. He had pulled the drag a short distance but wasn't entangled at all. When we appeared he snorted and crashed off through the brush about thirty yards before climbing a tree. This looked like a fine candidate for my experiment but the problem was I already had a bear in my cage in the Blazer. Since the bear was freshly caught I decided to return in the morning to tranquilize him and haul him to my pens.

It was late when we arrived at the Olympia research center and unloaded the little bear into the holding pen. After filling the water trough and installing a pan of food, I headed for home and reached my friendly bed at 11:30 p.m.

The next morning we returned to Deer Creek to secure the brown colored bear and found him entangled in the salal brush about ten feet from where we had left him the night before. To my dismay I saw that he had been chewing on his foot in an effort to escape and since this would make him unsuitable for my study, I reluctantly pulled my revolver and dispatched him. This was a big disappointment and I wished we had returned in the dark the previous evening to immobilize him. Often, once a snared bear knows that he has been discovered, he grows frantic in his efforts to escape (just as we would!) and sometimes will chew on the snared foot.

Four days later I rendezvoused with my hunter, Bernie Paque, and accompanied him to check his bear snares in the Clearwater River area. At one of the snares we found an adult bear of about 150 pounds tied up and waiting for us. The bear was freshly caught and of a mean disposition that didn't improve any when we approached. He would lunge at us, blowing and snorting, and we made sure we stayed out of the reach of his claws.

Kelly hadn't been able to come with me on this trip although he had left his tranquilizer gun and drugs in my Blazer. The cage was still behind my seat. Leaving Bernie to guard the bear, I drove down the valley to the Clearwater fire station and using an outside pay phone, I made many calls trying to locate one of the game department biologists, or Kelly, to come tranquilize the bear for me. Since it was Sunday, I got no response.

I desperately wanted to use this bear in my food preference tests and so I dug into Kelly's box of equipment, looking for an instruction manual. After reading it, I thought, "I can do this." Selecting a large dart and cylinder, I placed 15.5 cc's of Ketamine Hydrochloride in it, which was the amount that seemed appropriate to immobilize the 150 pound bear. Now I needed some water to finish filling the cylinder and the only water available was in a clear rain puddle in the graveled parking lot. Scooping some up, I filled the dart, loaded the gun, and headed back up the valley where I found the bear waiting and in no better humor than when I had left him. Bernie helped me carry the heavy cage up into the woods and when all was in readiness, I fired the dart into the bear's ham. Three minutes later the bear was asleep. Quickly obtaining a blood sample, we then caged the bear and dragged our prize down through the woods to my truck. The bear was a male and would do very well for my study.

By the time I reached Olympia after an 125-mile drive, my bear had revived and didn't seem to like the confine of the cage any better than he had liked the snare. Recruiting my boss, Bob Dick, to help me, we unloaded the bear into the holding pens in the dark. After placing food and water for both bears I headed for home, arriving just before midnight.

The next morning I drove to Olympia to check on my bear "inmates" and found yesterday's bear in a very bad mood. He had disarranged everything that was movable in his pen and made no attempt to hide in his enclosed sleeping area when I arrived. Instead, he lunged at the chain-link wire that separated us, huffing and blowing his defiance. He had eaten quite a bit of the food I had placed for him and seemed none the worse from his water-puddle drug mixture. I nicknamed this bear "Bernie."

During the next three days I caught two more bears but none suitable for my feeding study.

On May 27th, Memorial Day, Velma was planning a picnic at our house and had invited about thirty friends to attend. This also happened to be the day that my snares a few miles north of Aberdeen were due to be checked. These snares were set on the tree farm of Erich, a German friend of mine, who was experiencing tree damage in his young, pre-commercially thinned, fir plantation.

Assuring Velma that I would check the two snares and be home in plenty of time for her picnic, I headed for the woods.

Erich walked with me and finding the first snare undisturbed, we hiked in to the second one which was quite a distance back in the mature timber at the head of a marshy area. The snare was a trail set, firmly anchored to a large alder. When we reached it I saw immediately that I might be a little late for Velma's picnic. Standing there, hair-bristling, but docile compared to "Bernie Bear," was a huge 300 pound male bear.

Erich had been very angry when this bear had peeled his trees but as he stood looking at the big fellow, I could sense he was feeling sympathy for the bear. "Never haf I been so close to a bear!" he said in his broken English, and added, "Vot you do mit dis bear?"

Remembering the long hike through the swamp between my truck and the bear and also the thirty guests due to arrive at my house, I was caught between a rock and a hard place. I very much wanted to use this bear in my feed formula tests and so, against my better judgement, I told Erich if he could round up some help to carry the bear from the woods, I would contact Kelly and have him bring the tranquilizer gun.

In due course Kelly arrived and shortly after, Erich's volunteers; we now numbered fourteen people! With four carrying the empty cage, we slogged back through the swamp and found our bear (that I dubbed "Buford") patiently waiting. I darted him and in six and a half minutes he tumbled over. I removed the snare from his big paw and noticed that some of my crew started to put a little distance between themselves and the bear. After drawing a blood sample we wrestled the big fellow into the cage and his bulk completely filled it.

It took six of us to carry the 300-pound bear in the 100-pound cage, but with lots of help we eventually reached my truck. Loading my caged prize into the Blazer, Kelly and I roared off toward Olympia.

Since I had only two holding pens, I planned to release my little bear and put "Buford" into the pen. This meant I had to tranquilize the little bear, remove him from the pen and lay him unfettered on the grass while we got big Buford out of the cage and into the pen. Then we could put the little guy in the cage. We hoped we could perform all of this quickly before the little bear revived from the drug.

But Buford had other ideas. We had put him into the cage head-first which meant he would have to "back" out of it. This he didn't want to do for he had no idea what was behind him. Casting worried glances at the little bear, we prodded and poked at Buford but he wouldn't budge. Finally, growing desperate, I grabbed the water hose and sprayed water in his face. Little by little he backed up to escape the water and soon found himself in the holding pen.

After caging the little bear I headed for home, arriving too late for the picnic but finding our thirty guests patiently waiting. Taking the caged bear 100 yards from our house, I released him at the edge of the woods and he loped off to freedom.

Now that I had two adult male bears, Buford and Bernie, in my holding pens it seemed that every snare I checked held an adult bear. During the next four days I caught five bears, all adults, three of which were large males. All of these bears were caught in tree-damaged areas. After they were shot, I had to work quickly to obtain blood samples while there was still some pressure in their arteries. One big male bear that I snared near Leland Lake gave me a bit of a start. After shooting the bear with my revolver, I immediately rolled him onto his back and stuck the needle of my syringe into his groin, aiming for the femoral artery. As soon as the needle entered his flesh, the big fellow reacted and attempted to get up, causing me to jump to one side, grab my revolver, and give him another round. This settled his case and I was able to secure my serum sample.

I had obtained a centrifuge and was now able to harvest the blood serum at home, spinning the vials of blood for thirty minutes and retaining the clear serum that separated from the hemoglobin. During the summer and early fall I was able to collect serum, hair or tissue samples from twenty-four bears and these were kept frozen a maximum of six months before delivery to Dr. Foreyt for analysis. The analysis of bear sera and tissues collected during the period May-August 1985 was completed by the toxicology group of the Washington Animal Disease Diagnostic Laboratory at Washington State University. This analysis showed considerable variation in individual values but no significant differences between spring and fall samples, with the exception of manganese. This element was present in inadequate amounts in all but one of the serum profiles, with the late fall samples showing a greater deficiency. Early spring magnesium deficiency was not evidenced as supposed; sera analysis of spring and fall bear taken in damaged areas showed little difference in magnesium levels with spring bear actually showing higher levels. (Spring samples 24.16 parts per million average; fall samples 22.30 parts per million average.) Since the time lapse between collection of spring and fall sera samples was only one month (August) it is quite possible that insufficient time had expired to produce significant changes in the sera profiles for profitable comparison. Nevertheless, it was evident that all the bears were lacking in one trace element or another and I made sure that my feed formula contained the correct balance of vitamins and trace elements necessary for the bears' needs.

After my bears "Bernie" and "Buford" had been penned up for two weeks I felt it was time to experiment with variations of my "basic" pellet formula. Although a minimum of six and a maximum of eight bear utilized my feeding stations in the field and devoured the basic pellet offered there during the two-month study period, it was noted with interest that my captive bears, who also devoured the basic pellet with gusto when it was the only food offered, completely ignored it when variations of the formula were offered.

It has long been assumed that bear have unrestrained appetites, indiscriminately devouring anything availing itself to them. This is, in part, true of free-roaming bears in the natural state who must be opportunists, taking advantage of whatever provender presents itself, with little regard for principles or ultimate consequences.

My feeding studies with captive bear showed this assumption to hold true only when the bear was offered no choice. Being hungry and only one food offered, the bear would eat it. However, when multiple choices were offered, it was immediately noted that bears became individuals as regards food preferences. My first captive bear, an emaciated 40-pound yearling, was offered three choices: bread, Friskies Sauce Cubes, and the basic food pellet. He refused to eat the bread, devoured the Friskies with delight and ate sparingly of the basic pellet. When bread and Friskies were not offered he at the basic pellet without hesitation.

Bear number two (Bernard), an adult male weighing 150 pounds when captured, had a voracious appetite. Nevertheless, he had preferences. This bear opted for Friskies Sauce Cubes as first choice, regardless of which pellet formula variation was offered with it. He, too, ignored the basic pellet once multiple choices were offered.

Bear number three (Buford), an adult male weighing 300 pounds when captured, had, for his size, an abstemious appetite. When compared with bear number two, who was only half his size, he ate an equal amount (bear two consumed 233 pounds of food in twenty days; bear three consumed 234 pounds). Unlike bear one and two, bear three held Friskies Sauce Cubes in disdain and opted for the new variations of the food pellet.

I concocted ten variations of my basic pellet formula and placed an equal amount of each in a row of feed troughs in their cages. I returned each morning to weight the pellets remaining in each of the ten troughs to determine how much of each variation had been consumed. After eliminating formula after formula, I hit upon one that both bears preferred over all the others and decided that this would be the formula to use the following year.

Meanwhile, in the woods, it was found that the basic food pellets kept well during the damp, rainy weather as long as they were protected from direct contact with rain, or moisture finding its way down the tree trunk and subsequently wetting the feed. Wetting caused an immediate hairy-growth of mold on the pellets and rejection by the bear. In late June it was found that some of the feeders, where feeding rates had slowed, contained slightly moldy pellets. These were replaced and feeding resumed. Despite the availability of red huckleberries and salmonberries, bear continued to visit the feeders until they were removed on July 8.

During the two-month field study 317 pounds of basic pellets were consumed at the feeders, averaging 63.4 pounds per feeder visited. I had hoped for a better acceptance and higher consumption rates of the pellets, but felt certain I would see a big difference the following year when the new formula pellet was used.

After pulling the feed stations from the woods, I recruited a crew and set about running the two-acre test plots to determine if my feeding program had any effect on tree damage levels. The findings were encouraging, inasmuch as all five test plots showed marked improvement. The decrease in number of trees peeled, 1985 over 1984, ranged 18%, 39%, 58%, 100%, and 100% in the individual plots. Plot number one showed the least improvement (18%) with twenty-seven trees peeled before the bear located the feed station. Once it started utilizing the feeder, peeling stopped.

Supplemental feeding of bear in areas of tree damage appeared to be cost-effective, inasmuch as bear needed only be fed during the critical two-month period, May-June; a few feed stations could take care of a large geographical area; pellet cost and quantity consumed per animal per day seemed minimal when compared to the monetary loss in timber destroyed by hungry bears.

Chapter 11

Hungary

THE WASHINGTON FOREST PROTECTION ASSOCIATION'S ANIMAL damage control service's members, all timberland owners, had been closely observing this first year of the study and many of them volunteered their tree farms for an expanded study in 1986.

This added acreage included all of the west side of the Olympia Peninsula (which would eliminate all spring bear hunting in that area), the Olney Creek tree farm near Skykomish, the Bremerton City Watershed and Cavenham's acreage in the K-M mountain area near Cathlamet. This encompassed a total area of 793 square miles! This intensification of the feeding study would be undertaken with the assurance that any bear utilizing the supplemental feed and still persisting in peeling trees would be removed. The objective of the second year's work was to produce the new formula pellet and field test it at the original 1985 feeding sites, to see if the presence and use of these pellets by bear reduced tree damage. Tree damage test plots would again be laid out in 1986 for comparison of damage levels. Noting that in the 1985 study several bear had peeled trees before discovering and utilizing the supplemental feed, it was hoped that the bear's memory would direct them to the feeders much earlier in 1986. This could result in a further decrease in damage levels and should prove that second-year benefits of supplemental feeding in a given area would surpass first-year results.

I had been doing some snaring on K-M Mountain during the summer and had caught a big male bear in one of my trail sets. The bear had pulled the drag two hundred feet into a thicket of eight-feet tall salmonberry bushes in his efforts to escape and that is where I found him hopelessly entangled. He was plenty mad and was thrashing and crashing violently amid the inextricable confusion of broken and twisted salmonberry stalks. I quickly dispatched him with my revolver and began the tussle of dragging the big fellow through the confusion of bushes, toward my Blazer 150 yards away.

Two weeks later I caught another bear, also a male, in this same trail set. Since it was late in June, within a week of the time that bears usually quit peeling trees, and also realizing that I would be feeding bears in this area the following year I decided to tranquilize the bear and release him. Once he was sedated I drew a blood sample, placed numbered ear tags in his ears and set him free. Taking the snare with me, I proceeded on my way to the next snare, which was located a couple miles away on the far end of the mountain.

This snare was also a trail set, and I had placed it in an open-grown, mature stand of timber. When I neared it, I could see that the set had been disturbed and the snare cable and drag were missing.

Fresh gouges in the forest floor duff indicated which direction the bear had gone with the drag and the sign was easy to follow. After about fifty feet the drag marks led me up an embankment and halfway up it there was no more sign to follow. I was standing under a sixteen-inch diameter hemlock tree, trying to figure out the mystery of where the bear had gone, when I happened to look into the tree's limbs just above my head. There, on the first limb, about thirty feet up, stood my bear, quietly watching me! She wasn't entangled and the drag pole dangled loosely along the tree's trunk.

Quickly returning to my Blazer, I loaded the tranquilizer gun with 10 cc of Ketamine and hurried back to my bear. Luckily for me, she had not moved from her perch. The bear gave a start and blew a spray of mucous from her nostrils when the dart hit her rump.

Now I had a problem. I could tell by the bear's position that when the drug took effect she would fall on the opposite side of the limb from the drag pole. Should the drag pole happen to snag up on the limb the bear would be left dangling by its snared foot, over twenty feet above the ground. Not wanting to see this happen, I shinnied up the tree trunk and using my wrench, removed the cable clamps that held the drag, allowing it to fall to the forest floor. I had just finished this chore when the bear teetered on her perch and fell to the ground. Seeing that she was out like a light, I removed the snare from her paw and after securing a blood sample, placed tags in her ears. The bear had landed on its side when it fell and had rolled down the thickly duffed embankment unharmed. Within 2 ½ hours both bears revived and staggered off into the dark, mysterious thickets and lived to roam there many more years.

Now it was time to release "Buford" and "Bernie" bears. Both bears had gained weight while in captivity, with Bernie now weighing 162 pounds and Buford 312 pounds. After sedating the bears we placed ear tags on both animals and also installed a radio transmitter collar on big Buford. My plan was to release them near the point of capture and then, in late summer, recapture them for more blood analysis.

After placing the bears in separate hauling cages, we loaded Bernie bear in Paque's truck and placed big Buford in the back of my Blazer. Bernie bear had remained feisty and aggressive from the time he was captured and retained his irascibility right to the end. When Paque reached the Clearwater release site and opened the door to Bernie's cage, the bear left the cage but remained in the road, huffing and chopping his jaws for several minutes before entering the woods.

But big Buford had remained passive and shy, spending all of his time in the dark sanctuary of his cage's den or sleeping area, usually leaving it only to eat or drink in early morning, late evening or at night. If caught outside his den he would immediately race into it at full speed as if he had been caught naked. Once, when closed out of his den, he retreated to the far corner of the exercise area and sat passively on the edge of the water trough, head down, avoiding eye contact and showing no sign of aggressiveness.

Not wanting to release Buford back in Erich's tree farm where he had earlier done so much damage, I hauled him to the head of Helm Creek, which was seven-and-a-half miles northeast of the point of capture. On a timbered ridge at the road's end, I backed my Blazer up to the canyon's edge and after dragging the bear's cage out onto the tailgate I climbed atop the cage and lifted the door. Seeing daylight without bars for the first time in two-and-a-half months, he shot out of the cage like a black torpedo and his second jump took him over the canyon's edge and out of sight. After a few moments the sounds of his noisy departure faded away far down the brushy canyon.

Two days later Bernie Paque accompanied me on a bear damage flight on the west side of the Olympic Peninsula. Since our flight route would take us over the area of Buford's release I had Bernie bring his electronic receiver to see if we could pick up a signal from Buford bear's radio collar. After a few minutes of monitoring the receiver chirped loud and clear as we passed over the Wedekind Creek area, indicating that Buford had traveled 6 ¾ miles south since his release and now was just three-fourths of a mile east of Erich's tree farm!

On August 5th, just one month after Buford bear's release, I decided to attempt a recapture to secure more blood serum and also to remove his radio collar. Consequently, I was up and ready to go at 4:30 that morning, accompanied by my hunter Paque and his efficient pack of hounds. Around 5 a.m. we drove to Bear Gulch, put Bernie's strike dogs on the hood of his pickup and began our search for Big Buford. It was a beautiful summer morning that promised to turn hot and we hoped for an early chase. After hunting through the lower Donovan-Corkery country where we had picked up Buford's signal earlier, we headed up into the Helm Creek area. Bernie was using his electronic receiver but so far had received no signal that Buford bear was anywhere in the area. Heading south, we hunted down into the Van Winckle Creek area, but still no signal from our radio-collared bear. Then at 7:25 a.m., the strike dogs exploded into an uproar of bawling that meant only one thing: hot bear scent!

We piled out of our vehicles and I began looking for bear tracks while Bernie operated his receiver in hopes that this bear might be big Buford. Just then I espied the bear's tracks, big tracks, on the loose road-bank dirt and their size made me think they must have been made by Buford. When we still could not pick up a radio signal we wondered if maybe the bear's transmitter was not functioning or if possibly the bear had slipped the collar off. Deciding to find out, we released the hounds and the chase was on, headed down into the Bear Gulch country.

The chase faded out of our hearing and it was not until 8:15, forty-five minutes after the chase started, that we reached a high point from where we could hear the dogs barking, "treed".

Grabbing the equipment I would need to obtain some blood serum, we dived into the brush and headed down toward Bear Creek. Just before we reached the hounds and the treed bear we stumbled onto an old cat' road which made our going much easier.

We found the bear treed down in a steep draw just off the cat' road. Bernie tied the dogs back away from the tree while I studied the bear, looking for its collar and ear tags but could see neither. This bear was an enormous 300-pound critter that would have passed as a twin for Buford but it sure was not the one we were looking for.

After securing the dogs, we made our way back to our trucks and left the woods, as the day had grown hot. We then drove to Bowerman field near Hoquiam where I chartered a small plane, hoping to locate Buford from the air. We flew for an hour and twenty minutes but could pick up no signal from our bear. Deciding to search farther northeast, we headed the plane toward the Canyon River country and finally picked up a signal, loud and clear, from our radio-collared Buford bear. He was directly under us, in the west branch of the Satsop country, and nearly twenty miles northeast of Erich's tree farm!

The next morning we were up at 4 a.m. and on our way up the Wynoochee for another try at Buford bear. While I had him in captivity in my holding pens, my wife had become quite fond of the big, bashful bear and when we left for the hunt that morning she admonished me, "If you kill Buford, don't come home!" I had no intention of killing him but you never know when a darted bear will scamper to the very top of a tree and when the drug takes effect, topple from there to his death.

We headed up the Wynoochee valley in the dark that morning and turned east onto the Cougar Smith road. From a high point along that road we again picked up Buford's radio signal and he was still in the same general area where we had located him from the plane the previous day. While it was still dark but not far from daylight we explored all the old roads in the area but none of them would put us close to the bear. Reaching the end of the little-used forest road not far from the Satsop River, we decided that Bernie should take three dogs and the receiver and hike through the woods towards the bear's signal until he could get close enough for the dogs to scent the bear. Once the chase was on, I could keep track of the bear chase from the road and determine where they were headed until Bernie could hike back out to his truck.

This decided, Bernie headed into the woods and after quite a long wait I heard the hounds open up, red-hot! It was a good thing I stayed by the truck for the chase headed southwest, crossed the Cougar Smith road, and circled down into the hilly heads of Carter Creek. After radioing Bernie, I drove to the end of an old grade, following the hounds' voices and soon heard them baying the bear, who had stopped to defy them. While I was preparing the tranquilizer gun and collecting my vacutainers for the serum, Bernie arrived and ran towards the sound of the bear fight. The bear, sensing his approach, broke and ran and the sound of the chase faded out of my hearing. When Bernie did not return, I started patrolling the area, listening for the dogs, but could hear absolutely nothing. Leaving the area, I drove five miles down the Wynochee road to a logging road that headed east into some higher ground. Reaching a high point near the top of the divide, I stopped to listen and could faintly hear the hounds, but so far away I could not determine if they were bayed up or barking treed.

Finally, after an hour, I decided to take a chance and hike in that direction. Taking a compass reading, I dived down into the canyon and in a few seconds could no longer hear the dogs. I continued on, and once in awhile, from a high ridge, I could hear the dogs. The country was rugged, steep up and down, and forested with second-growth timber.

After an hour and ten minutes and two miles of hiking I reached a fairly level stretch of ground with scattered timber and lots of bracken ferns as high as my head. But now I could hear the hounds clearly, barking treed just ahead of me. When I reached the tree, I found Bernie and all the dogs patiently waiting for me. Bernie had followed the dogs through the woods all the way to the tree.

Buford was sitting on a big limb about twenty-five feet up a limby three-foot diameter fir, and acting his usual passive self. Bernie tied the dogs and I took aim at the bear's rump with my tranquilizer gun, hoping that he would not get alarmed when the dart struck him and climb high up into the tree. I was remembering Velma's admonition and I certainly did not want to see this big bear killed, for I had grown attached to him myself.

Much to my relief the bear merely flinched when the dart struck him and he remained on his perch. I held my breath while I waited for the drug to sedate him, praying that he wouldn't climb any higher!

In four minutes, the Ketamine took its effect and Buford's hind parts began to grow numb, causing him to slip from the limb and hang perpendicular to the tree trunk with his front claws supporting all his weight. Thus suspended, he was only about seventeen feet from the ground. Almost immediately the drug took effect and he dropped to the ground in a big, fat ball; unhurt.

Quickly removing the radio collar, I drew a blood sample and while Bernie headed out of the woods with his dogs, I sat down to wait for Buford to revive. After another two hours the bear was standing on his front legs and making an effort to regain the use of his back ones. It was getting late and with another mile hike to the road by the shortest route, I bade farewell to Buford, wished him a long life and many girlfriends and made my way out of the woods. Velma would be proud of me; Buford was unhurt.

My plan was to attempt to also recapture Bernie bear for blood analysis although I knew he would be much harder to locate than big Buford was. Since the bear was not equipped with a radio collar and realizing the vast area traveled by an adult male bear, there was no way of predicting where he might be. The nearby Olympic National Park and Quinault tribal lands being off limits to us, we would be out of luck if our bear had wandered there. Still, it was worth a try and August 9th found Bernie and I headed for the Clearwater country.

A light rain was falling as we left the blacktopped road and started up a graveled road in the Deception Creek area. Tethering the strike dogs on the hood of Bernie's truck, we proceeded slowly along the road in search of our bear. I followed Bernie in my Blazer along the old road that wound through areas of all stages of timber growth from six-year-old clear-cuts to mature stands. The rain had stopped but the sky remained cloudy; a perfect morning for bears to be out feeding.

One particular clear-cut looked especially good to me, being bounded on the lower side of the road by a steep, brushy draw with a little creek rattling unseen along the bottom of it. The area had been logged probably six or seven years previous and was acquiring a thick cover of huckleberry and salal bushes. One hundred yards above the road was a mature stand of timber with berry-laden huckleberry bushes growing right up to its edge.

Ahead of us I could see the road's end on an old landing. I was traveling along slowly, about 150 yards behind Bernie and was scouring the hillsides with my eyeballs for any sign of game. Just as Bernie reached the end of the road, I noticed a slight movement in a tall huckleberry bush, right at the timber's edge. Stopping my truck, I saw more movement and caught a fleeting glimpse of a bear as he ran from the bush where he had been feeding on red huckleberries and disappeared into the dark, shadowy timber. The morning had been warming and cold air was rising from the canyon below us, carrying the bear's scent toward the timber and away from the hounds' noses.

When Bernie returned from the road's end, we walked the dogs up to the timber's edge and they roared off on the chase like a bunch of schoolboys on the last day of school.

The bear turned out to be a "runner", covering eleven miles in four hours and as the day turned hot and humid, the dogs began dropping out of the chase. Finally, we called the last dogs off and made plans to try it again the following day.

The next morning dawned clear and 6 a.m. found me rendezvousing with Bernie on the Clearwater road. This time we headed for the area where yesterday's chase had ended and almost immediately started a chase.

Apparently the bear was still a little tired from the previous day's chase for he ran only about a half hour before treeing in a huge old-growth hemlock right in the bottom of a deep canyon. One side of the canyon was old-growth forest, the other side an open clear-cut. As we descended the steep clear-cut canyon side we could see the bear sitting astraddle of a big limb with his forelegs hugging the tree. He was about one hundred feet up and impossible to see when we reached the bottom of the tree to tie the dogs back. Climbing back up the open canyon side, we stopped at a point that put us within one hundred feet of the treed bear and just a little below him. It was a long shot for my tranquilizer dart but I decided to give it a try. Loading my dart with 7 cc of Ketamine I took aim at the bear's backside, which was facing us. With the gun rested over a stump to steady it and Bernie shading my eyes from the sun with his cap, I aimed high to allow for the distance, hoping to place my dart in his rump. With the bear's head in my sights I squeezed the trigger and watched the dart arch through the air, dropping as it went, and plunk perfectly into the bear's rump!

When the dart hit, the bear left his perch and backed down the tree to a limb only twenty feet above the rocky canyon floor. All this seemed too good to be true but when, after ten minutes, the drug had not taken effect, the bear climbed back up the tree to his original 100-foot-high perch. There he sat another five minutes until, finally, he began to teeter on the limb. We watched in dismay as he toppled from the limb and plunged one hundred feet to his death on the rocks below.

Hurrying down there, it immediately became apparent that he was beyond being revived and so I drew a blood sample and we headed out of the canyon. The bear, a seventy-pound yearling, having been drugged was unsafe for human consumption and we were forced to leave him.

At this writing, seventeen years later, there has been no report of Bernie bear being taken during a hunting season for his ear tags have never been turned in. He could still be out there; bears live to be 30 years of age and Bernie would now be 23!

That same summer, 1985, I received a letter from my friend, Franz, in Austria. I grew excited as I read it for he stated, "I have organized a wild boar hunt in Hungary for you. You are invited as a guest of the Wildlife Management Institute of the University of Yodollo near Budapest. You have to pay nothing! Do come, now that you have the chance! I also bought for you a short hunt in southern Hungary on boar, red deer hind and a young red deer stag (spikes or four or six points) lasting three days. You won't have any expenses.

"After that we will hunt in Regelsbrunn on small game and roe deer. Don't take bright or red colored clothing for hunting; it is not the custom in Hungary. Camouflage is _not_ allowed. Green, brown or dark colors (perhaps without spots, lines, etc.) are advisable for hunting clothes. Come somewhere from perhaps the 20th of November to mid-December. I will take you to Hungary and you can take one of my rifles. I shall attend you all the time to advise you."

"And," he added, "Velma, you _must_ join us, if you can't go with us on the hunt we leave you with our friends for a few hours. I fetch you from the airport. See you here."

Such an invitation sounded like high adventure and certainly not one to be turned down. After contacting Franz and assuring him that both Velma and I would join him in November for the hunt, I set about finalizing my bear-study work for the summer. I still had a few more bears to recapture for the collection of blood serum and tissue samples and on the morning of August 13 I crawled from my warm nest at 2:30 a.m. for another hunt.

I arrived at the Port Blakely tree farm near Bremerton at 4:30 a.m. and found Bernie and his hounds waiting for me at the gate. We started our hunt before daybreak but a couple of hours passed before we got a chase going. Then the dogs "struck", red-hot, and Bernie released the eager dogs on the spoor. Roaring like a pack of banshees, the hounds vanished into the thick brush, their voices echoing and ringing deep down in the canyon. After a bit we could hear a couple of the hounds' voices leading away from the main pack and it became evident that we had a "split race" going. While Bernie followed the main pack I tried to keep within hearing of the two dogs that were heading in the opposite direction.

After losing the sound of their baying I traveled the old roads for a half hour before locating them again. They were barking "treed" down in the timber on the point of a ridge. Hiking in to the tree I found an eight-month-old cub of the year staring down at me from the upper limbs of a hemlock. I had no desire to kill this little fellow and so I leashed the hounds and led them from the tree to my truck. When I finally located Bernie and the main pack of dogs, the chase was over. Bernie related that the bear had treed three times but would climb down and run each time he drew near. Finally, at the third tree, the bear stayed put and I was able to collect my serum sample.

A couple of weeks later I was up at 3 a.m. for a hunt near Naselle in the Brookfield area. My game department friend, Kelly Lund, arrived at 3:25 and after rendezvousing with Bernie at a café in Aberdeen, we headed south in two vehicles. My plan was to recapture the two bears that I had earlier ear-tagged at Brookfield and to collect blood samples from them for comparison.

The morning was foggy and overcast when we arrived there at 5:30 a.m. and it felt like a perfect morning to get a chase going. Nevertheless, it was five hours before the hounds picked up their ears and set up an uproar from the hood of Bernie's truck that signified one thing—bear! Once the hounds were released the sound of their voices faded in and out as they pursued the bear through the deep canyons and rough terrain. The Brookfield tree farm hills rose up abruptly from the banks of the Columbia River and the chopped up maze of hills and ridges made it easy to lose track of the dogs.

This bear took the dogs on a long and circuitous chase, but a good one, and as the hours passed so did the fog and clouds. As the day warmed, the chase slowed a little, but the bear showed no sign of wanting to "tree". I had driven my Blazer on a side road to a high point from where I could both hear and observe and had just arrived there when I saw the bear cross the main logging road nearly a mile away from me. It appeared to be a big bear and not in any particular hurry. Shortly after he disappeared in the brush, the hounds crossed the road on his trail. The chase continued another half hour and then we heard the music we had been waiting for—the hounds were barking "treed"!

We found them barking up a big hemlock tree and only forty feet from the logging road. It was a big bear, a boar, and weighed 225 pounds but it was not one of the ear-tagged bears that I had hoped for. Since the summer bear season was now open and Kelly desired some bear meat, this bear was shot and taken from the woods. After depositing the bear in a trout hatchery cool-room, we returned to the woods to round up a hound that was off on a bear chase of his own. Finding the hound walking the road in the August heat, we loaded him and headed for our cabin at Naselle.

The following morning we were up at 5 a.m. to make ready for another hunt at Brookfield. We were all hungry as a bunch of bears but to our disappointment we found none of the cafes in the little village open at that hour. So, with no coffee and stomachs growling, we headed for the woods. After "roading" the dogs for three hours, they struck a "hot" bear track and we released them all. The chase circled in the same area all day, a pre-commercially thinned stand of hemlocks on the south side of K-M Mountain. The dogs held the bear at bay many times but before we could reach them in the crisscrossed mess of downed trees, the bear would break and run! It crossed the roads and the power line right-of-way many times and we were able to determine that it was one of the ear-tagged bears that I desired but it was impossible to get close enough to dart it with the tranquilizer gun. Had we wanted to shoot and kill it, we could have done it many times. We kept hoping the bear would "tree" but when it had not after an eight-hour chase, we picked up the dogs and called it off at 5:30 p.m. By the time we reached Naselle we were more than ready for some food!

With this hunt I terminated my bear chases for the season and set about preparing a progress report that summarized the results of the first year of supplemental feeding. This was finally accomplished in mid-November, its completion held up by a quick trip to Maryland to visit my folks, many meetings with game department and forestry personnel, a trip to Washington State University to deliver serum and tissue samples and a side trip while there to harvest a fine mule deer. Then, with bears retiring to their winter dens and my workload easing up, I made ready for the trip to Europe. The date for our departure was set for November 21.

We awoke that morning to face a white world for three inches of snow had fallen during the night and the lead-gray sky gave promise of more. This was realized just as we left our driveway when the snowstorm hit in earnest. The trip to Sea-Tac airport usually takes one and a half hours, but this day required four hours and 4-wheel-drive and we arrived at the parking garage with twenty minutes to spare before our plane's departure time. The same storm that had made us late had also delayed every flight that morning and we made it into the plane only to sit there 4 ½ hours while the ground crew worked feverishly, but without success, to de-ice and de-snow the wings and allow us to take off. Finally, at 6:30 p.m. they announced that the airport was closed and we were lodged for the night in a nearby motel. By now six inches of snow had accumulated.

The next morning dawned cold and 20 degrees but the snow had ceased to fall. We boarded our plane but were delayed another 2 1/4 hours while the crew de-iced the plane. Finally, at 4:20 p.m. we roared off the runway and headed for Copenhagen, Denmark, arriving there after a nine-hour flight. After a connecting flight to Zurich we changed planes again and headed for Vienna. Most of Europe was covered with snow and the fading light of evening made the landscape below us appear inhospitable. It was dark when we arrived in Vienna as well as cold, snowy and foggy but we were soon transported to Franz's warm farmhouse by his dad and sister. By 8:45 p.m. we were snuggled under the fluffy goose-down quilts and soon asleep for our "day" had been twenty-seven hours long.

We must have slept like zombies for we did not awaken until Franz called at our door at 11:45 a.m. to announce that lunch was ready. Over our lunch of wiener schnitzels and chicken, cake, coffee and mineral water we visited and discussed the upcoming hunt. A little after 4 p.m. Franz decided we should go for a duck hunt and a few minutes later found us trudging across an open field in nine inches of snow while the cold wind lashed our faces with sleet. The tracks of hare and roe deer were everywhere in the snow and a roe deer buck snorted at us for nearly an hour when we entered the woods that bordered the Danube. An "arm" of the Danube extended into the woods at this point and we sat there until dark watching for ducks. Four did fly over but kept well out of the range of our shotguns. Hoot owls livened up just at dark and the woods echoed with their eerie calls. It was still snowing and sleeting when we left the woods and returned to the farmhouse.

The next day we enjoyed a lunch of roast pork, chicken, huge bread dumplings, sauerkraut, white wine, cake and coffee at Franz's table and enjoyed a good visit with his mother and father. That evening we accompanied Franz to Vienna and shopped at an open market in the falling snow while Franz attended to some business. Christmas lights were strung and lit everywhere in the open market and the fluffy snowflakes floating down added to the festive holiday feeling. After a while we became cold and went to a coffee house where Franz joined us in an hour or so. Visiting over coffee, Franz related that in late January he planned to make a trip to Zimbabwe, Namibia and South Africa and he invited me to join him. He had many acquaintances there from prior visits to the area, one of whom would loan us a car for our travels. Also, if I wanted to hunt, he knew several landowners whose land we could hunt on for a nominal fee. He would take his 7mm Sauer and some ammo and I would not have to ship my gun. The trip would last about three weeks. If I wanted to accompany him, I could fly to Johannesburg, South Africa and he would meet me at the airport there on the appointed date. Would I like to go?

I glanced at my wife and she was not frowning so I answered, "Yes, Franz, Lord willing, I'll go!"

I did not sleep much that night, a combination of things keeping me awake; jetlag, excitement over the next days' trip to Hungary and now the prospect of visiting and hunting in Africa! It was almost too much to comprehend as true!

We were up at 7 a.m. the following morning, finished packing, loaded our gear in Franz's little car and at 9 a.m. were headed east toward the Hungarian border. It was a pretty day, but cold, with a little sun and some blue sky. Large, Austrian hares were hopping everywhere in the snowy fields and I was enjoying the scenery, bleak as it was. After stopping in a small village to buy some fresh fruit as gifts for our hosts in Hungary, we continued on our way, soon arriving at the border between Austria and communist Hungary. Gates and barbed wire and machine gun emplacements were everywhere and guards swarmed our car like mad hornets. Franz presented the necessary papers and our visas, which the armed guards exclaimed loudly over, slammed their fists on the top of our car, and then disappeared with our papers into the border guard office.

I grinned at Franz and said, "Sure a friendly bunch, aren't they?"

"Don't laugh," Franz replied soberly. "This is serious."

The guards finally returned and handed the papers back to Franz with some conversation that Franz understood but not I. After searching our car we were finally allowed to proceed. After we were clear of the border and its guards, Franz said, "They think you are a very important person since you have official papers from Budapest authorizing this hunt."

With the border behind us, we stopped at the next village to get something to eat. The café was on the upper floor of an old wooden building and when we climbed the stairs and entered the place we found ourselves in a large, rather barren, open room furnished with rough tables and benches. Many of the tables were occupied and we selected one against a back wall. The place was noisy with conversation but as soon as I said something in English to Franz, all eyes turned in our direction and the place grew quiet, remaining that way until we had finished our meal and left. It was an uneasy feeling and I was glad when we departed that unfriendly atmosphere.

After a long day of driving and many wrong turns, we arrived at Marcali-

Boronko in southern Hungary. The whole journey had been through stark, snowy plains land with scattered leafless trees and gray buildings. All the buildings were gray, both large and small, making the country seem even more depressing.

Arriving in the village, we proceeded to the house of one Jozsef Németh who was the woods manager in that area and after instructing us as to the time and place of the morrow's hunt and where we would meet our guide, he took us to the house of our hosts, another Jozsef and his wife Marika. There we had dinner and shortly afterward went to our beds. It had been a long day and we were all very tired.

We were awakened the following morning by Marika who served us a little cup of strong Hungarian coffee. Stepping outside in the darkness we were jolted awake by the bitter cold air that penetrated our clothing as if we were wearing gauze. Driving to Boronko, we met our guide who was waiting outside the door of his little house. He was a young man and looked natty in his tight hunting breeches, tall fur hat, green hunting coat and tall black boots. Franz, with some knowledge of the language, was able to converse with him and in short order we were back in Franz's car and heading for the forest. Arriving there just before daybreak, we walked down an old grassy road through the trees while roe deer snorted and barked all around us.

I immediately saw that hunting in Hungary was definitely different than hunting in America. First off, I was not allowed to carry the rifle. If a stag or wild boar were spotted, the guide would determine if it met the specifications of my permit, and if it did only then would I be handed the gun. By then the animal would probably be gone, I reckoned. After walking quite some distance we arrived just at daybreak at an old clear-cut in the forest. In the middle of this clear-cut stood a high hunting stand, about thirty feet tall, supported by six-inch diameter poles. The platform at its top was open at the sides except for a railing of poles and was protected from the weather by a roof.

The dawn broke cloudy and raw. The ground was frozen and so were we as we made our way up the flimsy stick ladder to the platform.

Reaching the top, I surveyed my surroundings that were dim in the hazy first light of dawn. The clear-cut had grown up to the point that it provided good feed and a little cover for wildlife. I had hardly time to scan the area when a red deer stag materialized out of the haze and walked along the slope in front of us, completely unaware of our presence.

Red Deer is the common name applied to a deer (Cerfus elaphus) found in temperate regions of Europe and Asia. It is a handsome animal, resembling an elk, and stands four feet tall at the shoulders. It has a coat of dark red-brown, which becomes grayish in winter. The antlers are long and beautifully branched, a "royal stag" having twelve, if not more, branches.

My permit allowed me to shoot a female red deer, a spike, a four point or a six point stag. There was much whispered conversation between Franz and Frank (our guide) as they studied the animal through their binoculars. Meanwhile, the stag was getting farther away and closer to the timber while I stood, without a weapon, watching it fade away. Once it had disappeared, Franz stated that it was a two-point and not legal for me to shoot.

After the stag was gone we climbed down from our lookout and hunted the perimeter of the woods, next to the fields, looking for wild boar. Although sign was plentiful, we saw no boar. We did see three roe deer that I was not permitted to shoot. I was just getting excited about the hunt when, at 7:45 a.m., the guide said the hunt was over for the morning! I could not believe it! Quitting after only an hour and fifteen minutes and in the prime time of the morning! Reluctantly, I followed them back down the old grassy road to our car and we returned to the village. Our guide set a time for us to meet him for an evening hunt. This definitely was not my idea of a good hunt.

Marika had breakfast ready for us and we enjoyed some liver sausage, salami, cheese, bread, butter and tea. Then Franz and I went to the post office to file a report of our whereabouts, which we were required to do at set intervals, according to their communist law. Returning to Jozsef and Marika's house at noon we were treated to lunch; fried chicken, deep-fried chicken liver and hearts, chicken dumpling soup complete with chicken feet and lower legs. Also Hungarian Kraut, raisin and cherry pastry, red wine and tea, a delicious meal although I left the chicken feet at the bottom of my bowl. Franz said that the government had provided this food to Jozsef and Marika to impress us that this was normal fare for a communist family in Marcali.

On our way to pick up our guide late that afternoon we wound our way through an area of construction in the village. Apparently the town's sewer lines were being replaced and an army of workers was busily doing the job with picks and shovels. Not a piece of power machinery was to be seen; everything was done by hand and with wheelbarrows. A very labor-intensive project but it created work for the town's people. Horses and wagons and bicycles were more common than autos.

The evening hunt was to be for boar but it was no more productive than the morning's hunt. We saw three roe deer but no other game although we hunted for an hour after dark by the light of a rising moon.

After dinner we toured Jozsef's wine cellar, which was filled with barrels of wine, one particular white wine that had won him a gold medal. We sampled some and it was delicious. At 10 o'clock we were in bed with plans to be up at 4:15 a.m.

The outside world was freezing cold, frosty and moonlit when we picked up our guide at 5 a.m. As we headed for the woods we passed many workers headed for the fields in the darkness on their bicycles. On this morning we walked through the frozen fields, looking for wild boar by the light of the moon. No artificial light was permitted and I would have to rely on the rifle's scope sight to see my pig. This is crazy, I thought. What if I wound one in the dark? A wounded boar would be more vicious than a bear and I already knew from experience what a wounded bear could do! We hunted until daylight and saw no pigs although we did scare up a jillion mallards. After that we drove to the woods to look for a stag until 8 a.m. Although we saw lots of tracks of red deer, we saw nothing but a fox and two roe deer. By now our guide was getting desperate for if he did not produce a stag or a boar for me he could lose his job. I felt sorry for him although it was for sure that he was no hunter. Nevertheless, I could not set the rules and I had to follow his leading.

On returning to Marika's table that morning, we found a feast waiting for us. It was Thanksgiving Day whether she knew it or not, and she had set a table that did the occasion proud; roast duck, roast duck dumplings, chicken noodle soup and Hungarian fruit rolls.

Around 2 p.m. Franz and I picked up our guide a little earlier than usual, and headed for the woods. We had just arrived at the hunting ground and were still in the car when a fat red deer stag walked across the grassy road and stopped just inside the woods to stare at us. It was a spike, legal for me to shoot, and by this time in my hunt it looked pretty tempting. Franz and Frank passed comments back and forth in Hungarian while the spike stood, broadside, watching us. Finally Franz spoke to me in English and said they hoped to find me a better one and while he was talking the stag walked into the brush and disappeared.

That was a big mistake for we saw nothing more that evening but a pheasant. Just at dusk we climbed up into a huge oak tree that stood by a grassy field and posted there until dark. Down in a wooded draw to our right I could hear two red deer stags clashing horns but our guide refused to let me try to stalk them, possibly thinking I might shoot something that did not fit my permit. We climbed from our tree and left the woods in the dark, chilled to the bone. In the darkness I could hear laborers still working in the fields and marveled at the fortitude of these poor souls.

After dropping our guide at his house, we went to the woods manager's home. We were cold and hungry for the temperature had remained well below freezing all day. The manager's house was fairly large but unpretentious and was sparsely furnished with only the necessities. In a small room to the left of the entry was a rough table with benches on either side. A pot-bellied stove was glowing red hot near the table and when I seated myself on the bench behind the table near the stove, I quickly began to thaw out. Soon my heavy wool hunting pants and insulated underwear made me uncomfortably warm. A big pot of Hungarian goulash had been set on the table along with potatoes and rye bread and we tore into the food with gusto. It was delicious. There was no coffee or tea; in its place was a bottle of Hungarian beer at each person's place. Being thirsty, I drank mine and in short order the heat from the stove combined with the spicy goulash had me feeling a little giddy. Looking at the label on the beer bottle I saw that it was 10.5%! In European countries beer or wine is considered food, part of your meal, and you hurt their feelings if you refuse it.

When we returned to Jozsef and Marika's house we were surprised to hear something scratching at their back door. Marika opened it and in hopped a big European hare. He was a wild one but showed up every day for snacks! Marika called it Musika, which translated means "Jessica".

The following morning we were up at 5 a.m., met Marika at the bottom of the stairs for our morning coffee and then drove off into the frosty darkness to pick up our guide. We spent the morning in a high stand until 7:45 a.m. and saw nothing. By now Frank was so desperate he was trying to find a hind for me to shoot. On our way to our car I saw a roe deer. Thus I ended my hunt without even having my hands on the rifle.

After breakfast at Marika's we packed our gear, and said goodbye to our hosts. Velma had enjoyed her stay at Marika's, visiting with her and her mother, even though she could not speak their language.

Our guide was quite concerned that he had not been able to produce any stags or boar for us and was genuinely fearful of losing his job when we turned in our hunting results report at the Ministry of Wildlife in Budapest. Assuring him that we had enjoyed our hunt and would speak kindly of him at the Ministry, we took our leave. Even though he was a poor guide and hunter, he had tried hard and done his best.

The trip to Budapest was basically due north from Marcali and we arrive there in late afternoon. Sure enough, when we turned in our hunting report the official looked shocked and said, "But you did not kill anything! What happened?" We tried to impress him that it was not the guide's fault but he did not look as if we convinced him.

Budapest is Hungary's capital and largest city and occupies both banks of the Danube River; Buda on the west and Pest on the east. The city is ancient and foreboding at first appearance, with its colorless-gray buildings silhouetted against the leaden winter sky adding to its somberness.

Hungary is a predominantly flat country, partly encircled by the Alps on the west and by ranges of the Carpathian Mountains on the north and on the east. The Danube River, which forms part of the boundary with Czechoslovakia, flows in a southernly direction into Yugoslavia, dividing Hungary into two general regions. A low, rolling plain known as the Great Plain, comprises most of the region east of the Danube. Along the north border of the country is a region of highlands, which extend eastward from the gorge of the Danube at Esztergom and include the Bukk and Matra mountains. It was in this northeastern part of Hungary that my next hunt was to take place.

Since it is a great distance from the sea, it is marked by extremes in summer and winter temperatures. At one time Hungary was covered by vast forests of oak and poplar, but in time these woodlands were nearly depleted. Only about twelve percent of the total area of Hungary is covered presently by forests and one third of this consists primarily of various species of oak. The remainder consists largely of beech and other deciduous trees, as well as a small number of coniferous species. The country abounds in wildlife with the chief animals being rabbits, foxes, roe deer, red deer and boars.

After clearing things at the Ministry of Wildlife, we crossed the Danube and drove to Pecel, an eastern suburb of Budapest and went to the home of Gabor, our guide. Gabor was an instructor at the Yodollo University near Budapest and I was happy to learn that he spoke English fluently. The evening was spent visiting with his family as well as with his parents and in-laws. After a celebration dinner we retired to our beds at 8 p.m. with the admonition to sleep well and fast for we must be up at 1:30 a.m. for the long drive to the hunting area. This area was located about fifty miles from the Russian border and within three miles of the Czech border. We had to be there well before daylight since the hunt would be conducted at night. The wild boars tend to "hole-up" in the forests and thickets in the daytime and venture out at night to forage for food.

It seemed that I had hardly closed my eyes until I was awakened by Gabor's voice at my door. I quickly donned all the warm clothes I could pile on my body and followed him to the bitter cold and darkness outside. Gabor's dad, Andrei, and another friend, Janos, were to accompany us bringing our number to five. As we waited in the cold for Franz to arrive with his vehicle, I noticed something sticking out of Gabor's backpack and assumed it was the legs of a three-legged folding hunting stool that is commonly used in Europe. When Franz arrived and his headlights illuminated us, I saw that what I took to be stool legs were the necks of whiskey bottles!

At 4 a.m. we arrived at the hunting area and it was necessary for all of us to sign a registry at a small office building. Outside, lying half-frozen on the ground, were the carcasses of two red deer hinds that had been killed the previous evening. When I signed the registry the official exclaimed that I was the first American ever to sign the book.

After signing in, we drove up a rutted and frozen dirt road to some fields situated on a hill and surrounded by forests and thickets. It was frigid cold and the bushes were white with frost to the point that I imagined it to be snow. Parking Franz's car, we separated for the hunt; Franz with Gabor, Andrei by himself and I with Janos, each to high lookout platforms situated about one-third mile apart.

Janos and I reached our lookout "tower" at 4:30 a.m. and crunched our way up its snow-frozen ladder to the high platform. Here we stood in the bitter-cold darkness until 6:30 a.m., straining our eyes and ears for the sight or sound of boars. Some patches of snow remained in the thickets and this was where I watched, hoping to see a pig's silhouette against its whiteness. Again I thought, what a crazy way to hunt!

By 6:30 we both were shivering and when we heard a church bell ringing somewhere in a village nearby, Janos muttered, "Morgan" (morning) and motioned that it was time to climb down the ladder and end the hunt. I could not believe it!

Once on the ground Janos headed in the direction of the car but with daylight breaking, I separated from him and made a thirty-minute sneak hunt through the thickets, desperately hoping to scare up a pig. At least I had the feeling that I was actually hunting!

I arrived at the car to find the whole crew waiting for me. None of us had seen any game and the hunt was over!

The sky was leaden and foggy; the moisture freezing on everything and the Russian sun was a cold, white form as it tried to break through the overcast in the east.

Opening the hatchback of the car, my friends produced bottles of cognac, vodka and scotch which they lined up on top of the car. Then out came sausages, great loaves of bread, and a side of raw pork, all of this stuff half-frozen. Holding the loaf of bread under his arm, Janos carved off great slabs of it with his hunting knife while Gabor cut chunks of the raw, half-frozen pork for each of us. When in Rome, do as the Romans do, and I supposed that went for Hungary, too. I attacked the bread and pork and sausages with gusto and actually it didn't taste too bad!

With our frozen feast over with, we headed back towards Budapest but after only an hour my companions bade Franz stop at a bistro for coffee and cognac. It was Saturday and the place was crowded with the local peasantry, all standing and drinking and talking for there were no tables. Many horse-drawn wagons were "parked" in front of the place and I had the feeling that I had stepped back in time.

29. My Japanese friend Norio "Oyaji" Yamamoto and me at his Shiga Kogen mountain hut.

30. In a Hungarian field near the Russian border we feast on half-frozen cured pork and great slabs of bread after a moonlight hunt.

31. Kudu are about the size of a spike elk. I took this one near Kimberly, South Africa.

32. My red hartebeest, taken same day as my kudu.

33. This fine oryx, taken same day as my kudu and hartebeest, made for a perfect day.

34. Lion country on the banks of the Zambezi River in Zimbabwe.

35. Our Alaska Peninsula caribou camp on a rare sunny day.

36. My first caribou hunt on the Alaska tundra came close to being my last.

37. Over the first ridge from camp Franz and I spot a female brown bear with three cubs.

38. Despite our near-fateful first hunt, I returned to the tundra for another hunt.

39. Caribou on the skyline, 250 yards from our camp.

40. L-R: Myself and Ron Taylor with the spoils of our second hunt.

41. Marshall Tito's hunting lodge near Bugojno, Bosnia. L-R: The author, Sinisha and Djuro Huber confer with Ljupko Kuna.

42. Marshall Tito poses with brown bear in front of lodge.

43. We enter a hunting shack to observe brown bears at Bugojno feed lot.

44. *A European brown bear, this one trophy-valued at $20,000, comes out to feed.*

45. *Trails made by European brown bears in Bosnian forest.*

46. L-R: Sead Hadziabdic, myself, Sinisha, Ljupko Kuna (Photo by Dr. Huber) hold meeting to discuss supplemental feeding of Bosnian brown bears to reduce tree damage.

47. While at Bugojno, Bosnia, Ljupko Kuna set up a wild boar hunt for me.

48-49. Strategic pass above Kupres, Bosnia. A tank and air battle erupted here during war with Serbia and much of the forest was burned.

50. Dr. Huber, Sylvan and I climbed to top of Mt. Risjnak to radio-monitor brown bears.

51. My daughter, Sylvan, rests at entrance to brown bear's den on Mt. Risjnak near Slovenia border.

52. I carved this 6-foot tall cuckoo clock for my den after one of my trips to Europe.

53. The walls of my den bring back pleasant memories of past hunts.

54. More memories.

55. 360 pound bear taken in Kitsap County.

56. Velma says I need to be more selective; the walls are getting filled!

57. *In this 1960's photo, Vel poses with bears and cougar.*

58. *I still do a little control hunting for problem bears.
L-R: Kelly Lund, myself, James Lev.*

59. L-R: Sylvan, Velma, Ralph, Jacky; I'm a lucky man!

We eventually arrived in Pecel and after visiting at Janos' house we were informed that this was Andrei's name day and a big celebration dinner was planned at his house. Arriving there, we enjoyed a feast of Hungarian goulash, wiener schnitzels and all the trimmings with seventeen of us seated around the long table.

At 3:30 p.m. we left our hosts, crossed the Danube and headed for Austria. After a short stop at a little Hungarian restaurant where we enjoyed the music of a Gypsy violinist while sipping our coffee, we drove on into the night through falling snow and slick roads, arriving at Franz's farm around 8:30 p.m. The snow continued to fall. Franz's mom was upset when she heard the negative results of our hunt and summed it up in the two English words she knew, "Communist propaganda!"

The weather warmed during the next couple of days, softening the snow and creating a dense fog that restricted vision to seventy-five feet. On one of these days Franz and I went down by the Danube for a short hunt for roe deer, hare or foxes. Franz made a short drive for me while I posted on a slight rise in the forest. Soon I saw movement in the bushes below me, which turned out to be a large Austrian hare. As it bounded through an opening in the thicket I gave him a blast from my shotgun that tumbled him end over end. It was a big fellow, nearly ten pounds, and I wondered if this would be my only trophy of the hunt. Franz soon appeared and said that tracks in the snow indicated two roe deer had broken from the woods and escaped by way of the fields. The next day the hare graced our table along with gravy and bread dumplings.

After another chilly, foggy day, Wednesday dawned much warmer. The snow had softened and melted down to six inches and Franz decided we should have another try for a roe deer. We arrived near the hunting ground just after daylight and immediately got our vehicle stuck in the soft snow and mud of the field. Leaving our car, we trudged across the wide field toward the woods where I would be posted while Franz and his dog, Tasha, made another drive for me. Roe deer and hare tracks were everywhere in the snow and I had high hopes for this hunt. Franz had given me three shells for the rifle so I knew I had better "shoot straight"!

I also knew that Vel and I were scheduled to leave Vienna on a noon flight to Copenhagen and on to Seattle. If we got some game we would have to drag it ¾ mile to our car, which was stuck in the snow, creating another problem. I tried not to think about it as I trudged along behind Franz and Tasha. Nearing the woods, which dropped downhill to a flat along the river, Franz and his dog headed to the left through the field while I turned right and entered the woods. Selecting a good lookout point, I unfolded the little three-legged stool that Franz had provided and seated myself under a large tree. Here I would wait while Franz and Tasha walked down through the woods towards me. With the Danube on my right and the field on the left, I had a good chance of seeing a roe deer.

All was quiet for quite a while except for the calls of screech owls and the quacking of wild ducks. The snow made everything in the woods plainly visible and I kept my eyes busy, watching for any movement. I could hear jets roaring overhead as they left Vienna and was caused to realize that I would be on one of them in just a few hours.

Around 7:45 a cold northeast breeze started to stir and before long I was shivering. Just then I saw a movement in the brush along the Danube's bank. It was a red fox, working his way westward toward Franz's approach. I made ready to shoot but the fox kept himself in the densest thickets, making a shot impossible. In a few seconds he was gone.

After another half hour of shivering, I saw a roe deer come tearing through the woods towards me but angling towards the river. Just before he disappeared behind a slight rise that blocked my view of the riverbank, I found him in my 'scope and fired. In a flash I saw him reappear from behind the rise and run across an opening below me. I shot again and the roe deer piled up in the limbs of a fallen treetop.

Apparently the fox had met Franz coming through the woods and just as the roe deer fell, the fox zipped by me and escaped. Another minute and Franz arrived at the spot where the deer had been when I made the first shot. I saw him stop to inspect the snow at his feet then saw him point toward the river. I then pointed to the left where the dead deer lay, at which Franz called out, "Then you have two of them!"

Sure enough, when I walked down to join Franz I found a buck by the river and a doe in the treetop. This was the first part of December and the bucks have already shed their antlers in Austria. Thus, I thought I was shooting at a doe. The roe deer's mating season is in early summer and their antlers are hardened and polished by the first of May.

They breed in the summer but the fertilized egg is not implanted in the uterus until late fall. This phenomenon is know as delayed implantation and also takes place with bears, martens and some other species.

We had fun dragging the two deer up the steep slope in the slippery snow but soon had them at the edge of the field.

Franz then fetched some oak leaves and after dipping them in the deer's blood, put one in my hat. Another he placed in the deer's mouth and another he laid on their bodies. This is a ritual that is carried out all over Europe, whether the animal is roe deer, red deer, boar—whatever large game—and a sort of prayer is given, thanking the animal for giving his life and asking him to send many more in his place. The leaf in his mouth symbolizes his last food and the bloody leaf in the hat honors the hunter.

Leaving the two deer where they lay, we hurried across the field to our car. Franz's dad had heard my shots and had brought his tractor to retrieve my deer. Seeing our car was stuck, he had freed it for us.

Franz and I made haste to the village while his dad went to get our deer. Things moved rather quickly after that for I had to shower, change clothes, finish packing and have breakfast with the family. We arrived at the airport with no time to spare and followed the sun all the way home, arriving in Seattle around 5 p.m. after 11 ½ hours in the air. My Hungarian safari had not produced the stag or boar that I desired but certainly left me with many fond memories of a wonderful experience. I have always maintained that the success of a hunt is not always measured by a full game bag.

After arriving home I spent the rest of December on my job, drawing bear hunting maps for my employer as well as for the Department of Wildlife, preparing the annual budget for the animal damage control program, attending WFPA and game commission meetings, presenting supplemental feeding slide shows, doing interviews with the media regarding the new feeding program and finalizing arrangements for my upcoming trip to Africa.

I had been fortunate to be drawn for a cow elk permit and it became valid on New Year's Day. The hunting unit took in the area north of my house and sixteen permits had been issued to relieve crop damage in the Wynoochee, Wishkah and East Hoquiam river valleys. My daughter, Sylvan, had come from Oregon to hunt with me for a few days and we awoke on the first morning of our hunt to a blustery wind and heavy rain; an inch of it overnight. We headed for the woods before daylight and searched all day without finding a fresh track. We knew that any tracks we found would be "red hot", otherwise they would be washed out by the rain.

The second morning's weather was not much better; a cold north wind blowing through an icy rain in our faces. We hunted through the Helm Creek area until it started snowing and blowing. After a hunt through the Wedekind Creek country and finding no fresh tracks we called it quits for the day. On the third day Sylvan decided to go fishing and I hit the woods alone. It was a nice day, cloudy and cool with just a little misty rain and fog. Towards evening I drove up the divide between the Wishkah and East Hoquiam rivers. After about five miles I saw fresh tracks where a band of eight or ten elk had crossed the old logging road. They were headed east, down the Wishkah side of the divide and so I parked my pickup, loaded my .270 and started off on their tracks. The ground was bare but the tracks were easy to follow while the elk were still in a band and moving. I tracked them down to a tributary of Wyman Creek and noticed that they had slowed down, the tracks becoming scattered as the elk spread out to feed. It was now 3:30 p.m. and only an hour from dark in the woods so I decided to leave the woods before I spooked them and take up the tracks the next morning.

During the night there were more rain showers but not enough to obliterate the elk tracks. In the early morning hours the temperature had dropped below freezing and the ground was white with frost when Sylvan and I headed for the woods. We picked up the tracks again at 8:45 a.m. and headed down into Wyman Creek. The elk had been feeding and I had to keep my nose to the ground to sort out the tracks. Tracks would lead in every direction as they fed, then converge and move on to another good feed area where they would scatter again.

Over the years my hearing had been deteriorating from too many .357 Magnum and .270 rifle shots and so I depended on Sylvan's ears to alert me to any sounds of the elk. As she followed me, she kept her eyes and ears alert for the elk and I concentrated on sorting out the tracks.

The elk crossed Wyman Creek twice and fed on down the canyon almost to the Wishkah Valley road, then turned north up a ridge, then crossed a tributary of Wyman Creek and headed west again, in the direction of where we had started but on the opposite side of the canyon. At one point Sylvan heard the elk above us in a thicket of salal; they had doubled back to catch our scent and now they really moved.

After finally figuring out their route through the salal I was happy to see that the elk were continuing westward toward the divide. We kept after them and found that they had crossed the divide right by my truck and were headed down toward the East Hoquiam river valley.

The track was easy to follow here for they were running when they crossed the divide. After about a third of a mile we saw two of them moving through the timber above us but before I could get a shot, an alarmed old cow barked like a dog and off they went down the ridge. We hurried along on the track, which was leading us farther and farther down the ridges. The day was slipping by and I mentioned to Sylvan that if we did not catch up with them pretty soon we would have to give it up and try to find our way out of the woods before dark.

About twenty minutes later, at 2:20 p.m. I felt Sylvan tapping me on the back and I looked up to see elk moving among the alders and vine maples across the draw. I could only see two but they were broadside and starting to run. My first shot hit a vine maple limb and the elk really crashed the bushes in their escape. My second shot hit the cow in the shoulder and she fell behind the trunk of an alder. In a second all the elk were gone and our hunt was over. We had been on the track for five hours and thirty-five minutes.

We now were far down in the canyons and with only two hours remaining until dark, I quickly dressed out the elk, wondering to myself, which would be the closest route to a road. Seeing some daylight through the trees on a point off to our right, I walked up there to see if I could determine from that vantage point just where we were. Imagine my surprise (and delight!) when I reached the point and stepped onto a newly made logging road that ended right there! It was so new it had not even been graveled yet. Leaving Sylvan with the elk, I hiked up the road, knowing it must connect with the road on the divide. After a 1 ½ mile hike I reached my truck and drove it down the new road to within three hundred feet of our elk! Hanging a block in a tree, I ran the winch cable from my Blazer down through the woods to the elk and dragged the critter out whole. Once it reached the road I removed its head and lower legs, cut it in half behind the rib cage and then, with Sylvan helping, managed to get the halves loaded. With the hide still on, the front half weighed 235 pounds, the back half 185 pounds. We were very fortunate to get the animal out of the woods that evening for it started raining before we reached home and rained all night and the next day, turning the new road to mud. According to the Game Department's tooth analysis, the elk was 10 ½ years old.

Chapter 12

AFRICA

T**HE TRIP TO AFRICA WAS SCHEDULED FOR JANUARY 24 AND I** had already obtained my visa and airline tickets when word was received that my 85-year-old dad was hospitalized in Maryland. He had congestive heart failure and had also suffered a moderate coronary. This put me between a rock and a hard place and I decided we should visit my dad to determine the gravity of his condition, which would in turn dictate whether I should have to cancel my Africa safari.

That being the case, on January 12 Velma and I flew to Baltimore and traveled to my hometown of Hancock. We found dad returned from the hospital and seated in his favorite chair. I stayed seven days and he seemed to be doing very well except for some breathing problems at night. Velma and I discussed the situation and since Franz was already somewhere in Africa and I had no way to contact him, she volunteered to remain with my folks until I returned from Africa. Since I would be gone three weeks I was a little apprehensive about leaving but nevertheless January 24 found me boarding a plane in Seattle bound for London. Arriving there after a 9-hour flight I boarded a plane that would take me to Nairobi, Kenya, and on to Johannesburg, South Africa.

I was greatly relieved when I was released from the customs inspection area of the Johannesburg airport, passed through the security door and spotted Franz's face among the multitude waiting there. On the drive to Pretoria, South Africa's capitol, I was impressed with the lush green landscape. Being in the southern hemisphere, it was summer in January and extremely hot.

Pretoria is located in a low valley surrounded by hills and is a growing city. I could see lots of new high-rise construction in progress with huge cranes silhouetted on the skyline. We each obtained a room, with breakfast, for $11.00 in one of the hotels. Some of my luggage had been off-loaded in Nairobi and I had a two-day wait before it arrived. This time was spent visiting friends of Franz and touring the countryside.

One of Franz's friends was Johnny Wild, a Johannesburg policeman, and he offered to take us on a tour of Sowetto.

Sowetto is a black township about ten miles from downtown Johannesburg and at that time was home to 1.4 million blacks and coloureds. No whites were allowed. On an average weekend about twenty-seven murders occurred there. The populace was made up of many different tribes and languages, the main tongue being Zulu. About 250,000 of them commuted each day to Johannesburg by train, a two-hour trip one way, to work. They were not allowed to live in Johannesburg and had to be back in Sowetto and in their houses by 11 p.m. curfew. Sowetto is a miserable, filthy slum of one-story shacks and many riots occurred there.

We were safe, supposedly, while accompanied by our policeman friend and he took us on a five-hour tour of the place. We visited in three homes there, as well as the school and the police station and took photos. Huge piles of garbage were everywhere and the playground equipment consisted of old automobile tires. The shacks were piece-meal and constructed of cardboard, pieces of tin, and any other scrap materials that they could find. People from India were classified as "coloureds" and relegated to live in Sowetto. I was relieved when we left the place.

The next day we drove northeast toward the Zimbabwe (formerly Rhodesia) border, encountering a short-lived but refreshing rain on the way. Lots of wild game was in evidence along out route; blesbok, mongoose, monkeys and ostrich included. Around 8:30 that evening we arrived at Alldays, about twenty miles from the Zimbabwe border, at Bobbie Janson's "ranch", where I would have my first hunt.

The area was terribly dry, very little rain having fallen in the past seven years. The terrain was basically flat with a cover of thorny trees, prickly bushes and a low, ground-hugging type of cactus much worse than our western prickly pear. As I soon discovered, everything there seemed to stick, prick or bite. Janson's cattle shared the wide-open veldt with all sorts of wild game, including eland, blesbok, warthogs, jackal, impala, duiker, steenbok, oryx and others that I could not identify.

After meeting Bobbie and his family, we were treated to a dinner of sweet potatoes, a green bean-mashed potato mix, impala meatballs, eland roast, hominy, gravy, rolls and coffee. Around 9:45 I was shown to my quarters—a circular hut with a roof of deep thatch, containing a cot, small table and two chairs, shower stall and toilet. Six open windows around the circular walls offered some ventilation and a little relief from the heat. Franz warned me not to wander outside barefoot in the darkness, or for that matter inside, lest I step on a snake or a scorpion. He also alerted me to the fact that there were large black spiders that love to hide under the toilet seat and bite your backside, or worse, creating extreme pain and a festering sore. Shoes were to be kept on a chair at night and shook out each morning to eject any spiders or scorpions that might be hiding in them. After he left I spotted a spider moving near my bed but he escaped my stomp and crawled into a crevice.

Making ready, I crawled into my bed and lay there looking up at the thatched roof above me, wondering what sort of nasty creatures might fall out of it and onto me during the night. Fatigue conquered my fears and with a cool breeze wafting through the six open windows, I soon dozed off.

I was awakened at 6 a.m. when hot coffee and some sort of dry-cereal bar were delivered to my hut. Crawling from my nest I became aware that mosquitoes had been feasting on my legs during the night and I was glad that I had been taking medication to prevent malaria.

Shortly afterward we headed out for a hunt, accompanied by Bobbie's son and a black tracker. I did not really know what animals I wanted to hunt and decided to make up my mind when I saw something I liked. I knew the names of many of the animals but had no idea what they looked like. Franz had brought his 7mm Sauer (which is comparable to a .280) for me to use. It was a good gun and I knew that it shot true, but he had brought only fifteen shells for it. A couple of these were used to make sure the 'scope had not been bumped in transit and the remaining shells would determine the amount of game I would take.

Making our way through the thorny trees and bushes, we began to spot game; first, a small antelope-type animal of some sort, then a warthog with piglets, a jackal, a blesbok and about six eland. These all departed in a cloud of dust, offering no chance for a shot. A little later we jumped a band of about twenty gemsbok (oryx). Oryx are large animals about the size of spike elk, with long, thick black horns that resemble a unicorn when you only see one horn. Next we saw a couple impala does that leaped across an opening like they were flying.

The Janson's had no love for the jackals and encouraged me to shoot any I saw. I finally got a running shot at one and killed it but ruining the skin for mounting. They look much the same as our western coyotes, only smaller.

The morning was warming fast when we jumped a warthog from its hole beneath a termite mound. Warthogs root out a hole at the base of termite mounds and use them as a den of sorts where they can face their enemies without exposing their hind parts. These mounds are plentiful and sometimes reach the height of eight feet. These critters run like a blue streak, tail upright, and are a challenge to hit. Finding it in my scope, I fired and bowled it over. It had fair tusks but after seeing much bigger ones later in the hunt I wished I had waited. Leaving the warthog where it lay, we returned to camp for a breakfast of bacon, eggs and eland roast. Then, taking the "lorry", we returned to the bush to retrieve the hog.

The sun was high and hot when we reached the warthog and I was not surprised to see a big buzzard sitting on the carcass. Loading our prize we again returned to camp where the black tracker skinned and caped the animal for mounting. A taxidermist, Dirk Uijs, had a shop in the nearby village of Alldays and with the heat so oppressive we took the cape to him immediately before it spoiled.

By now it was scorching hot but being anxious to hunt I persuaded my companions to leave the shade and head back into the bush. We made a long, hot hike that showed us four warthog sows with piglets, a steenbok and a herd of seventeen or eighteen blesbok. We followed the band of blesbok around through the brush and I finally got a shot at a nice one, hitting it through the ribs and knocking him flat. It was a beautiful animal with 14 ½ inch horns. The African name blesbok actually means blaze buck, so called because of the white blaze on its face. The blesbok is a beautiful animal, dark reddish-brown with white lower legs and belly. The blaze on its face extends from forehead to nose and its horns resemble those of our antelope except they are not branched. Their body size is comparable to a deer.

It was so hot by now that I could not take any more of it so we quit, hauled the buck to camp, skinned and caped it and made another trip to the taxidermist. That evening we sat around an open outdoor fire and gnawed on some of my warthog's steaks that had been barbecued on the coals of our fire. The meat was dry and tough as shoe leather and I soon decided that we should have left it to the buzzard!

I put in a hot sticky night in my little thatch-roofed hut, sleeping naked with no covers and enjoying many mosquito bites. Finally, at 5:30 a.m., I got up, took a cold shower, shaved and made ready for the day, which promised to be another scorcher. Accompanied by the black tracker, Johannes, I headed for the bush at 7 a.m. The morning was clear and hot already and I hoped to find an impala buck, a springbok, a duiker or a steenbok before the heat got unbearable. We saw lots of eland, ostrich and game other than what I wanted. I thought the eland were ugly, looking too much like a big domestic cow, but wish now that I had opted to take one. I spotted a duiker laying in the shade of a tree trunk but with only his head as a target I did not shoot, knowing I would ruin the cape. We also jumped some springbok but could not get a shot at them. The ground was exceedingly dry with patches of dry grass in the more open spaces. There were some taller trees and lots of smaller woody bushes to block the view.

After breakfast I returned to the bush, this time accompanied by Bobbie's son and the black tracker. Hunting the south side of the area we saw lots of impala does but no bucks. Heading to the north end of the area, which was brushier, I kept my eyes open for an impala. Suddenly my heart jumped when I spotted not one but three impala bucks standing behind a tall thorn bush. They saw me at the same instant and bolted, creating a cloud of dust. I had only an instant to shoot but I managed to swing my rifle with them, find one in my scope and get off one quick shot. The dust cloud cleared and they were gone. Johannes, the tracker, was on their spoor in an instant but no blood could be found in the dust. Following their tracks in the hard, dry soil for another hundred yards, we looked ahead and saw the buck lying on the ground. It was a beautiful trophy with 23-inch horns. Janson advised me that anything over 22 inches makes the African record book.

Returning to camp, I lay in the shade while Johannes skinned and caped the impala. The temperature was now 105 degrees. A little later Dirk Uijs, the taxidermist, arrived to pick up the cape. He said he would mount the blesbok, warthog and impala for $100 each and ship them to me by water for another $100. This sounded good to me and relieved me of the job of transporting the capes and mounting them. I had seen his work and it was very good so I paid him the $400 and to this date, 2003, seventeen years later, I have seen no more of my trophies or my money. At least I have photos. Let the buyer beware!

The next morning I settled up with Janson for my hunt; $495 for two days of hunting, an impala, a blesbok, warthog, jackal, caping the trophies, three delicious dinners, two breakfasts and a packed lunch to take with us on our journey. I thought it was very reasonable.

We then headed north to Zimbabwe, formerly Rhodesia, and were stopped at the border town of Beithridge for a customs inspection. This procedure took over an hour, with many forms to be filled out. I was amused when one of the black customs agents looked at "Seattle" written on my passport and asked, "Where is this place?"

Entering southern Zimbabwe we found ourselves in an area of forested rolling hills, lush and green, with many open grassy spaces among the trees. Continuing northward, we located the old Zimbabwe ruins; an impressive and very ancient fortress and walled village made entirely by stacking flat stones without mortar. This type of construction was developed by the local Bantu tribes during the 14th and 15th centuries.

We then drove south and west on a narrow dirt road, miles and miles upward into a thick green jungle that spread out as far as the eye could see, with rocky outcroppings at the higher levels. The road was traveled by many blacks, all carrying a load on their head, but once we entered the thickly wooded hills we saw no one. Coming to a locked gate at the boundary of a National Park that Franz had wished to see, we were forced to retreat the way we had come.

Reaching the paved road we continued driving north until well after dark when we reached a small mining town with one old hotel. We had quite a hassle getting a room for they would not accept our traveler's checks. Customs rules forbade us from bringing South African rands into Zimbabwe, but luckily for us we had smuggled some in with us and finally found a small café owner who changed our rands into Zimbabwe money.

Returning to the hotel, we then procured two small rooms attached to the backside of the old building for $15 each. The rooms had no bath or toilet, only a single cot and chair.

It was Sunday night and all the blacks were drinking. We had not seen a single white person in town and it gave us a rather uncomfortable feeling. Just as I was preparing for bed a torrential rain came spattering down, cooling the air a bit. I crawled into my nest, leaving the window wide open, first making sure that my pants were on the chair and out of reach of the window. Sometimes they use a long stick with a hook on the end to reach in the window and snag your pants, wallet and all.

The rain continued all night, cooling and freshening the air, and I slept well. Shortly after 4:30 a.m., tea was delivered to my door by a black employee. We left in the rain before dawn and 5 a.m. daylight found us on our way to Victoria Falls.

As we traveled, the sky cleared and it grew very hot. Entering the city of Bulawayo, our accelerator cable broke, luckily right in front of a garage. There, three mechanics spent three hours repairing it and the bill, including part, was only $14.00 U.S. currency!

We had plans to visit a farmer-veterinarian friend of Franz that lived between Bulawayo and Victoria Falls but when we reached the place we learned that Franz's friend, his wife and a black worker had been murdered about a month earlier by black terrorists.

Arriving at Victoria Falls I could hear the roar of the cataract long before I could see it. A foggy mist hung in the sky over the falls, rainbows and reflections of rainbows arching in the midst of it. The falls were spectacular, three times larger than Niagara and the second largest falls in the world at ½ mile wide and 900 feet high. These falls are on the Zambezi River where it forms a boundary between

Zimbabwe and Zambia. The Zambezi is the third largest river in Africa. The falls have formed a deep gorge and the river flows parallel to and at the base of the falls until it reaches the Zambia side, where the river makes an abrupt turn and flows out of the gorge. A deep pool is formed at this turn and here the crocodiles love to wait and devour any hapless fish that come over the falls.

That evening we searched for a room that would suit our budget, steering clear of the posh tourist hotels in town. We finally located an old cabin in the jungle just upstream from the falls that we obtained for $16 for the two of us. It was a very hot, poorly ventilated shack with two beds and a cold-water-only bathtub. After brushing a 2 ½ inch long cockroach from my bed and observing lots of long-legged black biting spiders in the corners, I took a cold bath in the old tub, opened my window wide and collapsed in my bed. It was too hot to sleep but with the falls roaring below our hut I somehow dozed off, oblivious to spiders, roaches, scorpions and mosquitoes.

Shortly after dawn we were on our way up the Zambezi River, an hour's drive through jungle-y country rife with wildlife, to visit a professional hunter friend of Franz. This fellow was the head honcho of Westwood Wildlife Safaris and their hunts were conducted on a concession that consisted of 300 square kilometers in the famous Matetsi safari area. This area is known to be one of the finest hunting areas left in southern Africa. The concession has a fourteen-kilometer river frontage on the Zambezi and adjoins the Zambezi National Park on a twenty-five kilometer border. The area is completely wild and unfenced.

En route, we saw lots of trees freshly broken or pushed over by elephants, as well as fresh tracks and droppings. Bands of baboons and all sorts of animals bounded across the narrow road ahead of us. After having coffee with the safari guide, he took us with him in his lorry, along with a crew of blacks, to a site farther upriver where he was hacking a base camp out of the bush along the river. It was a beautiful spot, flat and level, heavily forested and right on the riverbank. We climbed out of the lorry and while the workers set to their tasks we stood admiring the beauty of the place. Near the riverbank the area was open and lush with short grasses. Huge three-foot diameter trees, gnarly and grotesque, were scattered through the park-like setting, with smaller eight-inch diameter trees growing from their base and twining around them like huge snakes.

The many reddish-colored termite mounds, some of them eight to ten feet tall, were worn smooth from elephants rubbing their sides against them.

The river at this point was very wide and ranged from six to nine feet deep, with many big rocks visible above the surface. Some small islets dotted the river and these were densely wooded. Franz and I were standing at the river's edge, observing a group of hippos far out in mid-stream which we at first thought were huge rocks, and also watching natives coming to the river for water from a small village on the Zambian shore, when our safari-hunter friend yelled at us.

"Get back away from the water! You cannot see them but there are crocodiles laying in wait under those lily pads, with only their eyeballs exposed. They will leap out of there in a flash, grab you and pull you under the water. They'll hold you there until you stop struggling and then either eat you or tuck you under a root to soften up!"

He did not have to warn us twice. We then wandered farther back from the river, following some cape buffalo tracks and looking for lion tracks. We had just entered an area of tall, reedy grass that grew nearly five feet high when we hear his voice again.

"Stay out of the tall grass and close to the truck or you will be lion bait!" One of his clients had been mauled there by a lion just three weeks previous, and it had torn all the muscles from one arm. Also, he said, two years ago one of his black trackers had been killed at this spot by a cape buffalo that had been wounded by a lion.

This would have been an excellent place to hunt if you could afford it but his hunts were set up on a ten-day minimum basis with the number and species of animal you could take dependent upon the length of your hunt; ten, fifteen or twenty-one days. He offered hunts that ranged $5,750 for ten days to $12,000 for twenty-one days. Trophy fees were added for each animal, these varying from $3000 for an elephant, $1,500 for lion, $700 for buffalo and the smaller antelope-type accordingly. Theoretically, a hunt with him for the same species and amount of game that I took on my entire hunt would have cost $7,180 while mine amounted to $1,800.

We left Victoria Falls around 2 p.m. and roared off toward Bulawayo, 430 kilometers away. We arrived there after dark, in the rain and with our fuel gauge registering empty for many miles, a very "hairy" experience in that location.

After arriving back in South Africa, we headed west from Pretoria through a very flat veldt-country; flat as far as the eye could see, and mostly farm land with crops of corn, sunflowers, and grass. Even here wild game was in evidence, ostrich and eland among them. We arrived in Kimberley late that evening where we located Albrecht Meylahn, manager of the huge Pniel Estates ranch at Barkly West. Albrecht was a stocky, sun-browned, friendly fellow, about my age and extremely likeable. Franz had arranged for me to hunt with Albrecht and I was really looking forward to it. After treating us to a steak dinner at a Greek restaurant operated by a friend of his, Albrecht drove us twelve miles out in the bush to the ranch house.

Here we learned that the Pniel property was once owned by Cecil Rhodes, who gave it to Queen Victoria. She, in turn, gave it to Kaiser Wilhelm, who then gave it to the Berlin Mission Church. The Church still owned the property at the time of my hunt but it has since been designated as a game reserve. The Pniel Estate consisted of 62,500 acres, nearly 98 square miles.

At the ranch house, where Albrecht lived alone, he showed us his mounted game trophies, which only tended to get me really fired up. I was particularly impressed with the Kudu and decided this would be the focus of my hunt. Albrecht also showed us a saucer full of rough diamonds that he had picked up from the ground during his time there as manager. He said that at one time the Estate had many blacks living there whose job was to scour the surface of the ground on the ranch and pick up diamonds. (Kimberley has one of the largest diamond mines in the world.)

The next morning I was up at 5 a.m., still tired after a hot, sticky night. After coffee at the ranch house with Albrecht, we set up a target and fired off a couple (of my precious few) shells at a target. Satisfied, we climbed in his lorry along with Ezok (Isaac), the black tracker, and headed off into the bush. In the daylight I could see that the area was very flat with some low, clumpy hills, lots of waist high tall grass, scattered acacia trees and occasional tangles of thorny bushes. Some sections of the ranch were covered to the horizon with nothing but low, scrubby bushes and rocks. Since I was interested in Kudu, Albrecht led me into an area of acacia trees and tall grass.

Our tracker, Ezok, had a limited vocabulary of English words and these consisted of the names of the animals and "Yah, boss", but what he lacked in words he made up for in eyesight. We had not gone far when Ezok pointed and exclaimed, "Kudu!"

Looking in the direction he was pointing I saw a cloud of dust in the distance marking the Kudu's departure route. We moved in that direction but they spooked again before we could get near.

Albrecht told Ezok to stay put while he and I tried to stalk the Kudu. After a long, circuitous sneak through the tall grass we found ourselves in a low depression that allowed us to crawl close to where we thought the Kudu had gone. Slowly raising my head above the grass, I spotted the animals a hundred yards away, four of them, and one a nice bull. They saw my movement and started to run but not before I found the bull's ribcage in my scope and squeezed the trigger. The Kudu dropped in his tracks, instantly dead, and Albrecht slapped me on the back in his exuberance.

It was now 7:30 a.m., already growing hot, and leaving me with the Kudu, Albrecht went to fetch the lorry. Returning with Ezok, we loaded the bull and headed for camp. There the animal was dressed, skinned and caped, the carcass weighing in at 250 pounds. After an early lunch we headed back to the bush. I now was intent on finding an oryx (gemsbok). We hunted an area with fewer trees and better visibility and at one point I spotted something on the horizon that looked like telephone poles. I could not imagine what phone poles would be doing away out in the middle of nowhere and a quick look through my binoculars showed them to be the necks of two giraffes! Their bodies were just behind the crest of the hill and only their long necks were visible.

Just then, off to my right about four hundred yards, I saw a lone oryx. We started toward it while it stood watching us for we had no way to conceal our approach. Catching a movement on a low hill to our left, I saw something round and black that looked like a bear but obviously could not be. It started to run and through my 'scope I saw that it was a big, black ostrich. The oryx saw the running ostrich, became alarmed and disappeared behind the hill.

We then moved off to our right, hoping to top the hill farther up and intercept him but before we had gone a quarter mile I looked toward the hilltop, about two hundred yards away, and saw a small group of red hartebeest. They were standing, observing us and offering a broadside shot but I could not see any bulls. One of the animals had its head and shoulders behind a bush and when it stepped forward I saw that it was a fine bull. One shot to the ribs and he fell, while his harem clattered over the hilltop in a dust cloud. It was an old bull, around fourteen years old and weighed 150 pounds after being dressed out and skinned. Albrecht said its horns made it well into the African record book.

We remained in camp through the heat of the day, returning to the bush around 4 p.m. It was still scorching hot, so hot that I could not touch my rifle barrel. Even in the heat we saw lots of game moving about. I wanted to get a springbok and when I saw two of them run up on a rocky outcropping and stop, I thought I had them in the bag. I took a good aim at the bigger one, squeezed the trigger and saw the bullet hit on a rock above him! I could not believe this and was equally surprised when they ran farther up the hill and stopped again! Another shot and again the rock dust flew above them. That time they vamoosed for good.

I could not explain these misses but Albrecht said that when the gun barrel and ammo are so extremely hot the powder burns hotter, causing the bullets to go high. I could not say whether this was the case or not but at least it gave me an alibi!

The day was growing late when we scared up a herd of oryx, about twenty or twenty-five of them. They were two hundred yards away and running like mad, creating a big dust cloud. I picked out a nice bull at the rear of the group, led him a little and fired. At my shot, the bull humped up, indicating that he had been hit, but he continued to run. In an instant he was swallowed up in the huge dust cloud and I lost sight of him.

The herd had continued on around the hill, which was evident by the dust cloud and in an instant were gone. Albrecht ran in the direction that they had gone, looking for blood. I followed Ezok who, with his nose almost on the ground, went directly up the hill instead of following Albrecht. How he could see tracks in that hard rocky ground I'll never know, but after one hundred fifty yards he pointed ahead and I saw a long, black unicorn-like horn sticking up from the grass and bushes. Drawing near I saw that I had not "led" the animal far enough and my bullet had struck a little far back, at an angle, but had gone through its liver. It was not quite dead and Albrecht had already warned me how deadly they can be with those long, pointed horns. Not wanting to ruin the cape, I put another bullet through his rib cage that finished him off. This time I slapped Ezok on the back and thanked him for locating the oryx for me. He did not understand the words but my actions were easy to interpret.

Albrecht returned and having heard my second shot, checked to determine if this was the same oryx I had originally shot at. Finding two bullet holes satisfied him and he hiked off over the hills to get the lorry.

The oryx had fallen in a terribly rocky place and we had to roll pumpkin-sized rocks out of the way before we could get the lorry to him. As we drove through the bush to camp the sun had dropped below the horizon and the sky was reddened by a beautiful African sunset, made all the more colorful by the smokes from many native cooking fires and dust. It had been a full and exciting day.

It was well after dark before the skinning and caping were completed and after that we sat around an open fire and chatted while the black women prepared our dinner. This consisted of grits, kudu liver (from the mornings kill), tomato and onion salad and a potato and onion cooked dish. After our meal we sat around the fire until 11 p.m. before calling it a day. The day's temperature had reached 110 degrees!

The following morning found me ready for another hunt and with only four shells left for the Sauer. This time we headed into an area of tall grass and scattered acacia trees in search of a springbok. We had not gone far before we jumped a duiker that was feeding among the small bushes. It ran like a rabbit through the tall grass and then stopped about sixty yards from us, partially hidden by the thick cover. Aiming at his rib cage, I got off a quick shot and the little animal disappeared. Franz was not certain whether I had hit it or not and asked where I had aimed. Walking over to where we had last seen the duiker, we found it lying very dead in the grass. The bullet had struck it through the rib section for which I was glad because a neck or headshot on such a small animal would have ruined the cape. Duikers are dainty little animals, weighing not much over twenty-five pounds.

After securing the animal we continued on and soon saw an animal smaller than the duiker go racing through the grass. I heard Albrecht say, "Steenbok!" and instinctively raised my rifle. By chance the steenbok stopped in the only opening of any size and I was able to get off a shot that dropped it in its tracks. Making my way through the tall grass to where it lay I was amazed at how small it was; it was not much bigger than a large jack rabbit and this was a mature buck! Luckily this little fellow had also been hit through the ribs, leaving the cape in excellent condition. I told Franz that if I had realized how small the animal was I probably would have missed it!

It was now 8:45 a.m. and growing hotter by the minute. Returning to camp, we skinned the animals, had some lunch and then spent the balance of the day in Kimberley. The temperature soared to 115º that day and was almost unbearable. Around 5 p.m. we returned to the bush for I was intent on trying for a springbok.

After a while Albrecht spotted a couple springboks that were moving through the bushes on a small hill nearly four hundred yards ahead of us. Motioning for me to keep down, we crawled along on our hand and knees, trying to get closer for a shot. After we had gone but a short distance I saw a shiny, glassy pebble on the ground by my hand and though, "That looks like a diamond!" but observing Albrecht crawling along and getting farther ahead of me, I passed it by and closed the gap between us. Just then Albrecht stopped, picked up a small pebble and examined it before dropping it and exclaiming, "I thought I had found a diamond…" To this day I wonder if what I had passed up was a diamond!

We never got close to those springbok so we headed out into a vast, flat expanse with no trees, only rocks and scattered clumps of grass as far as the eye could see. Far out on the flat land we could see large bands of springbok but the sad thing was they could see us, too! They reminded me of bands of Wyoming antelope and they were just as wild, bounding across the landscape like they had springs in their hooves. I now had only two shells left for the Sauer and I did not dare waste them on a "flying" shot.

Instructing me to lie prone on the ground, Albrecht went after the lorry and then tried to "herd" the springbok bands toward me, hoping they would pass near enough for me to get a shot. There were hundreds of springbok running about in many different herds but none would come within ½ mile of me. We left the hunt at dusk and returned to the ranch where we spent another evening around an open fire, barbecuing sausages and roasting ears of corn. Around 11 p.m., the air cooled a little and I headed for my nest. This was to be my last night at the ranch but I intended to have one more try for a springbok in the morning.

Dawn broke clear and bright with promise of another scorching hot day. Albrecht, Franz and I climbed in the lorry shortly after daybreak and drove to a part of the ranch that we had not yet been. We immediately began seeing springbok, a herd of them, running as usual. We followed then quite a distance in the lorry, then got out and stalked them for a mile but they always kept just out of range. At one point in our stalk I saw five zebras in a little side draw about two hundred yards from us. Drawing a bead on one, I was about to pull the trigger when I thought of my horse-loving daughters who would probably disown me if I brought a zebra home. I lowered my rifle and the striped beauties trotted off. Finally, while stalking, we spotted two lone springbok rams standing on a steep, rocky hillside about three hundred fifty yards away. Putting the crosshairs on top of the back of one that stood broadside, I shot and saw the bullet strike the rocks just under its belly, a clear miss. Thus ended my hunt, with one shell to spare.

The De Beers diamond people owned the land adjoining the Pniel Estate acreage and as a consequence the manager of De Beers diamond mine near Kimberley was a friend of Albrecht's. Since we were guests of the Pniel Estate, Albrecht was able to obtain a special permit that would allow Franz and I to tour the mine and factory. As a rule, tourists were not allowed in the mine and so we felt this was a rare opportunity for us.

Arriving at the mine in the 115º afternoon heat, we were ushered into a small room and briefed on what we could and would see, what the rules were, and asked to sign an agreement stating that they would not be responsible for possible injury or death. After giving us special shoes to wear, as well as white hard hats and long white jackets that made us look like USDA meat inspectors, we were escorted out to the elevator cage that would lower us into the mine.

The cage was suspended by a huge cable that wound through a series of pulley blocks overhead. The whole system, including the cage, looked antiquated to me but nevertheless I followed Franz, our guide and some black workers into the contraption. The cage was enclosed on three sides while the front was an open-mesh wire gate and once that was closed, we started our descent, straight down into the mine. Friendly daylight soon disappeared and as we dropped into the dark depths we would occasionally pass a flash of light that indicated a side tunnel of the mine.

We passed quite a few of these side tunnels before our cage stopped abruptly and bounced up and down several times from the stretch in the long cable before remaining still. We were now one-half mile below the earth's surface and when I stepped from the cage into the dimly lit and narrow tunnel I thought that I had died and gone to the wrong place. The heat was heavy and unbelievably oppressive, even exceeding that above ground and I wondered how anyone could survive working in such conditions.

The main tunnel was about seven feet high and not much wider while side passages about four feet high branched off from it at intervals. Ore cars sat on a narrow gauge set of rails that continued the full length of the main tunnel. An electric wire ran along the rock ceiling of the tunnel and suspended from it and quite a distance apart were bare light bulbs that emitted a dim, orange light. There was no bracing for either the walls or ceiling. At one location along the stone wall was a water spigot with a communal tin drinking cup chained to it.

The place was a cacophony of noises; drills running, explosions, draglines dredging ore (blue soil) from the side passages and ore being loaded. It gave me an uneasy feeling to realize that a half-mile of earth and stone hung over my head while all this shaking and blasting were going on around me.

The work force was made up entirely by blacks and they were good at what they did. They were seemingly oblivious to the terrible heat of the mine. As the blue rock that contained diamonds was blasted loose, workers dredged it from the low ceilinged side shafts to the main tunnel where it was loaded onto the ore cars and sent to the surface. At places the walls of side tunnels sparkled like Christmas glitter and I wondered if these were tiny diamonds. After each shift the workers were searched and subjected to x-rays to determine if they were trying to smuggle diamonds out of the mine by swallowing them.

It was quite an interesting and fascinating experience but I was glad when the old cage brought us safely topside and into the blazing sunlight. I remember my great thirst when I left the cage for I had become dehydrated during our netherregion tour and had passed up the for-sure germ laden communal tin cup.

A "pebble" picked up by a child on the banks of the Orange River in South Africa in 1866 and identified as a 21-karat diamond (this made me wonder again about the "pebble" I passed up on my hunt at Pniel!) was the first step in opening the diamond fields of the region, which had become the greatest in the world. Around 1871 "dry diggings" were discovered in the district near present day Kimberley. As the miners dug deeper in the clay soil they found below it a hard, bluish rock, which also proved to be productive. This "blue ground", scientifically identified as Kimberlite, was the tops of the funnel-shaped "pipes" which continued downward for an undetermined distance. These "pipes" are believed to be of volcanic origin.

The original mine workings at Kimberley was an open pit and was worked to a depth of more than 3600 feet before it was closed in 1914. The area of this hole at the surface is 42 ½ acres. This huge pit produced 14,504,566 karats of diamonds, or

5,988 pounds, before the mine was abandoned and "shaft" type mining was initiated. We viewed this huge hole in the ground, the bottom of which is now filled with water to a depth of 755 feet. It was probably the largest man-made hole on earth at the time it was dug.

From there we entered the factory where the ore was crushed fine before traveling down a wide conveyor belt to a second and wider belt that vibrated while running at right angles to the first one. This second belt was slanted downward from its top edge and was heavily greased. As the crushed ore dropped onto the vibrating greased belt it was continually flushed with water. Somehow the water caused the finely crushed rock to wash off the belt while only the diamonds, which are water repellent, separated from the ore and adhered to the grease. It was almost mesmeric to watch that continuous stream of precious stones moving down the belt.

They were then carried off into a glassed-in and sealed room where they were collected and distributed to workers sitting at a long table. These workers sorted the diamonds into piles according to grade; industrial or gem, and these in turn were graded into different categories.

After this tour we returned to Pniel, settled up for my hunt, and made arrangements with Albrecht to have my trophy capes dried and air-freighted to Seattle. After observing Ezok's thin sandals that offered little protection from the thorny bushes, and his tattered britches, I gave him my boots and hunting pants, which evoked a huge smile from him.

We then headed west into Namibia, or Southwest Africa as it is known today, intent on seeing the Fish River Canyon. The Fish River has carved a mile deep and winding gorge into the high plateau area of southern Namibia that reminded me of a "young" Grand Canyon. To reach it we drove two hundred miles on dirt roads through a barren, rocky country that was devoid of humans and animals. There was no traffic at all on the road and it would have been a formidable place to have car problems. Nearing the canyon we were brought to a halt by a gate across the road. From a small hut beside the gate a very surprised black guard emerged and had us sign and date a registry book. I noted that the last persons to enter had registered the previous October and it was now mid-February!

After leaving the canyon we backtracked on the dusty road and crossed the Namibia Desert, another long, hot drive through sand storms and drifted dunes and eventually arrived at Luderitz on Africa's west coast. Luderitz was a small port town with refreshing sea breezes and we welcomed the opportunity to shower and change clothes for we were a filthy, dirty, dusty and sweaty pair. Our dusty hair felt like wire.

We explored the diamond-mining ghost town of Kolmanskop, which was situated in the desert near Luderitz. At the time the mining town was active, diamonds were so plentiful in the desert that workers crawled on their bellies in the moonlight, picking up diamonds. Sand dunes are now consuming the old buildings and the search for diamonds in that area has now moved to the ocean beaches and the area near the beach is patrolled by armed guards.

Our next destination was Windhoek, the capitol of Namibia and to reach it we had to traverse the desert again. The heat was terrible, 115º, and most of the journey was on dirt road. Reaching Keetmanshoop, we headed north on the only north-south highway in Namibia. We covered long stretches of nothingness but flat earth, thorn bushes and wandering herds of domestic goats, the distance between villages being 150 miles.

After a night in Windhoek Franz drove me to the city's airport which was located thirty-five miles out in the veldt, in the middle of nowhere. Bidding farewell to Franz, for he intended to stay longer in Africa, I boarded a plane for Johannesburg, another from there to London, and eventually Seattle, where I was met by Velma and Sylvan, after a total of 22 ½ hours flight time.

The temperature was 39 degrees when I arrived in Seattle, a far cry from the 115-degree heat behind me. Africa was also behind me, but its memory will always be with me. Incidentally, my Kimberley trophy capes and horns arrived as promised and the mounted heads on my den wall never fail to remind me of that trip of a lifetime.

Chapter 13

Bosnia

With February nearly gone, April arrived quickly and I once again set about producing bear food-pellets for the second-year research. Using the improved formula that had been favored my both of my captive bears, I cranked out 825 pounds of pellets to get the season started.

The 1986 feeding study was enlarged to encompass nearly 800 square miles of timberland in five counties and on seven different ownerships. Noting that in the initial 1985 study several bear had peeled trees before discovering and utilizing the supplemental feed, it was hoped that the bear's memory would direct them to the feeders much earlier in 1986. This could result in a further decrease in damage levels.

By late April twenty-one feeders had been placed in the new 750-square-mile study area lying north of the Hoh River, while six had been installed at Kalaloch, three at Olney Creek (in Snohomish County), two in the Bremerton Watershed and two on K-M mountain in the Wahkiakum county. This amounted to a total of thirty-four feeders, increased to thirty-seven by mid-June. Feed station distribution ranged from one in thirty-six square miles to one in one square miles. The variation in number of feed stations relative to area was determined by the existing bear population, type of habitat, age and species of timber, and volume and location of damage in evidence from previous years.

The theory that bear would remember the feed station sites and return to them early in 1986 was substantiated when I arrived at the first feed station site to install the 1986 feeder and found that the bear had already been there, looking for the feeder. Finding it not yet installed, the bear proceeded to peel five young firs within fifteen feet of the feeder site and two others in the two-acre test plot surrounding it.

By May 10, all of the Kalaloch feeders were being visited by bear and as a consequence of heavy use, three more feeders were installed. Bear feeding remained constant at all nine feeders until they were removed from the study site on July 7. The bear's preference for the new feed formula pellet over the basic pellet offered in 1985 was readily noted. During 1985 in the Kalaloch study area 317 pounds of the basic pellet were eaten at the six feed stations during the two-month feeding test, an average of 63.4 pounds of pellets per station during the 1985 study. This computes to about one pound per day per station.

In comparison, during the 1986 two-month feeding study at Kalaloch, 3,470 pounds of pellets were consumed at the nine feed stations for an average of 386 pounds per station or 6.4 pounds per day, per station. The only non-target animals to utilize the feeding stations were an occasional raccoon or civet cat. Their visits were not consistent and volume consumed by these animals was insignificant, averaging one pound per month, per feeder.

In the five study areas only one bear had to be removed for persistence in tree peeling.

When the test plots were surveyed in July it was found that all the Kalaloch second-year feeding sites showed a decrease in damaged trees, ranging from 80% to 100% in the five plots. This was exciting and I recommended that the feeding study be continued in 1987, maintaining all the established feeding areas for continued comparison and data, and incorporating new areas in the state as well. A two-acre control plot had been established outside the Kalaloch supplemental feeding study unit, six miles airline from the nearest feed station. This control plot was monitored to compare damage levels between the feeding study area and an area where no feeding activities were being carried on. Heavy damage occurred in the control plot with forty-nine trees documented as being peeled between late April and early June. The entire plantation suffered comparable damage.

Meanwhile, my supplemental-feeding experiment had come to the attention of the news media. They were intrigued by the idea that after nearly thirty years of killing bears for peeling trees a non-lethal method of tree-damage control might be in the offing. It was a great public interest story-opportunity for them and I was besieged by television crews, radio, magazine and newspapers, including Time and

The Wall Street Journal. My work also drew the attention of animal-rights activist Cleveland Amory (Funds for Animals). Mr. Amory appeared on a Portland TV program and announcing the intention of his group to get a court injunction to halt the snaring of bears in Oregon, which would force the timber industry to initiate a bear-feeding program.

I tried in vain to persuade him that I was in the middle of my three-year feeding study and it would be unfair to force a bear-feeding program on Oregon until ours had proved itself effective and acceptable. This got me nowhere and a week later found me at the Corvallis, Oregon courthouse where the hearing was to be held.

There I found Cleveland Amory, his attorney and a large constituency of Funds for Animals folks, as well as representatives of the Oregon timber industry and their attorney. I also found myself in the enviable position of being smiled upon by both plaintiff and defendants. I felt that my testimony would be true and fair to both factions for I would only state that although the feeding experiment showed great promise, it was, nevertheless, still in the research stage. I was greatly relieved when the judge cancelled the case on a technicality—the plaintiff had not notified the Bureau of Land Management of the hearing.

In October I managed to squeeze out a 2 ½-day mule deer hunt in eastern Washington that showed me 183 does and no bucks, not even a spike! On another deer hunt two weeks later, Kelly Lund and I were driving down a logging road in the Satsop River drainage when we espied a bushy-bearded logger standing in the road. As we drew near he flagged us down and asked if we could take him to Shelton. We could hear the sounds of logging nearby and he indicated that he had been working with the crew when his saw-chain broke, whipped into his leg, cutting it and knocking him down, breaking his thumb in the process. Loading him into my Blazer, we headed for Shelton, post haste. When Kelly said that we would take him directly to the hospital the logger snorted and replied, "Hospital? I don't want to go to the hospital. Just drop me off at the Fir Cone tavern, I want a have a few beers! I've got some dental floss and a needle, I'll sew my leg up myself!"

It had been another busy year for me—supervising the animal damage control program, setting up hot-spot hunts, finalizing the annual aerial survey of damage areas, presenting public information slide shows, doing field trips with the media, snaring bears in non-feeding areas, producing bear-feeding pellets and conducting the bear-feeding study field work.

After a mid-November trip to Maryland to check on my dad's health, I returned to the chore of preparing a progress report on my research and the task of preparing the annual budget for the upcoming year's animal damage control activities.

Even though I was only fifty-eight-years old, I was beginning to feel weary. I penned a notation in my daily journal stating that, "This bear study is a full-time job in itself, without my other duties…"

In the early morning hours of Sunday, November 30, it happened. I had been asleep about five hours when I awoke at 4:15 a.m. with a feeling of pressure on my left chest, both front and back, that made breathing difficult. It felt as if a heavy weight had been placed on my chest and I suddenly became nauseous, with cold sweat on my forehead. Not wanting to disturb Velma, who was sleeping peacefully, I eased from under the covers and sat on the edge of the bed for a few seconds. Feeling even more nauseous, I made my way to the bathroom and looked in the mirror. What I saw looking back scared me (although it does that on a good day!) so I headed back to my bed and laid myself down on my back. The pressure was still there and by now I had a pretty good idea that whatever it was wasn't good. I breathed a prayer to the effect, "Lord, I don't know what is happening but whatever it is I don't especially like it and wish you would take it away…" In a couple more minutes the pressure subsided but I lay perfectly still, afraid that it would reoccur, until I dozed off. Velma had slept through the whole thing and did not learn what had happened until early afternoon. While having our lunch she inquired, "Did you sleep well last night?" to which I answered, "Not especially."

"Why not?" she asked.

"I think I had a heart attack," was my casual reply.

Velma nearly choked on her food and gasped, "You what? And you didn't wake me?"

"Didn't think there was much anyone could do," I replied.

Velma insisted that I see our doctor but since it was Sunday (don't toothaches and sickness always strike on weekends?) I opted to wait. I had my budget prepared and so the following day I delivered it to the WFPA's Olympia office, took care of other business and finally made it to the doctor's office on Tuesday. She sent me immediately to a cardiologist who determined that I had suffered a slight heart attack, due to a restricted coronary artery. A good warning, he said, and suggested I take some time off and get lots of exercise to get the old pump working. He advised that I walk about three miles a day and not wanting to do this along a paved highway, I took my machete and chopped out a 2 ½-mile long trail in the timbered canyons behind our home. I enjoyed this hike, up and down the steep hills, along the creek and above the beaver ponds, observing deer, ducks and herons on my way.

The doctor's diagnosis was that I had coronary artery disease and was a candidate for a serious ventricular dysrythmia, whatever that is. At any rate, up to this writing sixteen years later, I have had no more heart problems.

Early in the spring of 1987 I learned that the Department of Agriculture laboratory pellet mill would not be available for my use. Since the demand for bear feed had outgrown the small mill anyway, I started searching for a larger mill. Two commercial feed mills were contacted but they were reluctant to produce the pellet due to its high moisture content, which tended to plug their machinery. I finally located and purchased a used pellet mill in Canada that was capable of churning out 1 ½ to 2 tons an hour. Using this mill, which I set up in my shop, Velma and I produced 20,000 pounds of pellets in 1987 to supply fifty-two bear feed stations. This third year of bear feeding proved very successful in curbing tree damage and 1988 saw the feeding area expanded to include 1,600 square miles of western Washington forest land. Feed consumption that year at the one hundred sixty feed stations increased to 40,000 pounds. In 1988 the tree damage test plots showed improvement in damage levels averaging 80%. Thirteen timberland owners were now using supplemental feeding as a means to curb bear damage. At a WFPA steering committee meeting and feeding critique held early that fall, fifty attendees all had good reports for the feeding program.

On August 24, 1988, at age sixty, I retired from my Washington Forest Protection Association job, after twenty-nine years of bear damage control work. During this time I had personally dispatched 1,127 bears and it was a good feeling to realize that my supplemental feeding program now provided an alternative to killing bears for peeling trees. There still remained the need for population control but this could be effected through regular sport-hunting seasons. The habitat can only support so many animals, whether deer, elk or bear, and an over-population causes problems for both animals and humans.

My first year of retirement was certainly not spent idly; I continued to make bear feed, Vel and I producing 80,000 pounds during the April - June feeding period. I was also retained on contract by WFPA as consultant until my replacement got "settled in". That same summer we logged forty acres of our tree farm and I cut thirty cords of stove wood from the debris. Each year thereafter the feeding program expanded and the spring damage bear season was eliminated. Oregon joined in feeding bears in 1992, using twenty feed stations and 2,100 pounds of feed while Washington used 210,250 pounds in 350 feeders. By this time I had changed the pellet formula to create a harder pellet that could be produced in a commercial feed mill, giving my aching back a much-needed rest! At this writing (2003) 890 feeders placed throughout western Washington and Oregon use 500,000 pounds of pellets each summer (April—June). In 2002, Japan initiated a feeding program, using my pellets, in the mountains near Nagano.

In 1989 an international conference of bear biologists was held in Canada and among those attending was a young Croatian professor from the University of Zagreb; Dr. Djuro Huber. It seemed that the European brown bears in Bosnia had acquired a taste for tree cambium and were causing considerable damage to the fir and beech forests near Bugojno in the Dinaric Alps. The total forest area around Bugojno is 2,000 square kilometers (or 771 square miles; roughly an area of 25 x 31 square miles.)

Of this area, two hundred square kilometers or seventy-seven square miles compromises the Koprivnica Hunting Preserve, which was originally Marshall Tito's private hunting area. The tree species in the forest include beech, birch, maple, oak, fir, spruce, elm and pine.

The brown bear population in Bosnia had been nearly wiped out by the end of World War II, but careful management had seen their numbers increase in the reserve to ten to fifteen bears by 1970. The plan was to increase their numbers by supplemental feeding and a program was initiated that year. Twelve feed lots were established by clearing all the trees and bushes from half-acre plots, covering the ground with crushed white limestone and placing piles of corn, slaughter-house offal and road-killed animals for the bears to eat. This food was available for the bears year round, and the practice was continued for nearly twenty years, with seven hundred tons a year being consumed. The bear population increased dramatically to the point that, by 1987, there were one hundred fifty to one hundred seventy bears in the seventy-seven square mile reserve.

In 1982 the first bear damage to forest trees was documented there and it was first noted around and directly adjacent to the feeding sites. In 1985 and 1986 the damage became a real problem and the first steps at damage control were implemented in 1987. Up to this time about twenty bears were being shot each year at the feed lots by trophy hunters who paid $4,000 to $50,000 per bear, according to size.

Bosnia, at the time, was a socialistic state in the then Yugoslavia and a forest manager was responsible for its timber resource while a game manager was accountable for the wildlife. As could be expected, this bear-inflicted tree damage created a conflict between the two managers. Ljupko Kuna, the "bear manager", considered the bears to be as valuable as the timber while the forest manager, Hadziabdic Sead, wished all the bears could be eliminated.

During the fall—spring hunting seasons of 1988-1989 and 1989-1990, ninety six bears were killed by trophy hunters in an effort to reduce the population. This was done reluctantly, at the urging of the forest managers who had, during the preceding two years, removed 26,000 damaged merchantable trees from the area.

Dr. Huber was a bear biologist who dearly loved the European brown bear and championed their preservation. He was quite impressed when he learned of my supplemental feeding program from one of his American colleagues at the conference. Upon returning to Zagreb he contacted professor Nadazdin of the veterinary faculty at the university in Sarajevo, suggesting to him that I be contacted to set up a feeding program for Bosnia's bears. The professor took umbrage at this, stating that, "We don't need this American coming over here to help us. I can develop a food pellet that will do just as well as his."

And so he did, and the bears loved it. The only problem was they were consuming one hundred twenty tons of the stuff in five months and continued peeling trees! About this time I received a letter from Mr. Kuna inquiring "why my bear-feeding greatly reduced tree damage while theirs did not? If they paid my airfare and all my expenses would I be willing to come to Bugojno, Bosnia, and set up a bear feeding program for them?" I felt sure I could solve their problem by making two changes in their current approach but deferred divulging my theory until I had seen their problem first hand. I accepted their invitation and prepared for the trip.

I invited our oldest daughter, Sylvan, to accompany me on this adventure and September 7, 1990 found us on a polar-route flight to London. After a night in London, we continued our journey to Zagreb, Croatia where we were met at the airport by Dr. Djuro Huber. I was quite impressed with Djuro who was genuinely and intensely dedicated to the welfare of "his" bears, and I liked him immediately. We loaded our stuff in his little vehicle and roared off on the five-hour drive to Bugojno. The first part of the route was through flat land with gently rolling hills that became more mountainous as we turned south into the Dinaric Alps.

Darkness fell and limited our view to the narrow, two-lane road under our headlights but slow-moving trucks laboring up the steep, serpentine road were no obstacle to Djuro, who whizzed around them on blind curves with the daring of an Indy 500 driver. Somewhere near Banja Luka we stopped at the ancient village of Jajce and stretched our legs on a stroll along its cobblestone streets. Needing to find a restroom, we spotted a tavern, of sorts, that basically was nothing more than some tables and chairs set up under a huge, overhanging rock formation. No walls, except the natural rock, and a dirt floor. A cave with a sloping, dirt floor had been dug farther back under the ledge and this, we were informed, was the restroom. No toilet, no urinal, no water, only the floor and at a glance you could see that it had been well utilized. The stench was abominable.

One and a half hours later as we were nearing the Koprivnica hunting reserve, Djuro glanced in my direction and said, "Tonight you will be sleeping in Marshall Tito's bed." I laughed at this, but Djuro was serious. "Really, you will," he said. "You will be staying in Tito's old hunting lodge during your time here!"

It was 11:30 p.m. when we arrived at the lodge and found Nikko, the chef, waiting for us with a late dinner prepared. After our meal and a visit that ended around 2:30 a.m., we retired to our beds. Sure enough, I was settled in Marshall Tito's room and bed (he had been dead for eleven years at this time) and Sylvan was across the hall in Mrs. Tito's room. After a long journey and an equally long day, I snuggled under the feather quilt and slept soundly.

The morning dawned overcast and a little raw. A light rain had fallen in the night but the day showed signs of improving. After enjoying a good breakfast and being introduced to a young biologist from Sarajevo University, I went outside to view my surroundings. Visibility was good and the vista from the lodge was spectacular. I could see why Tito had chosen this spot as his private hunting reserve.

The lodge was situated at the head of a long valley between the mountains and a forest of tall firs dominated the hills behind and above it. Across the valley, to the right, was an open, rocky, meadow-like mountainside and this clearing extended far down that side of the valley until it reached a dense forest of fir and beech trees. At this spot stood a huge lodge, more like a long, modern, three-story hotel that had been Tito's retreat just prior to his death. Behind it the terrain dropped off sharply into the timbered depths of the valley below.

Directly in front of the old lodge where I stood was the game manager's residence and office. The house was of two stories with a dark-wooden porch on the second level contrasting with its white plastered walls. The forest grew in tightly around it and its ancient stone outbuildings. On the uphill side of the lodge and tight against it was an outdoor cooking area consisting of a roof, open sides and concrete-cobbled floor. A heavy iron grill sat over a bed of coals and nearby was a huge, cast-iron Dutch oven where bread was baked and delicious stews were brewed. Nikko, we soon discovered, was a master chef who had served Marshall Tito and his guests. At one dinner, he related to us, he accidentally spilled something on a visiting dignitary and Tito had him taken outside and beaten!

The old lodge where we were ensconced was rustic and comfortable, though not large. A huge picture of Marshall Tito standing with his rifle by a dead brown bear occupied a prominent place on a wall near the stairs. The dining room was a cozy place with a long table that seated ten, running the length of the room along one wall. A highly finished wooden bench and backrest was affixed to the wall while chairs were situated around the rest of the table. Comfortable chairs were scattered over the rest of the room while a smaller table, generously laden with bottles of whiskey and wine, stood just inside the door. The upstairs was divided into four rooms; Tito's room where I slept, Mrs. Tito's room where Sylvan slept, a larger "communal" room with several cots for other guests, and the bathroom. Toilet paper was not supplied in rolls but in a stack of thick four-inch square sheets. After a few days

I remarked that Bosnia was the only country I knew of where the money falls apart but you cannot tear the toilet paper!

Sylvan and I were watching five chamois that were feeding on the open mountainside when Ljupko Kuna, the game manager, arrived. He was a stocky, middle-aged man and very likeable even though I could only converse with him through Djuro, our interpreter. After introductions the five of us crowded into his vehicle and drove to Bugojno where we picked up a forest warden. Ljupko had a tour of the reserve planned that would allow me to see the lay of the country and the magnitude of the bear damage. As we wound up and down the dirt forest roads through the hilly terrain I was reminded of our forests at home.

The main difference was that in western Washington our forests are stocked primarily with conifers—fir, hemlock, spruce and cedar—while at Bugojno the forest was a mixture of conifers and deciduous trees.

We made frequent stops to hike through the woods and inspect "hot-spots" of tree damage. What I saw was comparable to damage inflicted by our black bears, with one exception—the brown bears, not being climbing bears, created only basal damage to the trees and this usually not more than four feet above the ground. And, as at home, open-grown, fast-growing trees were more susceptible to peeling than trees in dense stands.

We visited some of the feedlots and found heavy damage adjacent to them. Huge bear tracks, day beds, and well-padded trails were everywhere, giving one a feeling of being watched while you wandered through the woods. The Bosnian brown bears are comparable to our Alaska brown bears but lacking the abundant food sources of our American bears, they do not grow as large, reaching a maximum of six hundred pounds. Their temperament is not as irascible as our brownies; they are usually nocturnal, shy and reclusive but they have proven themselves to be unpredictable if threatened, surprised or traveling with cubs. In a 23-month period just prior to my arrival in Bosnia four people were killed by bears.

The first incident occurred near Bugojno where a small group of farmers were planting potatoes in a field next to the woods. A bear suddenly charged out of the woods and chased a woman who ran for the protection of the barn. While she was attempting to open the barn door the bear caught her and clawed her severely, causing her to be hospitalized. The bear then attacked and killed a six-year-old girl. The farmers beat the animal with clubs and axes and the bear died with the girl's head still clasped in its jaws. When the bear's carcass was examined it revealed fresh shotgun pellet wounds and parts of a steel snare were embedded in both front legs. Rabies inclusion bodies were found in the brain, which confirmed the first case of rabies in brown bears in Yugoslavia.

The second attack occurred in Slovenia where a woman in her sixties was killed while picking mushrooms. She was killed by a bite to her neck before being dragged over 185 yards into the brush where she was fed upon and partially buried. The offending bear was tracked down and killed and weighed only 135 pounds.

The third incident occurred in Bosnia where a 13-year-old boy was found mauled and killed by a bear after he had gone in search of his sheep that were foraging in the woods.

The last attack occurred in late March, in the afternoon of a very foggy day when a man was walking in dense woods about 650 yards from a small town. Tracks in the snow indicated that he was killed near the shallow den of a female and her cub. His eviscerated body was found 105 yards downhill from where he was first attacked.

After our woods tour we returned to the lodge for lunch and conversation. I had noticed small cabins or elevated hunting stands at all the feed lots we had visited and it was explained to me that in the northern socialistic republics—Slovenia, Croatia and Bosnia—bears were hunted exclusively from elevated or ground level stands using bait, during moonlit nights. The hunter is always accompanied by a guide, who is a member of the local organization that manages bears. The guide waits in the stand with the hunter and determines whether the bear that approaches the bait is suitable for harvesting. If it is, the hunter and the guide agree to a hunting fee based on the trophy value of the bear. They shake hands on the deal and the hunter shoots the bear. The hunter gets the pelt and the skull as a trophy. The average sized trophy bear cost, at that time, $20,000. Since the hunting organizations that manage bears are responsible for damage inflicted by bears to livestock and agricultural crops, in some areas over 25% of the income from bear harvests is paid in damages to farmers.

Around 4:30 Ljupko announced that we would return to one of the feedlots and wait in the hunting cabin to observe the bears when they came to feed. Leaving our vehicle at the end of an old road, we walked a half-mile up a trail to the feedlot. This particular lot was completely encircled by the fir and beech woods and one hundred eight feet from the center of the lot, snuggled into the forest's edge was a small, one room cabin. The entrance door was at its rear and once inside I saw a small bunk along the back wall while the front wall facing the lot was fitted with a long, narrow sliding glass window. A "shooting shelf" was built at the proper height just under the window and comfortable chairs were placed there for the hunter and the guide. On another shelf, higher up, sat an assortment of bottles of whiskey.

Sylvan, Djuro and I positioned ourselves by the window while Ljupko relaxed on the bunk. Around 5:30 p.m., while still daylight, a huge brown bear walked out of the forest and commenced eating at the bait pile. Ljupko commented that this was an average, $20,000 bear. I wondered what the $52,000 variety would look like.

At 6 p.m. another bear, comparable to the one already feeding, made his way onto the lot and fed at a pile a respectable distance from the first bear. This bear was very dark brown and almost looked black. Then a small bear appeared and fed at the far end of the lot but he was soon displaced when another larger bear mosied over in his direction. The small bear went back in the woods and then reappeared at the opposite end of the lot. Another big bear crowded him back into the woods where he could be seen moving about, looking and waiting for an opening at the feast.

Darkness fell and more bears appeared, their forms plainly visible against the crushed white limestone in the moonlight. A total of twelve bears showed up and nine were feeding at one time on the lot. Two wild boars also appeared and fed at the far perimeter of the lot. These boars really caught my attention for I had planned to go to Austria when my work was done in Bosnia and hunt boar with my friend Franz.

What a sight to see all these huge bears in the moonlight and realize that we had been walking among them in the woods all morning! On our way into the lot I had seen seven or eight beaten down bear trails crossing our path and heading for the lot and as we hiked back to our vehicle through the dark woods that night, I had the feeling that we might encounter one of the huge beasts at any moment. Especially so, since I was bringing up the rear of the procession in the darkness! Ljupko was armed with a .38 special revolver that would have about as much effect on a brown bear as a switch.

Back at the lodge, Nikko was waiting for us with a superb dinner prepared. A meeting was planned for the following morning, one that the forest manager Hadziabdic Sead would attend, and at which I would present my recommendations concerning a solution to their bear damage problems. After preparing my presentation notes, I crawled into my nest, tired after a fun day in the woods.

Morning arrived sunny and beautiful as only a September day can be and 10 a.m. found me in Ljupko's little office where I was introduced to the very businesslike forest director Hadziabdic Sead. Also attending were Professor Huber and Sinisa the biologist. The meeting got started and I saw immediately that it was going to be a laborious process, not only because each word had to be interpreted, but also for the fact that each participant came to the table hoping to see his individual goals realized, while their objectives differed to the point of not being amenable. Director Sead wished to see the bear population decreased to almost nil to curb the tree damage, while Ljupko wished the bears' numbers to increase to make the hunting enterprise more profitable, and Professor Huber would be happy if no bears were killed. That left me in the middle and they looked to me for the "magic" solution. Once again I found myself in my old role of mediator, just as I had been at home on my job striving to strike a happy medium between the timber industry, the Department of Wildlife and the organized sportsmen.

First, I learned from them the ingredients in their Sarajevo produced bear food pellet formula and as I had suspicioned it was high in protein but lacking in carbohydrates. The bears loved the taste of the stuff but continued to attack the trees to obtain sugar; the tree's cambium contains four to five percent free-floating sugars. I advised them how much to increase the sugar content in their formula and it was determined that the altered formula feed could be produced for thirty-three cents a kilogram or approximately $320 per ton.

Due to the high elevation of the area (600 feet to 6,890 feet) tree damage occurs late, during June and July, and the bears density in the reserve increases during that critical time period due to adjacent hunting groups stopping baiting at the end of May, which marks the end of the hunting season. Thus, many bears migrate into the reserve where feeding is carried on year-round.

My second suggestion was for them to produce fifty self-feeder barrels and scatter them throughout the reserve, keeping them filled with pellets during the June-July tree- peeling season. After having observed the bears at the feedlot on the previous evening it was quite evident that the larger, dominant bears crowded the smaller and more submissive bears from the lot. These ousted bears hung around on the periphery, just inside the forest, and peeled trees while they waited in frustration for a chance to feed on the lot. Having barrels of feed scattered throughout the reserve would give these bears an opportunity to feed and obtain the sugar they needed. I presented Ljupko with a scale-drawing plan for constructing the feeder barrels.

Ljupko agreed to this plan and I finally persuaded Director Sead to concur with it and allow a three-year trial of the experiment before making any conclusions. His consent was gained only when I convinced Ljupko to increase the annual bear harvest to bring their numbers down to a more realistic figure for the available habitat.

After four hours of discussion we arrived at this mutual agreement and with handshakes all around, adjourned the meeting. We walked over to the lodge where we found Nikko preparing a feast of young wild boar, potatoes and carrots in his Dutch oven, along with fresh tomatoes, bread dumplings and all the trimmings. Director Sead shared lunch with us and as the meal progressed there was much agitated and un-interpreted discourse that I could not understand. I soon came to realize that they were exchanging views and opinions regarding the possibility of a revolutionary war erupting in Slovenia, Croatia and Bosnia as those areas sought to be independent and self-governing republics and no longer under Serbian Belgrade control. The Yugoslav National Army was on the Serbian side and along with civil Serbian extremists would attempt to subdue the uprising with any radical means that they could devise. Croatia was already defiantly flying its new independent Republic of Croatia flag and things did not look good for the immediate future.

After our lunch, Djuro, Sinisa, Sylvan and I drove out to a mountain pass and climbed a high meadow-like ridge that gave us an excellent view of the town of Kupres that lay far below us. Little did we realize that a terrible tank battle for control of Kupres and this strategic pass would take place one year later. On such a peaceful and sunny Sunday afternoon it was hard to even imagine such an event.

That evening Ljupko came to the lodge and stated that in appreciation for my assistance he wanted to offer me a free hunt for a $2,000 wild boar. "At the feedlot last night I noticed that you were more excited over the wild boars than you were over the bears."

"Well," I grinned, "I've seen a lot of bears in my time but very few wild boars. I accept your offer—you could not have given me anything I wanted more!"

The hunt was set for the following evening and I went to bed excited over the prospects.

At dawn the persistent barking of a dog just outside my window announced the passing of a bear on its way to a nearby feedlot. After this uproar there was not much sleep and soon the place was astir with bodies gravitating toward the dining room. My work here was done and Sylvan and I had plans to try to locate some Croatian relatives of her husband; relatives that had not been heard from since before the onset of World War II. All we had to go on was an old letter and photograph and the name of the village where the relatives lived. Ljupko looked at the postmark and remarked that Metkovic was about three hours down the road, by bus.

After many telephone calls he came to the lodge and announced that he had located the family and they were eagerly awaiting our visit! Djuro was due back at the university in Zagreb and to help us travel "light" we loaded some of our duffle in his car to take home with him. Before he left a date was set for us to meet him in Zagreb to accompany him on a bear radio-tracking foray in the mountains around Gorski-Kotar, near the Slovenia border.

After breakfast, and bidding farewell to Djuro, Sylvan, Sinisa and I spent the morning hiking through the woods near the lodge. The hills were crisscrossed with wide bear trails that were so padded down they resembled cattle paths. Around 3 p.m. Ljupko came to the lodge, bringing one of the forest wardens, his .300

Weatherby magnum rifle, a chair and a bear-profile target. After setting up the target, I seated myself on the chair, rested the rifle on the porch railing and squeezed off a shot. Being used to my little .270 rifle I was not prepared for the recoil that took the hat right off my head. This drew a laugh from my audience and when a second shot relieved me of my hat again I thought I had best quit before they died laughing. At any rate, the bullets hit the "bear" in his vitals and being satisfied that the rifle shot true, we prepared for the evenings wild boar hunt.

Ratco the warden loaded us in his little vehicle and with Sinisa along as interpreter we drove to an area northwest of Bugojno. The area of the hunt was beautiful; rolling hills heavily timbered, a Karst outcropping appearing stark white against the greenery while multiple waterfalls cascaded down its face, through clumps of ferns, into a deep pool. From this pool the water escaped underground through eroded limestone caverns to reappear as a sparkling stream farther down the valley.

Parking the vehicle, we walked down a dirt road past some tall piles of hay stacked around center poles and soon reached a small clearing near the creek. Here we were met by two more wardens who were headquartered in some buildings at the far side of the clearing, close by the hill. The evening air was cool and a small fire had been built on the creek bank next to a rustic picnic table. Here the six of us sat, conversing, with Sinisa interpreting, and no mention was made of the hunt. From time to time one of the wardens would leave the table and disappear up a trail leading into the woods. As the evening grew later and just as I was beginning to wonder when the hunt would ever get underway, the warden reappeared from one of his walks and said simply, "It is time."

At this, he handed me the rifle and Sinisa, Sylvan and I followed him up the trail and into the woods. There had been no briefing as to the method of the hunt and I had no idea what to expect. All I knew was that Ljupko had stated that the hunt was for a $2,000 trophy-valued boar and from my experiences in Hungary I knew it would be the warden's decision as to the animal I would be allowed to shoot. With the language barrier and the necessity of Sinisa interpreting the warden's remarks, I figured that any hog we did see would escape by the time it was determined shootable and permission to shoot translated into English. At least I was allowed to carry the gun!

I was a little surprised when we were led to the back door of a little hunting shack perched on the top of a brushy hill. Admonishing us to be quiet, the warden ushered us into the shack and motioned me toward the open window. Peering out, I was shocked to see at least fifty wild hogs foraging in a small clearing in the timber, about one hundred yards away. There were wild hogs of all sizes from piglets up to 400-pound boars, rooting, squealing, slashing at each other with their wicked tusks and moving about in such a confusion of activity that it was hard to keep your eye on any particular one. The warden was studying them with his binoculars and finally selected the boar I was to shoot. By the time his comments were interpreted, the boar would no longer be at the same spot and I sure did not want to mistakenly shoot a $5,000 trophy! Finally, in exasperation, Sinisa said, "It is the one with something white on his face!"

Then I spotted it, at the far side of the clearing, at the forest's edge. It was hard to get a clear shot without another hog getting in the line of fire, but when he turned facing me and gave me a "three-quartering" view of his body, I found his rib cage in the crosshairs and squeezed the trigger. This time my hat stayed on but to my dismay the hog did not fall! I saw dust fly directly behind it and moaned inwardly when, at my shot, all the hogs took off as one and headed into the woods.

I kept my eye on my hog as I cranked another round into the rifle chamber and was about to shoot again when Sinisa informed me, "It isn't necessary! It isn't necessary!"

By this time I noticed that my hog had swung out of the herd and was running erratically back down the hill toward us. He started up the hillside where our shack was situated, then tumbled down the hill and fell dead at the clearing's edge. Hurrying down to inspect my trophy, we found that my bullet had entered his rib cage just where I had aimed and had passed through him shattering his heart and liver! I was amazed at how tough these wild boars were.

It was a dandy hog, two hundred pounds, with heavy tusks that measured nine inches overall. It was also very ugly with a face that only a mother could love but I was thrilled with it and could already envision his ferocious looking head on my trophy room wall! After dragging the animal to the creek and dressing it out, the warden placed a small fir bough in each side of its mouth as its last food, and, dipping another bough in its blood, placed it in my cap.

Back at Koprivnica lodge the boar was skinned and caped for mounting. To make sure it was caped properly, I stayed and watched the procedure until Nikko's second call to dinner pulled me away. After a delicious (and appropriate!) pork chop dinner I made it to bed at 11:30 after entering the notation in my diary, "I have finally got an European wild boar! Hunting in Europe sure differs from hunting in America!"

It rained all night and continued into the morning. After our breakfast Ljupko appeared and presented me with the tusks from my boar. The cape, he assured me, would be waiting at the Zagreb University when I arrived there. Then, much to my surprise, he handed me a thick packet of Yugoslav money, which he said was per diem for the rest of my journey. When I protested, he insisted I accept it, stating that

I should have to pay nothing for my stay in Yugoslavia. He also gave Sylvan a huge package of frozen roe deer meat for the relatives we were going to meet. We said our goodbyes and Ratco drove us to the Bugojno bus depot where we obtained our tickets to Pocitelj for $4 each.

The bus wound its way down the mountains through a beautiful landscape, often having to back up several times to negotiate corners in the narrow-streeted villages. The rain had ceased shortly after our departure and the three-hour journey passed quickly. We were now heading down into the sub-tropical region of Croatia and the thick stands of timber gradually disappeared, limestone-Karst hillsides and low vegetation replacing it.

At Pocitelj we were met by Matto Celic, his wife and his brother's beautiful, English-speaking girlfriend. They had no trouble recognizing us for Ljupko had told them to watch for a man wearing a green cap; certainly not the standard head gear in Yugoslavia!

We were then taken to Matto's home in Metkovic where many members of the Celic clan awaited our arrival. The next couple of days were spent traveling the countryside around Metkovic to meet and visit more relatives in outlying villages. Everyone wanted to feed us and I recall eating five meals in one day!

Our visit over, we boarded a bus and headed for Split, a city on the Adriatic coast, and our journey led us on a pretty route through more mountainous country. When we arrived at the bus depot in Split, we found several matronly women waiting there, each "hawking" rooms in their private homes. I thought this would be more fun than staying in a hotel so we agreed to follow one of the ladies to her home, which was situated on the fourth floor of an older building, above a busy street. The room had two hide-a-beds, the bathroom was clean and the place was within walking distance of the train station. The price was a little exorbitant at 400 dinars ($40 American) but I paid the large, stone-faced and all-business lady and we settled in.

Split was situated right at the water's edge but a walk along its waterfront was anything but delightful. The water was polluted with city and boat sewage, with natural sulphur in the water adding to the stink. After a relaxing dinner with Sylvan at an Italian restaurant across the street, we retired to our nests and despite the noisy traffic on the street below, soon nodded off to sleep.

The next morning we walked to the train depot, had a roll and some coffee, bought our tickets to Zagreb ($13.40 each), and boarded the 10:30 a.m. train for the 8 and a half hour trip. The train was filled with passengers but we finally found an empty compartment at the rear of the car. Four young Serbian men soon joined us, and the train moved off. The train made numerous stops and we soon learned why our compartment had been empty—the train's toilet was located directly behind us and like most other public toilets in Yugoslavia, the odor was atrocious, permeating our compartment each time the train stopped.

The train's route crossed many rivers and passed through numerous tunnels as it snaked its way through the mountains. The scenery was spectacular. We arrived in Zagreb a little after 7 p.m., bone weary and hungry. There had been no food or water on the train but the stench from that toilet wasn't conducive to enjoying a meal, had there been one.

We spent the night in a hotel near the depot and were picked up by Djuro the following morning for our trip to Gorski Kotar. Our destination was the Risnjak national park lodge, which was having its grand opening that day, and Djuro had somehow obtained free lodging and meals for the three of us for two days.

Gorski Kotar was the prettiest spot I had seen in all Yugoslavia, even surpassing Bugojno. It reminded me somewhat of Alpine Switzerland. Djuro was engaged in a bear study in that area and had placed radio-transmitter collars on quite a few brown bears. We accompanied him on a climb up Mount Risnjak and onto its summit, all the while monitoring movements of the bears with his receiver and directional antenna. Leaving the summit, we climbed around the rocky-faced side of the mountain to inspect a bear den that Djuro had located earlier. The entrance to this den was right on the face of a rocky cliff and led back into a cave that made an abrupt right turn into the den's "room." A female with cubs had used the den the previous winter, but since it was now early for denning we found no one at home on our visit.

Our search for one female bear led us into Slovenia where we finally located her far up on a rocky mountainside. While in the area we stopped in a village on the Croation side of the border. The forestry and wildlife manager of Gorski Kotar had his office there and had voiced a desire to meet with me and discuss some concerns that he had regarding the brown bears. Over coffee, he voiced his alarm about the recent and unprecedented human fatalities inflicted by brown bears and his belief that research methods of capturing bears with snares, administering anesthetics, and collaring bears with radio transmitters were changing bears and making them more aggressive toward people.

I shared with him the fact that hundreds of bears had experienced the same indignities and treatment at the hands of our western Washington biologists but, to my knowledge, none had acquired hostile or inimical attitudes because of it. On the contrary, it tended to make most bears more wary and fearful of human scent.

After radio-tracking bears all day through some of the prettiest September-colored woods you could ever imagine, we left the Slovenia border and headed back toward Zagreb. At Karlovac, a military-base town not far from Zagreb, Sylvan and I spent the night in a Zimmer, or guest house, while Djuro continued on to Zagreb.

The following morning we watched the gentleman of the house building bee-boxes in his workshop until one of Djuro's students arrived to take us to Zagreb. A day of touring the city, and evening and night with Djuro and his family, and it was time to say our farewells. It had been an exciting and rewarding trip. I was anxious to see what the results of the next year's feeding program at Bugojno would be and was optimistic that the report would be good.

On June 26 of the following year (1991) war broke out in Slovenia and spilled over into Croatia by July. We learned that because of the military base, much of Karlovac including the Zimmer where Sylvan and I had stayed, had been destroyed. In early 1992, Bosnia was under attack from the Serbs. Correspondence from Djuro informed me that Ljupko had purchased over 55,000 pounds of pellets made with the amount of sugar that I had advised and placed it in feeding barrels throughout the reserve in June 1991. Ljupko proudly reported that the new feed reduced the tree damage by 90% that summer! The only areas experiencing damage were locations where the food was not placed in time. This was good news.

The bad news was that a more serious threat was facing the bears and the reserve. Because of the political situation and war only three hunters came to hunt during 1991 when they had expected 40. By fall, all of the funds for the reserve had run out. This meant they couldn't buy any more food for the bears, they had no fuel for vehicles to distribute food and manage the reserve, and no more money for salaries for their 18 employees. When, in mid-March of 1992, the war exploded in that area no special feeding was even attempted. Even if funds had been available it would not have been possible to get the pellets from outside of Bosnia.

Great battles occurred in the town of Kupres until it was taken over by the Serbian army. The next major Bosnian fight was for the pass above Kupres—the nice meadow-like ridge where Djuro, Sinisa, Sylvan and I had walked and enjoyed just eighteen months previous. This strategic pass was also taken by Serbs after a tank and air battle. From there they headed on to Bugojno, right through the core bear habitat. Some 372 square miles of forest was burned, mined, shelled, and the bears shot on sight.

Fifty years of bear conservation down the drain!

Chapter 14

Alaska

After retiring from the Washington Forest Protection Associaton at the end of 1988, I did very little bear hunting. I had once thought that the bear hunting "fever" that had burned within me for so many years would never expire, but it was happening. It was hard to get excited over a bear hunt after having made 1,161 kills. Besides, I would ask myself, what would I do with another bear? Although each year I continued to buy a bear tag, I was expending so much time and effort during the summer months on the supplemental feeding program that I gave no thought to a bear hunt other than to capture an occasional problem bear for a timberland owner. I have taken only five bear in the past two years.

Now my hunting interests have turned to other game that I had little time for in past years; mule deer, antelope, whitetail deer and caribou; and with my 75th birthday approaching I still pursue these with a passion.

My first caribou hunt was during the last week of September 1991 and it came close to being my last one. I had become acquainted a couple of years previous with a 49-year-old Alaskan, Ron Taylor. Ron had read my book *The Education of a Bear Hunter* and, being a sport bear-hunter himself, had contacted me on the 'phone to comment on the book. Through subsequent correspondence we laid plans for an unguided caribou hunt on the Alaska Peninsula.

September 24th found me on a plane to Anchorage where I was met at the airport by my new, but never before seen, friend Ron. After shipping our camping gear by air freight to King Salmon, we drove to Ron's log cabin for the night, returning to Anchorage the following morning for our flight over the Alaska Range to Dillingham and on to King Salmon. Our air-freighted gear had arrived safely and was waiting for us at the terminal. A young fellow from the local flight service hauled us down to the river dock and we soon had all our stuff stowed in the float plane.

The plane left the river with a mighty roar and we headed down the peninsula. I was surprised, to say the least, at the landscape that passed beneath the plane. It certainly held up to its name "barren ground" for there were no trees to be seen anywhere, only moss, lichen, rocks and small lakes. This was the tundra and it certainly didn't look to me like any animal could or would live in such a place. We flew at a low altitude and I kept my eyes busy looking for game but saw none. After about 50 miles and just as I was about to despair, we reached a series of low ridges and I began to see small bands of five or six caribou. Then larger groups appeared and I nearly jumped from the plane when I spotted a dandy bull among them. We flew on until we found a lake big enough to set the plane down and sufficiently long to allow for a takeoff. Idling the plane to the shore, we unloaded our gear in a big heap and after instructing the pilot to return for us in four days, we watched him roar off the lake and disappear in the distance.

Surveying our surroundings, we looked for a good spot to set up our little two-man tent. Any place that was level was squishy wet so we were forced to erect our tent on a slight slope to allow for drainage. By now rain had started to fall and we worked quickly to get our gear under cover.

We couldn't hunt the same day we were airborne but we took a short hike around our camp to get our bearings. By now the rain was pelting down and we crawled into our tent to prepare our freeze-dried dinner. Then it was into our sleeping bags to wait for dawn. My entry in my journal that evening reads, "There are absolutely no trees here, no bushes. Only rocks, moss, lichen, patches of swamp grass, lots of little pot-hole lakes. No wood at all for a fire. No landmarks; everything looks the same. We will have to be careful lest we get disoriented. Our camp is in a swale by the lake and not visible from any distance. Sleeping bag feels good tonight, but rain water is making its way along the tent floor. Lots of rocks under the tent."

The cold wind and rain that had lashed our tent all night hadn't abated at daylight. In fact, it had become worse and a peek out the tent flap showed a thick blanket of fog had blown in from Bristol Bay, reducing visibility to practically nil. We finally persuaded ourselves to leave our warm nests at 9 a.m., don our rain gear and hip boots and face the elements. We prepared our breakfast outdoors and by the time it was ready my hands were so cold they had lost their feeling. We decided to go for a hunt anyway, noting that as the wind whipped the fog across the tundra it sometimes thinned enough for us to see nearly 100 yards. The rain was constant and being wind-blown, it came almost parallel to the ground. Hunting into the wind brought the rain splattering into my face and on my glasses, binoculars, and rifle scope. So far, I thought to myself, this isn't much fun.

Then, like gray ghosts in the fog, we saw the forms of about forty caribou moving around a small ridge across from us. They faded in and out of the swirling fog but I was able to pick out at least three bulls despite the rain streaming down my glasses. I had hopes of finding a trophy bull, one with a double shovel, which occurs in only 40% of the bulls.

We continued to hunt all day and as the fog cleared we moved farther out from our campsite. Even so, we saw no game until around 6 p.m. The rain had stopped by then and we had a good view of the river plain below us. Then, about a mile away, and moving away from us, we saw a group of around 100 caribou. Through our binoculars we saw one impressive bull with antlers that stood out above all the others, but had to be content to watch them fade away in the distance for there was no way to get near them.

The next morning dawned quiet and clear and we were up early to greet it. Before we could fix our breakfast I spotted some caribou coming over a hill at the south end of our lake. Grabbing our rifles, we dropped down a small bank and waded along the lake's edge, keeping a low profile, hoping to get within range of them. By now the entire group was feeding along the face of the hillside and a couple of bulls were having a sparring match, pushing each other around with their antlers meshed. Ron and I remained crouched by the lake and enjoyed the show until the caribou band moved around the hill and disappeared. Then, taking a round-about route, we, too, made our way around the hill. Ahead of us we could see that the caribou were now bedded down, with only a few remaining standing.

Crawling on our bellies we managed to get within shooting distance without being detected. We then "glassed" the herd, which numbered thirty-five or forty animals, and found nothing but small bulls. Leaving them to their cud-chewing, we hunted farther out on the tundra, forgetting about breakfast as the day became prettier. Then, on a high ridge far out in front of us, we saw caribou scattered along its top and on its flanks for a mile! They were moving over the top so we skirted around past our camp to get a view of the other side. What we saw stopped us in our tracks. The river plain was covered with hundreds of migrating caribou, a half-mile away, and impossible to approach unobserved. Caribou were all over the ridges above us, watching us. When we would try to approach a band that hadn't seen us, another band would come over the ridge, spot us and spook all the animals. We couldn't get within a half-mile of them on that wide-open tundra. We saw three exceptional bulls among them but could only watch and drool.

Hunger drove us to camp around 6 p.m. After our dinner I walked up on the hill above our tent and spotted a herd of caribou moving along the skyline at the north end of our lake and only 250 yards away. They quickly disappeared behind the hill while Ron and I hurried around the hill to try to ambush them. By the time we skirted the lake and climbed the ridge they were still 250 yards ahead of us and it was too dark to see horns. The sunset had been beautiful and red and the day a perfect, sunny one. Maybe tomorrow would be my lucky day!

Morning arrived quiet, cold and frosty. We had our breakfast, pulled on our hip boots (which were worn everyday because of the squishy-wet tundra and pot holes) and headed in the direction of yesterday's hunt. We had gone about one and a half miles when we saw a cloud bank moving in from the east that signaled a change in the weather. We also began seeing caribou, although not in as great numbers as the day before. By 11 a.m. we were watching five different bands of caribou on the hills in front of us. Honing in on the nearest bunch, we crawled to the top of a low ridge, peeked over, and saw that they had bedded down about 225 yards away.

Remaining prone with just our heads above the ridgeline, we studied the group with our binoculars. There were quite a few nice bulls in the herd but nothing spectacular. A few were bedded out of our sight. We watched them until noon and when it started to rain I decided I would take one of the bulls, knowing that the fog might move in again and I could end up with nothing.

About then the caribou began getting to their feet and moving around. It was then I saw a nice bull, with double-shovels, that I hadn't noticed up to now. When he turned broad side to me I targeted his rib cage and squeezed the trigger on my 41-year-old .270 Remington. The gun roared, the bull fell dead in his tracks, and his companions ran off a hundred yards and stood watching. Ron didn't opt to take one of the bulls, which he easily could have done, but waited in hopes of finding another double shovel.

As the caribou trotted off into the distance, Ron and I walked to the fallen bull. I set about gutting it, removed the lower legs and was starting to cape it out for mounting when I noticed a movement by the pile of entrails. Straightening up from my task I was surprised to see a red fox, ten feet from me, feeding on the gut fat! After snapping a photo of him I continued with my work and when I glanced in that direction a few minutes later, he was gone.

After skinning and caping the bull and removing the antlers and skull plate, we loaded all of this stuff on my back and with Ron carrying the boned-out hind quarters we headed for camp, all of this in a down-pour of rain. Far off on the horizon, many miles east of camp, lay a mountain that had the shape of a huge turtle with its neck extended. We had dubbed it "Turtle Mountain." Close behind camp was a small hill of the same shape that we called "Little Turtle." When these two hills were aligned it was easy to determine the direction to our camp.

Even though it was raining the visibility was good and we reached our camp without problem. After dropping our loads and stowing the meat under a tarp anchored down with rocks, we crawled into our tent to escape the rain and also the wind that had suddenly begun. Our plan was to have some lunch and then return for the rest of our meat but before we had finished our snack the rain increased and an east wind suddenly began, gusting up to fifty miles per hour. By 5:40 p.m. the storm was getting worse instead of better, and being concerned for the safety of the meat remaining on the caribou carcass, we decided to make a quick run and get it back to camp before dark. Donning our long rain coats and shouldering our pack boards and meat sacks we started on the mile and a half trek to where my caribou lay. We were walking directly into the wind and this slowed us down considerably.

The wind was so strong we had to lean into it and force ourselves forward. At one point we saw a red fox trying to negotiate his way around a hill and it looked like he was trying to hold on by his toe-nails while his tail was blown out at a right angle to his body. We pushed on and eventually located the carcass. I had brought my rifle along for protection just in case we might find an ornery brown bear trying to claim our prize but the meat was unmolested.

Hurrying as best I could in the icy rain and wind, I finished boning out the carcass and secured it in two heavy, white meat sacks. Tying these to our pack boards, we started back to our camp. By now the day was about gone and we knew we had to hurry to beat the darkness.

Ron took the lead and I followed along behind him with my head down to protect my glasses from the wind-driven rain. About this time we noticed the fog coming in and we quickened our pace as much as we could, considering our hip boots and load of meat. When we got to the top of the ridge we looked for Turtle Mountain to be sure of our bearings, but to our dismay, the fog obscured it from our view. Dropping down off the ridge we trudged on but somehow nothing looked familiar. Then we saw a small isolated hill ahead of us and Ron said, "Do you think that is Little Turtle?" But when we drew nearer we knew it wasn't. Things weren't looking very good for us at that moment and we knew we were in big trouble.

We hurried on, desperately trying to locate our lake, knowing that darkness would soon be upon us. Nothing looked right, especially in the wind and rain and swirling fog. Coming to another small domed hill, we climbed to its top but saw nothing we could recognize. Ron, at age 49 and fourteen years younger than I, was still doing well but my heavy load of meat, along with my rifle and hip boots, was beginning to slow me down.

Dropping my sack of meat I remarked that I didn't think it was worth having another heart attack over and besides, if we were going to locate our camp before dark, we had to hustle. Ron opted to carry his meat as long as he could and we hurried on, looking in every direction for something that might give us our bearings. With only a few minutes left before dark, we saw what appeared to be some water up ahead. Hurrying toward it like two drowning men clutching for straws, we reached it only to find it wasn't "our" lake. Our hearts fell. And at that same moment, darkness fell. We had been walking, lost, for two hours and now had absolutely no shelter, and no fuel for a fire. It is hard to imagine the feeling of hopelessness that came over us.

Ron dropped his load of meat and we sat down on some big moss-wet rocks to rest, turning our backs to the wind. The wind slammed the rain against our slickered backs until it sounded like rain hitting a tin roof. Although we had been warm and sweaty from our hike, and so weary that we almost dozed off while sitting there in the blackness, soon our bodies cooled and we began to shiver.

"Ron!" I said. "We're going to have to keep moving to keep our body heat!"

"Where will we go?" Ron asked.

"I guess we'll just have to walk around this lake all night," I answered and with that we stumbled off along the lake's edge. Thank God, Ron had brought a little 2-cell flashlight in his pack and this guided our path until we stopped to rest again. This was going to be a long night, twelve hours until daylight, and I didn't know if I could walk that much longer. And if we could, would the light's batteries last that long? The rain and wind continued relentlessly.

This time when we stopped to rest, Ron laid on the ground on his pack sack while I seated myself on another big rock. We both kept dozing off until I roused and realized I was shaking from hypothermia. My hip joints were aching and my voice sounded squeaky when I roused Ron and said, "We've stopped here too long! We gotta get up and walk and try to warm up!"

When Ron answered me I could hardly recognize his voice. We roused ourselves and stumbled along the opposite lake shore in the darkness but when our shivering intensified, Ron suggested that we climb the hill above the lake to see if that effort would warm us. Once on top the hill and still shivering, we struck out across the tundra again, using the little flashlight's beam to avoid the deep trenches made by bears digging for ground squirrels. We had no idea where we were headed and you can be sure we both did some praying.

After a long while of stumbling across the tundra and through the rocks we began to make out something ahead that looked a little faint but somehow different than the darkness around us.

Continuing on we began to realize that it might be a body of water with what little light was in the sky reflecting on its surface. This spurred us on and after dropping down a long ridge we found ourselves on the shore of another lake. Could this be ours?

We followed around its edge for a great distance but in the dark nothing looked familiar. After awhile we could hear water running and remembering that a small stream ran into the north end of our lake, we moved toward the sound. On the hill above the stream we had dug our toilet trench and had impaled a plastic bag containing toilet paper on a bleached out caribou antler.

When we reached the stream, Ron shined the beam of his little light up on the hill and I was never, in my life, so glad to see a roll of toilet paper! Two hundred and fifty yards more and there sat our tent, looking at that moment like the Hilton Hotel! We thanked God for his guidance and made our way into our tent and out of the wind and rain. Our hands were so cold we couldn't light our lantern so we quickly got out of our raingear and wet clothing and snuggled into our warm sleeping bags. Almost immediately we were asleep. We had found our tent at midnight.

I was awakened at 2:30 a.m. by the wind buffeting our tent ferociously and the rain slamming against it in torrents as the storm intensified. I couldn't see Ron in the darkness but I knew he was awake, too. "Ain't you glad we're not lost out there now!" I asked. The rain continued to pour all night. It had been a close one.

The rain came down non-stop all night and into the afternoon of the following day. After our ordeal of the night before, we slept until 11 a.m., when nature forced us to leave our nests. All of our clothes were wet from rain and sweat except our pants. When I tried to get my boots on a sudden pain showed me a bursted blister the size of a fifty-cent piece on one of my heels, caused by a sweaty sock wadding up in my boot on our long trek. This pretty much put me out of commission as far as any serious walking was concerned.

In the afternoon the rain slacked off enough that I was able to flesh and salt my caribou cape before another storm hit. I had barely finished when the rain started pouring again and the wind, that had never let up, continued to blow.

We were both concerned about the meat we had left on the tundra, but my big raw blister nullified any chance of me searching for it. The plane was supposed to pick us up that evening but with the high winds gaining force, we didn't really expect him to show. Finally, Ron could take it no longer and said that he was going to the far side of the lake and hike in the general direction that we had walked in the night, in hopes that he could find the other lake and the sack of caribou shoulder meat. I was like a chained dog when I saw him leave and I wasn't able to go with him. I assured him that if he wasn't back by dark I would hobble up the ridge across the lake and carry the Coleman lantern for him to guide on.

It was with great relief that I saw him returning, just before dark, with his load of meat. After spreading the meat out under a tarp, we retired to our tent for another night.

Sometime during the night the stillness awakened me and I realized that the rain had stopped and the wind had died! But this wasn't destined to last very long for, at 7:30 a.m., the rain started again and a high wind came up that flopped and distorted our tent like a rag until I feared its seams would pop. We were just starting to make some coffee when we heard a plane coming. We hurried outside into the storm just as the Beaver float plane finished a circle of our camp and then practically hovered in the air just above our tent like a vulture, with the terrific wind holding him. We could see the pilot looking at us as we waved, and seeing that we were still alive and in camp, he flew on and disappeared behind a ridge. It was too dangerous for him to attempt a landing.

After a light breakfast we broke camp, except for taking the tent down, just in case the storm should subside and the plane return. But it wasn't to be for the wind roared all day and the rain came in squalls. Again we thought our tent would come apart and it started to do so around the door-flap seams. It finally calmed a little in early evening and a smidgen of weak sun actually appeared on the horizon. This lull came too late in the day for the plane to rescue us, so after blowing up our air mattresses again and changing the dressing on my huge blister, we crawled back into our sleeping bags. Shortly after 8 p.m. the rain returned and poured until after midnight before letting up.

The morning broke clear and cold with a slight breeze. We were just thinking about coffee when we heard our plane coming! Quickly dropping and folding our tent, we carried our gear to the lake shore, loaded it in the float plane and roared off the lake. We made a couple circles over the general area where I believed my sack of ribs and neck meat had been dropped but failed to locate it. Pointing the plane's nose toward King Salmon, we left the site of our adventure behind but the memories remained and served to form a lasting kinship between Ron and myself.

Before I left Alaska, Ron grinned and said, "Ralph, if you write another book, I hope you don't put this story in it for I don't intend to tell my wife about it." He spoke my mind for I hadn't planned on relating this experience to my wife, either!

Four years passed before Ron and I were able to get together for another caribou hunt. In late September of 1995 we headed once again for the Alaska Peninsula and our Turtle Mountain campsite, this time accompanied by Ron's brother, Jerry, and my Austrian friend, Franz. Being an alien, Franz couldn't hunt in Alaska without a licensed guide and he had joined us for the fun of the trip and to experience the vastness of the tundra country.

Using Turtle Mountain as our guide, we located our lake and previous camp site and soon had our two tents erected, close together with the entrances facing each other. The day was beautiful and actually warm and we worked leisurely, covering our tents with blue plastic tarps anchored to the tundra and adding another tarp to form a roof between the two tents. After all our gear was safely stowed inside, we walked to the top of the hill behind our camp to look for caribous. We couldn't hunt the same day that we had flown and it seemed the caribou knew it for we saw a couple hundred of them scattered over the low hills east of our camp. Around 8:30 p.m. a large herd with several trophy bulls paraded past our camp at 300 yards and we hoped that this was a preview of coming attractions. We also hoped this beautiful weather would last but those hopes were dashed when the wind came up and the rain started lashing our tent around 3 a.m. The blue tarps flapped and flopped all night, creating such a racket that sleep was hard to come by.

All hands were up and enjoying a cold pancake in the rain by 7:45 a.m., anxious to begin the hunt. On my way to the latrine trench that morning, and only 75 yards from our tents, I found fresh bear scat and the large tracks of a brown bear in the soil of a ground squirrel burrow.

Although the rain was still falling, the wind had abated somewhat by the time we separated for the day's hunt. This time Jerry accompanied Ron, and Franz went with me. And this time I paid close attention to my route. As we walked, Franz was intrigued by the creatures that existed on the harsh tundra and pointed out a ground squirrel, an eagle, a kite and a ptarmigan. We also noticed a type of huckleberry growing on a viny stem and flush with the top of the moss. The bear scat that I had seen was full of these tiny berries and although a bear would spend considerable time foraging on these to fill his stomach, he had nothing else to do and hundreds of square miles to do it in.

When Franz and I crested the first hill north of camp we immediately spotted a female brown bear and her three yearling cubs, two brown and one blonde, about a half mile away and feeding up the hill towards us. We watched as they drew nearer until the sow suddenly caught our scent on the breeze and started to run; in the opposite direction, thank goodness. We regarded their departure through our binoculars until the four of them reached the river plain where two more bears were observing their approach. These must have been sub-adults of the female for she joined them and they all galloped off together until they faded from our view.

There were no caribou in sight so Franz and I continued on, passing the site of my previous caribou kill, and climbed a high ridge to scan the hills on the far side. We had just topped the ridge when we saw the fog moving toward us, rolling in the wind. In a matter of minutes, we were surrounded by pea-soup fog that restricted our vision to twenty feet.

At this point I still was oriented as to the direction of camp and I told Franz that I was determined to wait right here until the fog thinned, even if it took all day. Travel a few hundred yards in that fog and you would lose all sense of direction. Retreating about forty feet down the hill to escape the wind and cold rain, we sat down on the moss and waited. And waited. After one and a half hours the fog began to thin, allowing us to see one hundred yards before closing in again. Finally, as quickly as it came, the fog blew past us and was gone.

Ever since my 1991 hunt I had wanted to return and locate the lake where Ron and I had spent so many miserable hours while lost, so when the rain ceased around noon Franz and I went on a search for it. On our way we spotted the tips of a caribou's antler silhouetted on the sky line just at the top of a low ridge. Since it didn't move, we felt sure a herd was bedded there, just over the crest. Keeping the wind in our favor, we crouched low and stealthily made our way to the ridge top. Then, easing myself up ever so slowly, expecting to see the animals very near, I stood up and laughed. Franz, who was behind me, joined me in my laughter for our caribou "bull" was a shed antler propped up against a rock. Silhouetted against the sky, it looked like the real thing. We were glad we were all alone on the tundra with no one to observe our "stalk."

Continuing on, we located the "lost" lake. In the calm daylight the area looked beautiful and serene and held none of the implications that being at this same spot under the wrong circumstances could kill you.

Around 4 p.m. the wind increased, driving the cold rain across the tundra and we made our way back to camp, having seen only one caribou the entire day! The entry in my journal that evening read, "Rain lashing and canvas flapping. Water in our tent. To bed at 8 p.m., half frozen."

The wind raged throughout the night, flapping the stiff plastic tarps so loudly that it was hard to sleep. Everything in our tent was wet except our sleeping bags which were slightly elevated by our air mattresses. Unknown to me, I was in the advanced stages of a prostrate problem, which caused me to get up at least three times each night to relieve myself. This entailed getting out of my sleeping bag and pulling on my hip boots without allowing my stockinged feet to touch the wet floor of the tent. This was all done from a sitting position while trying not to kick or otherwise disturb Franz. Then it was on with the still-wet long raincoat and hood before crawling out into the inky blackness of driving rain and wind. (Three months later my prostate swelled to the point that urination was impossible and the pain was excruciating, resulting in surgery. Had this occurred on the tundra I probably would have expired from pain and infection.)

The storm roared all morning until finally, at 12:30 noon I began to ache too badly to stay in the sack any longer. Despite the storm, I donned my clothes, took my rifle and set out for a short hunt around camp while my compadres slept on. It was too foggy to see over 150 yards and after awhile I headed back toward camp to get out of the wind. The fellows were rousing by now and Ron was brewing some coffee when I spotted some caribou on the skyline at the south end of the lake. Several bulls appeared, their antlers emerging over the hilltop before their bodies did. One bull was a nice one and I alerted the guys to grab their weapons.

The caribou were feeding toward us and it appeared that they would pass just to the east of our camp. Crouching down we climbed the hill and crawled the last twenty yards to the ridge top. The rain was still coming down and the fog settled in again, making it hard to see. Although it was early afternoon the leaden sky, rain and fog made it as dark as early morning.

The biggest bull was now moving toward us, slightly separated from the other animals, and about 175 yards across the draw from us. We could see that it sported only one shovel, but this a long one that extended past the end of its nose. Since Jerry, from Michigan, had never shot a caribou, we offered this one to him but he refused, hoping to find an even larger one with double shovels. Ron was waiting for me to take the animal so I eased myself into a sitting position and prepared to shoot. The fog would drift in and out making the bull appear like a phantom and hard to find in my rain-spattered rifle scope. Finally, the sight looked good, I squeezed the trigger and the big bull fell, a .270 bullet through his neck. The rest of the herd scattered and this being the best bull, no other shots were fired.

When we walked over to where the bull lay I could tell that Jerry was having second thoughts and wishing he hadn't refused the shot. The animal and antlers looked even bigger, close up. While Ron and Jerry returned to camp to prepare some food and finish brewing the interrupted pot of coffee, Franz and I dressed out the bull before hurrying to join them for an afternoon breakfast. The brothers then set out for a hunt while Franz and I skinned, caped and boned out the caribou and carried it to camp, only 300 yards away. After placing a tarp on the moss we spread the meat out to cool, covering it loosely with a second tarp. Ron and Jerry returned empty-handed from their hunt and after our dinner we crawled into our tents, tired, and enjoyed a good night's sleep. The sky was clearing, the wind was quiet and a few stars appeared overhead.

In the morning there was a little frost on the moss and the wind was now blowing from the east. Jerry admitted that he didn't sleep well, worrying about the bears and that big pile of caribou meat just outside the tent. It was a treat to be able to prepare a meal without being rained on and we enjoyed a good breakfast of eggs, bacon and caribou tenderloin. Around 10 a.m. Ron and Jerry left for a hunt and Franz accompanied them, while I stayed in camp to guard our meat pile against the bears. With the gut pile so near there was a good possibility that a bear would be attracted.

After the fellows left I spent four and a half hours leisurely fleshing the caribou cape and while at it, looked up to see a band of caribou staring at me from one hundred yards away. I sat on a big rock with my back to the wind, wearing my raincoat with the hood up to cut the chill. After a couple of hours, I looked over my shoulder quite often, thinking how quietly a hungry brownie could approach on the thick moss. Again the fellows returned with no meat, although they had seen and shot at some caribou. About this time the east wind intensified to gale force and the rain came again with an icy feel to it. By 7:45 p.m. we were forced into our tents and sleeping bags while the wind raged, not in gusts, but non-stop. I feared our tent would blow away with us in it and when I got up in the wee hours to obey nature's call I found that the canvas had blown off our tent and two of the ropes were broken. I tried to replace the tarp but the roaring wind kept tearing it from my hands. Finally, I awakened Franz who, amazingly, was sleeping through the whole commotion and got him out into the inky-black storm to help me. We finally got the tarp re-tied and pegged and weighted the pegs down with big rocks. A tough job in hip boots and underwear!

Rain had been forced through the tent's walls and my clothes were saturated as well as part of my sleeping bag. Relief came at daybreak when the storm passed through and all became calm. While Ron was starting our breakfast fixin's I walked up the hill toward the spot I had sat when I shot my caribou. I was stopped in my tracks when I saw the head and front end of a wolf as he stood staring at me. He looked black, but being silhouetted against the sky, it was hard to determine his color and didn't give me much time to find out. In a flash he was gone, streaking over the tundra until he became a dot in the distance. Apparently I had surprised him on his trip to the caribou gut pile.

Ron and Jerry headed out to hunt again and this time Franz remained in camp with me. The wind had picked up again but so far, no rain so we hung some of our wet clothes on the caribou antlers and tent ropes in an effort to dry them. I continued to flesh the caribou cape and while at it saw two big herds of caribou approaching on the far side of the lake. One group turned south and disappeared while the second herd headed north, skirting our lake. When they were 250 yards from us we could see that there were several big bulls in the group, one of them a real trophy. On our flight to King Salmon a native Alaskan had given me a caribou hunting tip that I thought I would now try. He said if you see caribou in the distance and you wish to stop them, even if they've already seen you, raise both arms above your head, imitating antlers, and swing them from side to side. If you are too close it will probably only serve to frighten them more but at a distance they will stop and mill about, probably thinking you are another caribou.

It sounded goofy but I decided to give it a try. Sure enough, when I raised and moved my arms, the herd stopped and remained on the hill staring at us until Franz had time to snap many photos! Too bad Ron and Jerry aren't here, I thought.

Around 6 p.m. Ron came in with a load of caribou meat and when Jerry appeared they headed back out to retrieve the rest of the meat and the antlers. Ron had scored on a fine bull. He related that, earlier in the day, he was watching a band of caribou through his binoculars, trying to determine if there were any bulls worth stalking. To his amazement, as he watched, he saw two wolves streak over a knoll, target a cow and after a thirty-foot chase bring her down and start feeding on her.

The rest of the band vamoosed and Ron followed them, but finding no bulls, he returned to the caribou kill and found the wolves still feeding on her. Seeing Ron approaching, they disappeared over the hill before he could get a shot at them.

Our plane appeared two and a half hours late to pick us up the following morning. Our lake being too small for a heavy load takeoff, the pilot took Franz and Jerry and half our gear to the huge Lake Becharof and dropped them off, then returned for Ron and I and the rest of our stuff. On the flight to pick up Franz and Jerry we saw another big sow brown bear with three yearlings, all of these blonde, running across the tundra beneath our plane. I can still see the fur rippling over the layers of fat on her body as she ran.

The fall months sped by, filled with deer hunting trips to Idaho, eastern Washington and Colorado that supplied us with venison for the coming year. These adventures were brought to a halt by my hospital stay for prostate surgery. One stormy winter evening in early December, while I was recovering at home and experiencing "cabin fever," an ocean storm blew in and the wind and rain raged so fiercely I began to imagine I was back on the Alaska tundra. The only thing missing was the constant flapping of the tent tarps. Just as we finished our evening meal the power went off and plunged the house into darkness.

We were cozy with our wood-burning stove doing its job so I lit the old kerosene lamp and we retired to my den. After starting a fire in the fireplace, I settled down beside Velma on the davenport and, influenced by the flickering lamp-light, the fireplace and the wind roaring outside, I looked at Vel and said, "Hon, I think this is a good time to tell you a story!" I then proceeded to relate to her my "lost on the tundra" experience while the wind and rain added all the authentic sound effects. When I had finished Vel asked why I hadn't told her this before and I replied that I wanted to go back to the tundra again and didn't want her to be worried.

And now that I had gone back and returned home without mishap I was itching to go back again. While the solitude of the tundra and the fickleness and unforgiving nature of its weather tends to discourage most hunters from returning there, it holds an attraction for me that keeps calling me back. In a year's time I tend to forget the leaky tents, wet clothes, violent wind and icy rain in the face, fog, rain clothes, hip boots and soggy-cold pancakes and seem to remember only the infrequent sunny days.

Consequently, the following September found Ron and me once again ensconced in a tent on the tundra, this time accompanied by two of Ron's Michigan friends, Bill and Roger.

On this trip the weather didn't even wait for us to get our tents up; in fact it was so foggy and rainy during our float plane flight that we couldn't locate Turtle Mountain, much less our old camp site. It was too dangerous flying over the foggy, hilly tundra of our previous hunts and we were forced to search the river plains for a lake big enough to set the plane on. Finally locating one, we quickly unloaded our gear in the rain and watched our plane take off into the fog.

The area was flat and swampy with a few patches of low-tag-alders and the lake much bigger than at our old camp. We finally got our tents up and everything out of the rain by dark and just as a strong wind commenced driving the rain. The wind velocity increased and blew all night, ripping our tent pegs from the tundra and breaking tie-down ropes. The storm continued into the next day, with the rain turning to sleet.

Around 2 p.m. the winds increased to gale force, ripping our metal tent pegs out and flailing them at the end of their ropes like knives, cutting slits in our tent walls and tarps. After resetting the pegs we retreated inside our tent only to hear the wind intensify to the point it was absolutely scary. The wind didn't come in gusts; it was a constant, steady roar like a freight train. The windward side of the tent was taking such a pounding that Ron and I had to take turns standing and leaning our backs into the canvas to keep our tent from collapsing. We kept this up for two hours until the wind slowed a bit and gave our aching backs and legs a rest. By this time all three of the tent's fiberglass supports were shattered, leaving our tent very saggy and floppy and with no means to repair it. Using duct tape, I attempted to repair the slits in the canvas, hoping to slow the leaks.

Around 8 p.m. the wind tapered off and being anxious to escape our "cage" for awhile, I climbed up the hill behind our tent to have a look-see. I was surprised to see some caribou moving in the distance, about 400 yards away, and with one nice bull in their midst. These were moving away and escaped just before dark without being shot at.

The next morning was bitter cold with hail and wind. After making a four-mile hunt around the perimeter of the lake and returning with nothing but a hip boot full of icy water, I had an early supper and called it a day. The wind and hail squalls had continued all day and only eight caribou had been seen by the four of us.

The hail showers continued all night and into the morning. After a fried egg sandwich breakfast, Ron and I were cleaning up the cooking mess when Bill came down off the hill and reported a herd of 150 caribou were about four miles south of camp and headed in our direction. Roger, in the meantime, had left for the opposite side of the lake for a hunt.

We watched the caribou for two hours and saw other bands merge with them until their numbers resembled the children of Israel making their exodus from Egypt. They were moving slowly and Ron, becoming chilled from the cold wind, left for a hunt elsewhere. About then the caribou started moving fast and four more herds converged into a group of hundreds and hundreds. When they reached the south end of our lake, they veered to their left and headed directly toward where we expected Roger to be.

Just then we heard Roger start shooting and saw most of the herd go off at a right angle to the lake and disappear over the hills to the west. Hearing Roger's shots, I ran back to camp, hoping that some of the animals might pass by on the opposite side of the lake. I had just reached camp when I saw five cows and a bull across the lake and running north. They were at least 500 yards away but I chanced a shot at the bull and missed. Holding a little higher and leading him more, I shot again and the bull slowed and fell behind. He was getting farther away but I kept shooting, guessing how high to hold, until my gun was empty. The cows disappeared over the hill but the bull hobbled into some tag alders and fell.

To reach the caribou I had to hike a mile around the swampy north end of the lake. Reaching the head of the lake I saw my bull, still 250 yards away, attempting to rise. Two more shots and it was over. Making my way over to him, I found that I had hit him six times; the bullets had dropped so far that my first shots had hit him in a hoof and two knees, while two hit his shoulder and one entered his rib cage.

I set about boning out the meat and was surprised at how little of it was damaged from my shots. While busy at my task Roger appeared with part of his caribou. He went on to camp with his load, then returned just as I finished my boning job.

Each of us shouldered a load and we got the meat and antlers to camp in one trip. We had just spread our meat on a tarp to cool when Ron came over the hill carrying a caribou quarter. A little later Bill arrived but with no meat.

After a quick supper we crawled into our sleeping bags. I enjoyed a good sleep until the wind changed to the north and I woke up shivering and couldn't get warm. Finally I put on my hickory shirt and an insulated shirt over my long johns, and then laid my wool jacket over my sleeping bag.

Morning came, sunny and cold, and after our usual egg sandwich and coffee, Ron and Bill headed out to retrieve the rest of Ron's caribou meat while I went with Roger to help bring in his animal. It took us an hour and twenty minutes to reach his kill, which we found unmolested by bears, wolves or foxes. While boning out the animal I spotted a lone bull moose hiking across the wide open tundra nearly a mile away. I don't know what his destination was but he seemed in a hurry to get there.

Five hours after we left camp we were back with Roger's meat. Just as we arrived, Ron and Bill showed up with Ron's meat and then headed back over the hills to bring in the meat from a caribou that Bill had shot. After getting all our meat taken care of we were able to enjoy a meal outdoors for a change and we sated our hunger with fried potatoes, hamburgers and caribou tenderloin. It had been a beautiful day after a 20° morning and our hunt was over. None of the caribou racks were spectacular but with the rotten weather we thought we had better not be choosy.

The morning arrived frigid and frosty with an icy north wind picking up. After breakfast we strung some orange marking tape around the lake's edge near our tent in hopes of attracting our pilot so we could make an early escape. We had nothing to do but wait and watch big herds of caribou passing by on the opposite lake shore with big bulls pushing each other around. It made us drool to look at their huge antlers but, sadly, it was too late for us!

Again, the wind changed to the south, the sky clouded, and the cold rain commenced anew. Our plane arrived for us the next afternoon and after cramming the sacks of caribou meat inside its pontoons, the pilot managed to get our five bodies and 1,000 pounds of loot off the lake and safely to King Salmon.

That was my last hunt there. Now, seven years later and at 75 years of age, I get the itch to return, even as I write this!

Chapter 15

Austria Revisited

After Franz had accompanied me on my second caribou hunt he invited me to come to his farm in Austria for a roe deer hunt. My earlier hunts there had taken place in the late fall and early winter and after the bucks had shed their antlers. This hunt would be for an antlered buck and would take place in late May, during the rut. At this time Franz was permitted to kill a roe deer buck every other year and 1997 was the year set for the hunt. I thought it was extremely unselfish of him to offer me his hunt when hunting opportunities are so rare in Austria. It was something that only a true friend would do.

I arrived at his farm on May 22 and the following day purchased my jag kart (hunting license) for 1,800 schillings or $200. This license is good for your lifetime. It had rained all night and this continued until late afternoon when it ceased and was replaced by a blustery wind.

Around 7:30 that evening we walked to a tree-stand "house" that was situated in a small grove of trees, adjacent to a field of rye. On the way to our hunting stand we saw a roe deer leap into the tall rye and disappear; the rye was taller than these little deer! After we were settled in our little observation post Franz remarked that hunting is never good on a windy day and his words held true, for although we stayed until dark, we saw nothing except two cock pheasants.

During the night the wind subsided and the morning dawned beautiful, clear and warm. Franz took me for a drive through the farm fields and we saw lots of roe deer tracks as well as the large tracks of a red deer stag. This was encouraging and I could hardly wait for the evening's hunt. Franz then explained to me that I couldn't shoot just any roe deer buck; only the spikes or the large *old* bucks could be harvested. The *prime* bucks were not to be killed but conserved for breeding. Only a certain number of the old bucks could be killed in this area and part of the quota had already been taken. This narrowed my chances down quite a bit for I certainly didn't want to travel all the way to Austria just to shoot a spike. I wasn't too sure what they considered a "prime" buck or an "old" buck but Franz assured me he would determine this for me when the time arrived.

Around 6 p.m. we headed out for the evening's hunt, this time going to a different hunting stand at the edge of a forest and facing the fields. After leaving Franz's car along a dirt road, we skirted the edge of the woods and climbed up into our little lookout post, which was elevated on poles about ten feet above the ground. The lookout "box" was just that—a small, roofed cubicle whose walls were boarded from the floor half-way up with the top half open for observation. A single board bench served as a seat and once inside and seated, you remained perfectly still, continually watching the area to the front and sides of the stand.

In front of us was a large field of tall rye, while to our right was a field of some sort of grain that had not grown tall enough to conceal the soil, and to our left, partially visible over the rye, was a field of peas. We hadn't been seated long until we saw three does cross the pea field and enter the rye. Once in the tall grain they completely disappeared from sight.

Around 7 p.m. the sky turned black, thunder rumbled and lightning began to flash. In a couple more minutes the storm was upon us. Rain came down in torrents and lightning stabbed down from the clouds, striking nearby with tremendous explosions. I began to feel uneasy, sitting in that open-fronted stand, holding a rifle, and hoped I wouldn't be the target for the next lightning bolt!

As quickly as it appeared the storm moved on, the rain stopped and silence settled over the area again. Just then I saw a movement to our right and nudged Franz as a roe deer buck left the woods and entered the field while Franz studied it through his binoculars. By the time he decided it was one we could take, the deer had trotted out of range of the little 5.6x50R. Mag that Franz had provided for the hunt. This buck was hardly out of sight before I saw another buck enter the field at the same spot as the first one. This buck looked good to me and I had the crosshairs of my scope on him while Franz looked him over. Franz speaks English very well but occasionally in sentence formation a mis-placed word can almost change its meaning. As I kept my sight on the deer, I heard Franz whisper, "I think we should take this one—not." Before he said "not," I almost squeezed the trigger! This was a buck in its prime and he continued to stand at the same spot, looking apprehensively in all directions. When it turned to face the woods and began to "bark" I whispered to Franz that it must have caught our scent and its barking would alert all the other deer. Franz shook his head and said that the deer wasn't barking at us but that this was a sign that a much bigger and more dominant buck was nearby in the woods.

Finally the deer moved to our right, following the forest's edge until we could no longer see it. By 7:30 p.m. we had seen five roe deer bucks and only one had been shootable. The odds didn't look very good.

Then, off to the left about 130 yards I saw the heads and upper bodies of two bucks that had just entered the pea field! Again I nudged Franz and nodded in that direction and while he appraised them with the binoculars, I found them in my rifle's scope. The one on the right was a spike while the other was a dandy buck. When Franz said, "The one on the left—I think we should take this one!" I slipped the safety off and prepared to shoot. But there was a problem, something Franz had warned me of earlier—the field of tall rye lay between me and the deer and I had to be careful not to aim too low lest the little bullet should hit the rye and deflect or disintegrate. There wasn't much of the deer's body showing above the rye but I took a careful aim, squeezed the trigger and the roe deer fell. "Good shot, Ralph!" Franz exclaimed, slapping me on the back.

Climbing down from our stand took only seconds, despite the fact that our legs and backs were stiff from sitting, cramped in one position for so long. Following the forest edge to get beyond the rye, we approached the fallen deer and found that the little bullet had done its job well.

Franz looked at the buck but a second before he remarked that he believed this deer's antlers were the biggest of any taken in this hunting area since World War 2! If I had been elated before, this put the icing on the cake. Before I could touch the animal, Franz said, "Wait here," and he disappeared into the forest, returning a couple of minutes later with three small green pine sprigs. Approaching the buck, he stood beside it, and after placing one of the sprigs in the animal's mouth and another on its back, he removed his hat. I, standing on the opposite side of the deer, did the same. Then Franz delivered the hunter's prayer over the animal, thanking it for allowing us to take its life and requesting it to send back many more of its kind to replace it. I can't remember all of it but I was moved by Franz's sincerity. Having done this, he dipped a sprig in the animal's blood and placed it in my cap.

By now the light was swiftly fading and so I wrapped the animal around my shoulders and headed for Franz's car. As we neared the road another buck and a doe dashed across in front of us. While still in the brushy cover, we heard a car leaving another part of the forest and as it would pass near us, Franz suggested we let it pass without observing us. Franz knew the fellow, who was also a hunter, and said if he saw our deer he would want us to go with him to celebrate the kill far into the night!

The buck was an old one and his antlers measured eight inches long and four and a quarter inches tip to tip. Doesn't sound very impressive when compared to whitetails or mule deer but he was grand enough that all the local hunters were aware of him and vied for the chance to make him their trophy.

The next day I attended a Roman Festival at some ancient ruins with Franz and his recent bride, Gabi. While there Franz was approached by the hunter that we had heard leaving the woods on the previous evening.

"I saw your car and heard a shot last evening—did you kill a roe deer?"

"Yes," Franz replied, drawing out the word. "My American friend got a very nice one!"

"He didn't get the big one, did he?"

Franz smiled and said, "I'm afraid so!" That didn't amuse the hunter at all but Franz thought it was great.

And that brings me to the conclusion of my narrative but certainly not to the end of my outdoor adventures. My retirement years have been fun, blessed with good health and many hunts that haven't been included in this book. I continue to hunt and to enjoy the out-of-doors, even though the hills tend to get steeper and the swamps seem deeper. And I am always finding something new and interesting in Nature, and a promise of even better days ahead!

Too often we tend to reminisce of days gone by and recall them as the "good old days." After you have lived a lot of years you begin to realize that there are no good old days.

The "good old days" are right now—today—and we are wise if we can grasp that fact. Yesterday is gone, forever, taking with it our youth and its heartaches, toils and missed opportunities. We can't go back, except in memory, which is too often deceptive, bringing into sharp focus happy events while paling the harsh experiences. We can't allow today to be a repetition of yesterday or we could possibly go through life defeated and chained by mistakes of the past.

Samuel Pepy was an English diarist (circa 1660) and I share his philosophy that still holds true today. He wrote, "The truth is, I do indulge myself a little more in pleasure…out of my observation that most men that do thrive in the world do forget to take pleasure during the time that they are getting their estate, but reserve that till they have got one, and then it is too late for them to enjoy it with any pleasure."

The hills get steeper and the swamps get deeper…

I feel sorry for those who are always going to do something adventurous, exciting, and exhilarating—some day.

Today is here for the living, new and fresh with each dawning, a clear stage in the drama of life. This drama has been going on for as long as man has stomped about on this earth. Your day to day problems are not unique to this day and age; they have always plagued mankind, even in the "good old days." Today is here! Make the most of it! Do the things you want to do.

Tomorrow may never come.

Epilogue

THE SUPPLEMENTAL FEEDING PROGRAM WAS NOT DESIGNED TO put a stop to bear hunting but to curtail the killing of bears for peeling trees; nonlethal control. Ideally, spring feeding was to work in conjunction with summer and fall sport-hunting seasons that would harvest over-populations of bears. Traditionally, in the state of Washington, 90% of the bears taken by sportsmen could be attributed to the hound-hunting method while only 10% were taken by "boot" or "still" hunting.

The combination of the two—spring feeding and late summer hunting—worked very well until 1996 when the voters in our state passed an initiative on the ballot that put an immediate ban on hound-hunting of bears, cougars and bobcats. This allowed the bear population to increase, creating bear-human conflicts in urban areas and a greater number of bears to be fed to prevent tree damage.

As a consequence, the sport-hunting bag limit on bears has been raised to two animals per season in western Washington. The Department of Wildlife has also reserved the right to issue special hound-hunting damage permits to the timberland owners when bears create a problem. Not all tree farmers use the supplemental feeding alternative and can't be forced to do so and as a result they continue to experience tree damage.

But where it is used it has been proved that supplemental feeding works and has been a timely discovery for the tree farmers of the Northwest.

Our trees are a renewable resource; our bears are not. Supplemental feeding has created a means for the two of them to coexist.

ORDER FORM

TITLE	QUANTITY
The Education of a Bear Hunter @ $14.95 each	
Bears & Flowers @ $16.95 each	
SUBTOTAL	
SHIPPING & HANDLING (*$2.00 per book*)	
TOTAL	

Please mail check or money order to:
Ralph Flowers
4802 Olympic Hwy
Aberdeen, WA 98520
(360) 532-5143